Music Therapy with Displaced Persons

of related interest

Music Therapy and Autism Across the Lifespan
A Spectrum of Approaches
*Edited by Henry Dunn, Elizabeth Coombes, Emma
Maclean, Helen Mottram, and Josie Nugent*
Foreword by Adam Ockelford
ISBN 978 1 78592 311 1
eISBN 978 1 78450 622 3

Social Work with Refugees, Asylum Seekers and Migrants
Theory and Skills for Practice
Edited by Lauren Wroe, Rachel Larkin, and Reima Ana Maglajlic
Foreword by Debra Hayes
ISBN 978 1 78592 344 9
eISBN 978 1 78450 674 2

Art-Making with Refugees and Survivors
Creative and Transformative Responses to Trauma After
Natural Disasters, War and Other Crises
Sally Adnams Jones, PhD
ISBN 978 1 78592 238 1
eISBN 978 1 78450 518 9

MUSIC THERAPY WITH DISPLACED PERSONS

Trauma, Transformations, and Cultural Connections

EDITED BY
Elizabeth Coombes, Samuel Gracida, and Emma Maclean

FOREWORD BY VIGGO KRÜGER

Jessica Kingsley Publishers
London and Philadelphia

First published in Great Britain in 2025 by Jessica Kingsley Publishers
An imprint of John Murray Press

2

Copyright © Viggo Krüger 2025, Foreword © Elizabeth Coombes, Emma Maclean, and Samuel Gracida 2025, Introduction © Hala Hamdan and Eva Marija Vukich 2025, Prelude © Emma Maclean 2025, Chapter 1 © Gene-Ann Behrens 2025, Chapter 2 © Bolette D. Beck 2025, Chapter 3 © Heidi Ahonen 2025, Chapter 4 © Sander van Goor and Evelyn Heynen 2025, Chapter 5 © Samuel Gracida, Diane J. Pitzer, Cordula Reiner-Wormit, and Alexander F. Wormit 2025, Chapter 6 © Mitsi Akoyunoglou 2025, Chapter 7 © Elizabeth Coombes and Saphia Abou Amer 2025, Chapter 8 © Andrés Salgado Vasco 2025, Chapter 9 © Danny D. Kora 2025, Chapter 10 © Elizabeth Coombes, Letitia Slabu, Anthony Mangiacotti, Tamar Hadar, and Fabia Franco 2025, Chapter 11 © Emma O'Brien 2025, Chapter 12 © Nigel Osborne 2025, Chapter 13

This edited book is dedicated to all persons who have experienced displacement due to war, political instability, or other reasons and any associated distress.

Contents

FOREWORD: MUSIC THERAPY TO MEET THE NEEDS OF FORCIBLY
DISPLACED PERSONS II
Viggo Krüger

INTRODUCTION 15
Elizabeth Coombes, Emma Maclean, and Samuel Gracida

PRELUDE: A SUDDEN DISPLACEMENT DUE TO WAR IN PALESTINE-
ISRAEL, AND ITS IMPACT ON PRESENT AND FUTURE PLANS. 24
Hala Hamdan and Eva Marija Vukich

1. A Critical Review of the Literature on Using Music and Music
    Therapy with Displaced Persons 31
    Emma Maclean

Section 1: Traversing Trauma

2. Impact of Trauma on Displaced Persons: Integrating
    a Neuroscience Perspective 49
    Gene-Ann Behrens

3. Homecoming: Resettlement and Acculturation Processes in
    Music and Imagery Therapy for Female Refugees Suffering
    from Post-Traumatic Stress Disorder 69
    Bolette D. Beck

4. Sounds of Pain and Hope: Storytelling with Music –
    Narrative Music Psychotherapy Through the Lens of
    Trauma and Recovery 86
    Heidi Ahonen

5. Safe & Sound: A Music Therapy Intervention for Refugee
   and Asylum Seeker Children 103
   Sander van Goor and Evelyn Heynen

Section 2: Supporting Social Transformations

6. Music Therapy Perspectives on Music-Based Interventions
   with Displaced Youth: The Heidelberg 'Bridges' Project 123
   *Samuel Gracida, Diane J. Pitzer, Cordula Reiner-Wormit,
   and Alexander F. Wormit*

7. Researching Safe Spaces, Addressing Ethical Challenges:
   Music with Children on the Move in Transit Camps 145
   Mitsi Akoyunoglou

8. Interactive Therapeutic Music-Making in Palestine: Insights
   and Considerations Amid Conflict and Displacement 163
   Elizabeth Coombes and Saphia Abou Amer

9. Music Therapy, Displacement, and Internal Conflict in
   Colombia. 183
   Andrés Salgado Vasco

Section 3: Co-Creating Cultural Connections

10. The Songwriters' Democracy 203
    Danny D. Kora

11. Music for Displaced Dyads (M4DD): A Music Therapy
    Feasibility Study for Displaced Ukrainian Parents and their
    Pre-School Children 212
    *Elizabeth Coombes, Letitia Slabu, Anthony Mangiacotti, Tamar Hadar,
    and Fabia Franco*

12. Our Humanity: Creating a Music Video with an Asylum
    Seeker While He Was in Mandatory Offshore Detention 232
    *Emma O'Brien with guest contributions from Blair Harris and Craig
    Pilkington*

13. Songs of Travel: Songwriting with Children Displaced by War: A Biopsychosocial Model, Methodology, and Possible Taxonomy – Music and Transformation 251
Nigel Osborne

A HOPEFUL FUTURE 267

ABOUT THE CONTRIBUTORS 270

SUBJECT INDEX 278

AUTHOR INDEX 285

Foreword

Music Therapy to Meet the Needs of Forcibly Displaced Persons

VIGGO KRÜGER

Increasingly, music therapy is being recognized as a sustainable approach for working with forcibly displaced persons, and this book supports this trend. By offering both theoretical perspectives and practical, real-world examples, the book explores how music therapy can address the complex neurological, emotional, psychological, and social challenges faced by individuals who have been forcibly displaced. It also highlights its potential to foster resilience and a sense of community among those with the resources and competencies to cope with everyday life. By integrating theory with practice, the book serves as a valuable resource for professionals seeking to understand and apply music therapy in this critical area of humanitarian work.

As the reader will learn, forcibly displaced persons are individuals compelled to leave their homes due to factors such as armed conflict, persecution, human rights violations, or environmental disasters. These individuals may become refugees, asylum seekers, or internally displaced persons (IDPs), depending on whether they cross international borders or remain within their country. The United Nations High Commissioner for Refugees (UNHCR) reports that the global population of forcibly displaced persons reached over 117 million by 2024, a record high driven by conflicts in countries such as Ukraine, Syria, and Afghanistan (UNHCR, 2024). This growing crisis emphasizes the need for international cooperation and sustainable solutions to ensure the safety, dignity, and well-being of displaced populations. It is important for readers to recognize that to be classed as an asylum seeker or refugee a person needs to be forcibly displaced. For the purposes of this foreword, however, the term 'displaced' will be used to cover all populations who are removed from or leave their country for reasons stated above.

The need for music therapy can be seen in relation to challenges outlined at a policy level. According to the World Health Organization, the status of displaced persons represents one of the main global challenges of our time (World Health Organization, 2023). Being displaced is linked both to health and democratic challenges and raises debates on identity, human rights, and legal issues. However, displaced persons and their cultural rights are protected under human rights law (United Nations, 1966). According to Article 27 of the International Covenant on Civil and Political Rights, ethnic, religious, or linguistic minorities have the right to enjoy their own culture, profess and practise their own religion, and use their own language. Additionally, the 1951 Convention Relating to the Status of Refugees stipulates in Article 22 that refugees should receive the same treatment as nationals with respect to elementary education, ensuring access to cultural education (United Nations, 1951). The Universal Declaration of Human Rights also reinforces these protections; Article 22 recognizes that everyone, as a member of society, is entitled to the realization of the economic, social, and cultural rights indispensable for their dignity and the free development of their personality (United Nations, 1948).

The notion that music therapy can be a vehicle for the realization of human rights is not a new one (Curtis & Vaillancourt, 2012; Klyve, 2019; Krüger, 2020; Stige & Aarø, 2012). This book can be seen as the result of a long tradition of using music therapy to engage in human rights discourses, serving as a vital tool for advocating social justice and promoting the rights of populations participating in music therapy. Reading this book offers a profound exploration of the intersection between displaced persons, music, and music therapy. Through examples from various contexts, such as educational settings, institutional care, and child welfare, the authors shed light on the transformative impact of music therapy on those forced to flee their homes. As the reader will discover, the experiences described in the book are marked by loss, trauma, and the challenge of rebuilding one's life in unfamiliar surroundings. As a vehicle for supporting human rights, music therapy, then, is described as empowering displaced persons by facilitating their self-expression and sense of community.

The book portrays music therapy as offering a holistic approach to addressing complex needs, leading the reader to a broader understanding of the subjects involved. A central theoretical perspective across many of the chapters relies on what is known as a narrative approach. Such an approach uses stories, in this case about various practices, to create meaning and understand the processes involved in this work. In addition to several chapters themselves utilizing a linear narrative approach, the book offers several accounts of how narrative approaches can be integrated into music therapy.

Opportunities for this are techniques such as songwriting and musical storytelling. Such narrative approaches play a vital role in offering individuals a means to express their experiences within a community and connect their past with the present (Bath, 2015). They allow displaced persons to share their stories in a safe and supportive environment, facilitating a process of meaning-making and reflection. In recent years, the significance of a narrative perspective in music therapy has gained recognition, through such models as Resource-Oriented Music Therapy (Rolvsjord, 2010). A narrative framework suggests that music not only provides emotional support but also serves as a vehicle for communal storytelling. By engaging in storytelling, participants can use music to reframe their experiences of trauma and loss, fostering resilience and a sense of agency over their narratives. This process not only validates their lived experiences but also helps to build connections with others, thereby reducing feelings of isolation.

This book highlights the necessity of adopting a self-critical view of music therapy research and professional development. By recognizing the complexities of identity and the socio-political contexts in which music therapy practice exists, music therapists can ensure that practice does not inadvertently perpetuate frameworks that are a product of their own preconceptions. Instead, as emphasized in this book, music therapists are in a unique position to foster an empowering therapeutic environment. This is essential for honouring the voices and experiences of individuals affected by displacement.

Harnessing knowledge from this book will help prevent burnout among music therapists working with this population, something that can be a result of such work due to the complex emotions expressed in music when working with our clients. As the book demonstrates, engaging in self-care is crucial for music therapists, due to the intense emotional and psychological demands of this work. By prioritizing self-care, therapists can foster their own resilience and maintain a healthy balance between professional responsibilities and personal needs, helping to avoid vicarious trauma and burnout.

Ultimately, this book is a powerful call to action, urging readers to recognize the profound impact music therapy can have on the lives of displaced persons. It emphasizes the importance of continued support for these efforts through advocacy and the provision of cultural resources. It illustrates the dedication of music therapists and their interdisciplinary collaborators in helping displaced persons not only survive but thrive and enjoy their cultural rights, even during times of crisis. The contributions in this book underscore the critical importance of grounding music therapy for displaced persons in evidence-based knowledge and professional experience.

REFERENCES

Bath, H. (2015). The three pillars of traumawise care: Healing in the other 23 hours. *Reclaiming Children and Youth*, 23(4), 44–46.

Curtis, S. & Vaillancourt, G. (2012). The children's right to music project. *Voices: A World Forum for Music Therapy*, 12(3).

Klyve, G. P. (2019). Whose knowledge? Epistemic injustice and challenges in hearing children's voices. *Voices: A World Forum for Music Therapy*, 19(3).

Krüger, V. (2020). *Music Therapy in Child Welfare: Bridging Provision, Protection, and Participation*. Gilsum, NH: Barcelona Publishers.

Rolvsjord, R. (2010). *Resource-Oriented Music Therapy in Mental Health Care*. Gilsum, NH: Barcelona Publishers.

Stige, B. & Aarø, L. E. (2012). *Invitation to Community Music Therapy*. New York, NY: Routledge.

UNHCR. (2024). *Global Trends: Forced Displacement in 2024*. UNHCR. www.unhcr.org/globaltrends.

United Nations. (1948). Universal Declaration of Human Rights, Article 22. www.un.org/en/about-us/universal-declaration-of-human-rights.

United Nations. (1951). Convention relating to the status of refugees, Article 22. www.unhcr.org/3b66c2aa10.

United Nations. (1966). International Covenant on Civil and Political Rights (ICCPR), Article 27. www.ohchr.org/en/instruments-mechanisms/instruments/international-covenant-civil-and-political-rights#:~:text=or%20other%20status.-,Article%2027,to%20use%20their%20own%20language.

World Health Organization. (2023). The health of refugees and migrants in the WHO European Region. www.who.int/europe/news-room/fact-sheets/item/the-health-of-refugees-and-migrants-in-the-who-european-region.

Introduction

ELIZABETH COOMBES, EMMA MACLEAN, AND SAMUEL GRACIDA

Human history is one of people on the move. While voluntary migration comes with its challenges, we must also face the fact that people have often been forced to move due to war, natural disasters, poverty, persecution, and conflict. Forced displacement has become a global crisis in the 21st century, with over 117 million people forcibly displaced across the world (UNHCR, 2023). There is a need for a range of support mechanisms for those who find themselves displaced.

This book directly addresses and responds to this situation by exploring how music and music therapy can assist displaced persons in a range of settings around the globe. It has been generated by a passion for working with this population by the co-editors and book contributors. The editors and chapter authors share a range of perspectives on how music and music therapy can be used to address the needs of people displaced across and within borders. The chapters cover a wide spectrum of music engagement, ranging from clinical therapy sessions to community-based programmes that include elements of training, co-production, and sustainability. In the midst of the complex and overwhelming experience of displacement, music provides a medium to hold spaces, build trust, and access whatever emotions and experiences need to be expressed. Musical experiences as well as music therapy offer a range of ways to communicate these emotions and provide support, connection, grounding and regulation, and comfort.

Readers of this text have the opportunity to learn about the diverse ways in which music can facilitate personal transformations and cultural connections for displaced persons. While there is certainly a great deal of interest and will to work using music and music therapy with this population in all parts of the world, there remains uncertainty as to how best to proceed. We believe that this book offers a further understanding of practice and the opportunity to stimulate critical exploration of this area of work.

THE CO-EDITORS AND THEIR POSITIONINGS
Elizabeth Coombes

A chance meeting with a publishing house at a music therapy conference gave me the impetus to think about what I felt could be an important addition to music therapy literature and led to the production of this text. My interest in working with displaced persons began in 2009 when I accepted a volunteer role in Palestine to run a music project there. Since then, I have developed music therapy work with displaced persons in the UK and internationally. My own musical training was grounded in Western practices with undergraduate, masters, and doctoral qualifications from the UK. Since my first experience of working internationally was not only in another culture but one in a conflict zone under occupation, my thinking and practice have developed significantly. I believe musicians and music therapists need to be alive to the danger that we could accept and promote a view of displaced persons that is homogenous and privileges this identity over broader cultural identities and individual needs.

Samuel Gracida

I have experienced first hand the challenges of living far from home, having resided in four distinct countries: Mexico, China, the USA, and Germany. While I do not consider myself displaced, these experiences have provided me with a unique perspective, allowing me to empathize with the struggles of the displaced youth I work with in Heidelberg. Through these experiences, I have developed what I believe is a 'transcultural identity' (Benessaieh, 2010) – an ability to morph and adapt to various environments and people – an identity that a lot of displaced persons assume just like me. This adaptability and empathy have been instrumental in my work with displaced persons, allowing me to connect and support them through their own journeys of adaptation and resilience.

Emma Maclean

While I now find myself at home in Edinburgh, I have English, Scottish, and Polish roots. My maternal grandpa came to work in the UK under what became the 1947 Polish Resettlement Act following World War 2. At this time, integration of Polish refugees was well resourced. He received funding to go through medical school and due to this always claimed that he was proud to be British. However, following his divorce from my Scottish grandmother, in his second marriage he rekindled many of the Polish traditions he had left behind. I often wonder about how these different parts of my family story have shaped me when thinking about the impacts of shifting environments, cultures, families, friends, and communities. So, when Elizabeth invited me to join her and Samuel as a co-editor of this book, I was interested in learning, alongside my colleagues, more about how music therapy and music can be shaped by and shape those who have experienced forced displacements, and their families, and the communities around them.

WHAT DO WE MEAN BY DISPLACED PERSONS?

We have chosen to use the term 'displaced persons' as an overarching term for this book. The Office of the United Nations High Commissioner for Refugees (UNHCR, 2024) describes a forcibly displaced person as someone who has been forced or obliged to leave their homes and cross an international border or move within a state or country. This may be due to having to avoid armed conflict, violence, human rights violations, or natural/human-made disasters. The concept of being 'displaced' encompasses a wide range of experiences and circumstances, often involving the forced removal from one's home and the subsequent challenges of adapting to new environments.

'Refugee' is a more widely used word, although this is a more specific term that does not include asylum seekers or internally displaced persons. While the term 'refugee' has been in use for centuries, it wasn't until the 1951 Convention related to the Status of Refugees that it gained a specific legal definition. A refugee is someone who has fled their country and has sought asylum internationally due to a well-founded fear of persecution. In contrast, the term 'displaced persons' encompasses a broader spectrum of individuals who have been forced to leave their homes for various reasons, and includes those displaced internally.

The process of seeking asylum and the policies governing it are deeply influenced by political considerations. Different countries have varying policies regarding the number of displaced persons they are willing to accept. Interestingly, some low-income countries, such as Uganda, have more welcoming policies compared to wealthier nations. For displaced persons, life is marked by uncertainty and the need for significant adaptation. This uncertainty can affect all aspects of life, from legal status to employment opportunities and social integration.

A common assumption in the literature on displacement is the association between losing one's home and experiencing trauma. This trauma can have profound effects on mental health, altering brain function, as noted by researchers like Gene-Ann Behrens in Chapter 2 of this book. However, beyond this shared experience of trauma, displaced persons are incredibly diverse. They can vary in age, nationality, and the specific circumstances that led to their displacement. Their journey and settlement processes also differ greatly, with some taking short flights and others enduring long, arduous journeys by land, sea, and air.

Some chapter authors also refer to asylum seekers. According to Amnesty International (2019), an asylum seeker is someone whose claim for international protection has not yet been finally decided by the country where it was submitted. Thus, not all asylum seekers will be recognized as refugees, but all refugees were initially asylum seekers.

Regardless of the terminology used to describe those who are at the heart of this book, we can assume that displaced persons most likely have experienced an event that was catastrophic or life-threatening and forced them to flee their homes. Those who are internally displaced may remain tantalizingly close to their former places of habitation, but unable to return to their homeplace. Many of those displaced will have embarked on a potentially dangerous journey that could have taken weeks, months, or even years to reach their host country. They now find themselves building new lives in countries that are likely to be very different from their own, thus facing new challenges in their host country.

Codrington, Iqbal, and Segal (2011) have written about the challenges of working with families from a refugee background and have proposed a discussion of the refugee journey. The refugee journey they propose serves to identify the possible life stressors in a refugee's life. It is divided into three sections: the country of origin, flight, and the new country (resettlement). In their country of origin, refugees can have experiences of grief, loss, war, and violence, as well as possible abuse or neglect. Biological predisposition to mental illnesses as well as developmental disabilities may have existed and exacerbated the effects of the stressors in their lives. As they leave their country and embark on a journey to a country of refuge, refugees may experience loss or separation from family members, loss of personal belongings, basic needs not being met, difficult experiences in their first country of asylum or refugee camps, and more. Lastly, as they arrive with or without their families in the new country of resettlement, refugees face new difficulties such as language and educational barriers, housing difficulties, cultural differences, social isolation, ongoing mental health problems, experiences of racism and discrimination, and ongoing effects of past trauma.

LITERATURE ON MUSIC THERAPY AND REFUGEES

There are currently no music therapy texts that directly address working with displaced persons as their main focus. Emma Maclean has provided a literature review of music therapy and displaced persons from the last ten years in the first chapter of this book. This provides a systematic analysis of recent work with displaced persons. Historically speaking, it seems that writings on this topic in music therapy only started at the turn of the century. Nigel Osborne, as he explains in Chapter 13 of this book, has been working with music in conflict areas since 1993, but writings about his work were only first published in 2009 (Osborne, 2009). Lang and McInerney (2002) also wrote about their work at the Pavarotti Music Centre in Bosnia which took place as early as 1998.

There were other sporadic writings on the topic in the first decade of this century. Orth (2005) summarized interventions he used in a clinical context with refugees. Storsve *et al.* (2010) gave insights into the different trajectories that children took in a music programme in a Palestinian Refugee Camp. Felsenstein (2012) operationalized a model to think about working through trauma with children from the point of view of music therapy. These are only a few examples from the literature that show that music therapists have been engaging with displaced persons for the last quarter of a century.

As mentioned earlier, displacement comes with many uncertainties and unpredictability. This is often the case for music therapists as well, and given that a big proportion of displaced persons live in the Global South, it can be assumed that there is work with this population that has not been documented, or not in academic publications at least. Zambonini and Tosto (2024) have written about the challenges of publishing from a Latin American perspective, for example. Historically, Latin America is a geographical area that has seen incredible amounts of displacement, but it was not easy to find a contributor from Latin America for this book. Eventually, Andrés Salgado Vasco was able to contribute a piece on internal displacement in Colombia. It is unlikely, though, that there has not been any work with people displaced across borders in Latin America. This is also the case in other regions of the world. While this work remains largely invisible in academic publications, we hope that in the future it may be made visible in these settings as well as through other platforms.

PUTTING THE BOOK TOGETHER

As with all journeys towards publication, there were many twists and turns in bringing this book together and the opening chapters aim to give voice to the context within which it evolved. Hala Hamdan originally hoped to offer some thoughts on trauma and displacement from the perspective of music therapy when she became displaced herself. She accepted our invitation to reflect on her lived experiences of displacement in the prelude.

Eva Marija Vukich, who was due to co-author, responds with important questions about how we include the perspectives of persons who have been displaced to shape ongoing transformations of practice and research. Following this, Emma Maclean shares a critical review of recent literature by music therapists and musicians working with displaced persons and some of the themes that this generated. Taking these contexts, and our ongoing critical discussions within the editorial team, into consideration we group the remaining contributions into three sections as follows: traversing trauma, supporting social transformations, and co-creating cultural connections.

Section 1: Traversing Trauma

The chapters in this first section all focus on trauma: what it is, how it might be experienced by displaced persons, and what might be useful for practitioners to keep in mind. In Chapter 2, Gene-Ann Behrens opens the section with a comprehensive overview of neuroscience perspectives with the aim of supporting practitioners to integrate knowledge about trauma in everyday psychosocial practice. She teaches the reader how small changes in tempo can support increasing resilience, and how reciprocal musical interactions might help to practise co-regulation. In Chapter 3, Bolette Beck, who has been involved in clinical trials researching the impact of Guided Imagery and Music (Beck *et al.*, 2017, 2018, 2021), details some case studies, sharing what is often overlooked in outcomes from randomized controlled trials. She invites the reader to travel with her and the persons she has worked with to learn more about the process of reducing symptoms of trauma and increasing well-being and safe attachments. In Chapter 4, Heidi Ahonen describes a Narrative Music Psychotherapy approach for refugees who are seeking help within community health centres related to their experiences of trauma. Finally, in Chapter 5, Sander van Goor and Evelyn Heynen outline their project, Safe & Sound. This aims to build preventative approaches for groups of children, young people, and individuals attending schools with specific provisions for new arrivals in the Netherlands. Their chapter echoes perspectives from neuroscience such as relaxation of the vagal brake with reference to 'alarm bells', and how musical responses may help to calm these.

Section 2: Supporting Social Transformations

The chapters in the second section, while still recognizing the importance of knowledge about trauma and resiliency, focus on broader themes of how music and music therapy can support increased connections, transforming both the displaced person and the context around them. Samuel Gracida and colleagues open this section in Chapter 6, providing an overview of the

Bridges programme in Heidelberg, Germany. They explore the importance of reaching beyond traditional trauma-focused interventions to offer displaced children a breadth of opportunities for therapy, and to encourage and support ongoing musical progress. Their writing suggests that each participant should have access to what they need at the right time, building towards social integration within the host country. In Chapter 7, Mitsi Ako-yunoglou similarly advocates for a community music therapy approach with refugee children in transit camps. She shares her aims to cultivate ongoing transformations from what might feel hostile at first into friendlier and safer environments. In Chapter 8, Elizabeth Coombes and Saphia Abou Amer unpick some evaluation data from training programmes in which international development aims to embed interactive therapeutic music-making to support ongoing social developments in Palestine. In the final chapter in Section 2, Andrés Salgado Vasco tells us about ongoing work in Colombia in a range of music therapy projects in which strengthening support networks and building increased community empowerment become central themes.

Section 3: Co-Creating Cultural Connections

The final section brings together four chapters that highlight the breadth of cultural connections and shared understandings that can be co-created through music. In Chapter 10, Danny Kora introduces the Songwriters' Democracy Method. The facilitator offers multiple choices for co-created songs, strengthening cross-cultural communication and guiding the displaced person to find a way to share their story through music. Elizabeth Coombes and colleagues, in Chapter 11, describe and discuss a mixed-methods research project working with displaced dyads from Ukraine now living in the UK. In Chapter 12, Emma O'Brien brings a more political perspective. Through the sharing of Moz's songwriting, recording, and distribution she invites the reader to experience how music can be a vehicle for increasing awareness of ongoing struggles faced by asylum seekers in the face of bureaucratic challenges. Nigel Osborne closes this section with his chapter, which he aptly names Songs of Travel. In this, he brings to life the cultural connections that can be co-created through musical moments between project leaders, volunteers, and children displaced by war. Here musical illustrations demonstrate how what may begin as fleeting connections can flourish into musical friendships through which moments of joy and deep despair can be shared in equal measures.

The book ends with a brief summary in which we pose questions about how this work may develop in the future and continue to offer hope for displaced persons and those who want to listen, connect, and build towards supporting ongoing social transformations.

Compiling the content of the book has been a rich and complex journey. The sheer range of experiences and sensitive nature of the work has at times felt almost overwhelming to read and absorb. Richard Gwyn, a Welsh poet, describes how immersion in the work of others can produce 'a kind of inner upheaval; a confusion brought about by plenitude for which the metaphor of sinking into sand might be appropriate' (2024, p.82). There have also been would-be contributors who have not been able to complete their submissions for a range of reasons. Sometimes work schedules have not allowed for time to write, or due to the complex life experiences of those with whom music therapists have been working, these displaced persons have been wary of their experiences being 'out there' in any form. We now invite you to read Hala Hamdan and Eva Marija Vukich's contribution about trauma and the role of music therapy in supporting the processing of displacement. Global events overtook the authors, and they tell us why they could not write what they had intended. Perhaps the publication of this text will facilitate further writing and sharing of such work; there are many more stories to be told.

REFERENCES

Amnesty International. (2019). What's the difference between a refugee and an asylum seeker? www.amnesty.org.au/refugee-and-an-asylum-seeker-difference.

Beck, B., Messell, C., Meyer, S., Cordtz, T., Simonsen, E., Søgaard, U., & Moe, T. (2017). Feasibility of trauma-focused Guided Imagery and Music with adult refugees diagnosed with PTSD: A pilot study. Nordic Journal of Music Therapy, 27(1), 67–86. http://dx.doi.org/10.1080/08098131.2017.1286368.

Beck, B. D., Lund, S. T., Søgaard, U., Simonsen, E., et al. (2018). Music therapy versus treatment as usual: Protocol of a randomized non-inferiority study with traumatized refugees diagnosed with posttraumatic stress disorder (PTSD). Trials, 19, 301. https://doi.org/10.1186/s13063-018-2662-z.

Beck, B. D., Meyer, S. L., Simonsen, E., Søgaard, U., et al. (2021). Music therapy was non-inferior to verbal standard treatment of traumatized refugees in mental health care: Results from a randomized clinical trial. European Journal of Psychotraumatology, (12)1. https://doi.org/10.1080/20008198.2021.1930960.

Benessaieh, A. (2010). Amériques Transculturelles. Ottawa, Ontario: University of Ottawa Press.

Codrington, R., Iqbal, A., & Segal, J. (2011). Lost in translation? Embracing the challenges of working with families from a refugee background. Australian and New Zealand Journal of Family Therapy (ANZJFT), 32(2), 129–143. doi:10.1375/anft.32.2.129.

Felsenstein, R. (2012). From uprooting to replanting: On post-trauma group music therapy for pre-school children. Nordic Journal of Music Therapy, 22(1), 69–85. https://doi.org/10.1080/08098131.2012.667824.

Gwyn, R. (2024). The Ambassador of Nowhere. Bridgend: Seren Books.

Lang, L. & McInerney, U. (2002). Bosnia-Herzegovina: A Music Therapy Service in a Post-War Environment. In J. Sutton (ed.) Music, Music Therapy and Trauma: International Perspectives (pp.153-174). London and Philadelphia: Jessica Kingsley Publishers.

Orth, J. (2005). Music therapy with traumatized refugees in a clinical setting. *Voices: A World Forum for Music Therapy*, 5(2).

Osborne, N. (2009). Music for Children in Zones of Conflict and Post-Conflict: A Psycho-biological Approach. In S. Malloch & C. Trevarthen (eds) *Communicative Musicality*. Oxford and New York, NY: Oxford University Press.

Storsve, V., Westbye, I. A., & Ruud, E. (2010). Hope and recognition: A music project among youth in a Palestinian refugee camp. *Voices: A World Forum for Music Therapy*, 10(1). https://doi.org/10.15845/voices.v10i1.158.

UNHCR. (2023). *Global trends report 2023*. www.unhcr.org/global-trends-report-2023.

UNHCR. (2024). *Who is a 'refugee'?* www.unhcr.org/uk/refugees.

Zambonini, J. P. & Tosto, V. (2024). Decolonial perspectives from Latin America: Initial core concepts and special issue announcement. *Voices: A World Forum for Music Therapy*, 24(2). https://doi.org/10.15845/voices.v24i2.4323.

Prelude

*A Sudden Displacement Due to War in Palestine-Israel,
and its Impact on Present and Future Plans*

Hala Hamdan

It was meant to be just another ordinary Saturday, the warmth of the morning sun gently caressing my face through the window. However, 7 October 2023 will forever be etched in my memory as a day of profound changes, both personally and professionally. The tranquility of my Saturday morning routine was shattered at 6.30am by the jarring cacophony of alarms, rockets, and frantic calls from loved ones.

Before that fateful day, my life had been marked by stability and routine. As a certified music therapist, I dedicated my weekdays to working with primarily Jewish Israeli children facing emotional, physical, and social challenges in a public clinic in Jaffa and Tel Aviv. Weekends were reserved for cherished moments with family and leisurely strolls along the picturesque streets of my hometown.

Being a Palestinian, I have grown accustomed to periodic disruptions caused by conflict and violence in my homeland. I was born in the Israeli territories, and I had already experienced some wars and other violent incidents in my country. I am 'used' to having my routine disrupted. I am 'used' to feeling internal conflicts. These inner conflicts are more frequent in times of war and violence between the Israelis and Palestinians. I am 'used' to the fears, sadness, and anger that rise up when things go badly. I am 'used' to being interrupted as a music therapist, to losing days of work, to knowing how to handle things with the children attending therapy online, when it is not safe to meet in the clinic. I am 'used' to recovering pretty fast when it is over, diving into my routine again and focusing on my future plans. Yet the magnitude and duration of this war are unlike anything I have experienced before.

As the weeks passed, it became increasingly clear that life as I knew it would never be the same again. Faced with the grim reality of an extended conflict, I made the difficult decision to seek refuge in Europe, yearning for a semblance of safety and stability. I was always passionate about the effect of music therapy on those who have been forcibly displaced as well as people who live in areas affected by war. As a result of this, I established the SADA project[1] along with Eva Marija Vukich. With this project, we aim to provide consultations for the integration of music therapy tools by psychosocial teams who work directly with refugees around the globe. I never imagined that I would one day be in the position of being displaced from my homeland, and writing a personal reflection on it for this book!

Even though I was thousands of miles away from home, my commitment to my clients remained unwavering. Through virtual sessions, I endeavoured to provide them with the support and solace they desperately needed amid the chaos. Despite the big challenge, I chose to continue these online sessions. I had to cope with the dissonance between my professional ethics and my personal feelings towards what my people were going through in Gaza. I felt a huge responsibility towards my clients, to be there for them in this scary and chaotic period. I felt privileged to be their anchor and to maintain some kind of routine for them from their previously normal life. Yet, the storm and grief I was facing inside my soul were always there during my work time, being a Palestinian who was witnessing massive violence towards my people. It was sometimes triggering and overwhelming for me when, for example, I was treating an Israeli child who might express a lot of negativity towards my people. But I was on duty; my ethics and my true love for my clients have shown me the path and given me the power to contain and hold them. I was able to feel empathy towards them, knowing that they were only scared children. I have also to confess that this helped me as well. I felt I could still do the thing I loved the most: music therapy. I felt that supporting them continued to support me and my well-being. Supporting my clients while I needed support as well empowered me as an individual and as a professional therapist during an emergency situation. It also helped me to feel significant and provided a sense of being in control, somehow, at a time when I felt I had lost any control over my own life. Added to this, most of the parents asked me to keep the sessions going, witnessing the challenges that their children were going through and asking for my therapeutic guidance and support.

Navigating the complexities of displacement while maintaining my clinical practice tested my resilience like never before. Suppressing my own fears and anxieties, I assumed the role of another caregiver, offering a beacon of

---

1   www.linkedin.com/company/90220158

hope to those in need. Each session was a delicate balance between providing emotional support and safeguarding my own mental well-being. Eventually, the need to prioritize my own mental health compelled me to bid farewell to my clients and embark on a new chapter in a foreign land. The transition was fraught with uncertainty and challenges, yet it offered a glimmer of hope for a brighter future.

As I grapple with the realities of rebuilding my life in a new country, I am reminded of the resilience inherent in every displaced person. Through my own journey, I have gained a deeper understanding of the profound impact of sudden upheaval on both personal and professional aspirations. I have been living in a new country for the last three months, and all I brought with me are some clothes and a guitar. I was moving between seven apartments during the initial few weeks and only recently settled down in a new home. I have not yet played guitar here; I find that I haven't had the capacity for it, with having to create a new life here from scratch. I have also been scared to let my feelings out through playing the guitar. As a music therapist, I know that music can do that, and I have not yet been ready to face these hard feelings. I can imagine now how displaced persons might not have the capacity to create and observe their feelings at a time when their lives are dominated by this struggle. Energy must be saved for settling down. The most significant need is to feel safe, to feel at home.

Throughout this period and building my new life, I have not had time for prior commitments, such as writing a chapter for this wonderful book. This was to be entitled 'Towards a Critical Self-Reflexivity in Music Therapy Practice with Refugee and Migrant Communities', and my colleague Eva Marija Vukich and I were intending to share case examples and recommendations for practice. There was to have been a salient emphasis on the responsibility of the music therapist to engage in constant self-reflection, while critically questioning their motivations, roles, and the power dynamics inherent in their practice, with the ultimate aim to enhance therapeutic outcomes and ensure dignified and ethical treatment.

Not having enough time, space, and capacity due to my sudden relocation in another country, I had to face the reality that I was not able to meet previous commitments, such as writing the chapter. This made me feel frustrated, that my life had been cut and interrupted by external circumstances that I had no control over. Although not able to contribute to the previous topic of this chapter, I am glad and feel a sense of gratitude that the editors invited me to reflect on my experience of going through a sudden relocation due to a war and to express how it affected me in my personal life, as well as my professional life as a music therapist.

I understand today how anxious people who are forced to live far away from their homes can be, how scary it is to adapt to a new culture and new language, to invent yourself from scratch, to be worried about your financial situation, and how unstable it feels to be forced to change so many plans that you had for the near and far future. I understand how hard it is to miss your mother's hug, your niece when she jumps with happiness when she meets you, miss the Zaatar and olives, the beautiful landscapes that only exist in your home. I miss anything that is familiar and, of course, family and friends.

Despite the upheaval and uncertainty, I remain steadfast in my belief that every displaced person possesses the resilience to forge a new path towards a more peaceful and fulfilling future. I trust that music therapy will be part of my new life and that I can use my own experiences to support new clients. While I work on this, my own resilience and understanding of myself continue to grow.

Eva Marija Vukich

Hala and I had intended to write a chapter on the practice of reflexivity as music therapists, motivated by our own meaningful processes of unpacking our intersecting identities and observing positionalities of power and privilege as it relates to designing and engaging in music therapy with those affected by armed conflict. Instead, the events of 7 October 2023 and onwards have painfully altered Hala's homeland, and millions of Palestinians are being subjected to life-threatening warfare while global powers refuse to intervene, despite tremendous demonstrations of anti-war solidarity and calls for ceasefire across the world.

My friend and co-writer experienced her world turned upside down, enduring ever-persistent cycles of grief, re-orientation of resources, and nervous system regulation, until taking the fateful steps to relocate to another country, a move which does not necessarily guarantee a lessening of those cycles. These are familiar processes; we intimately recognize the forced migration prognosis – and although it is profoundly heartbreaking to bear witness to such an experience, it is also an honour to breathe together and share the grief, singing 'no more pain, we've had enough'. In a way, our chapter and work aims were also put into the liminal space between life and death, embodiment and disembodiment, culture and politics, possibility and impossibility, love and hate.

In the spirit of reflexivity, it is worthwhile to pause and see in what ways our identities are tied to these devastating events, in turn rendering the chapter unwritable, and how this implicates the book in terms of representation (or lack thereof) of those directly impacted by conflict or other forces that compel migration and resistance. This unfortunate phenomenon is visible in much of academic writing about vulnerable people, wherein those of the ingroup are rarely the ones seen directing the research question nor publishing the articles about their group. This has prompted activist movements such as 'nothing about us without us' (Waldschmidt et al., 2015) as seen in disability justice spaces. Of course, it is not that those in the vulnerable group are not willing to reflect and theorize, particularly since their vulnerability is likely tethered to liberation and justice. Instead, the issue seems to be in part that our professional standards of publication, such as written texts and books, are intrinsically difficult formats to undertake during periods of instability. For contributors in processes of active displacement, it is most likely not feasible for them to sit down and write, in addition to considerations of pre-existing learning disabilities or other conditions that make this format of dissemination quite unbearable. However, these are voices and perspectives that are crucial in furthering this discussion within the music therapy community.

We have been observing a kerfuffle in our music therapy community as a few take more polarized stances in response to the siege on Gaza, while the vast majority, including professional associations, seem to tiptoe around clear statements that would align with international human rights experts in the United Nations and International Court of Justice, and those compelling reports outlining genocidal actions, including internal and transborder forced displacement (Albanese, 2024). How have we come to this moment where there is something contentious in health practitioners publicly stating that people should not be forcibly displaced within or outside borders? It feels like a revealing moment wherein our collective principles are being tested, ultimately presenting an opportunity for collective reflexivity. As this ambitious book centres on those who have experienced displacement and the socio-political processes of finding well-being, it calls the reader forward to recognize their political voice that co-exists with client advocacy, and which is at risk when the experiences of the displaced are de-politicized.

Hala and I offer these prompts to spur collective reflexivity:

- How might we transform solidarity and manifestations of mutual aid within our professional community and in our wider political network of music therapy users and advocates? Can you imagine an effective mutual aid model for our community?

- What does equity look like within knowledge production structures, particularly in research and learning about marginalized groups? What practical modifications might allow for increased inclusion and leadership by those with lived experience?

- As music therapists working within refugee and displaced communities, to what extent do we have an ethical responsibility to advocate for their rights on societal levels?

We hope these questions enable a deeper reflexive stance from colleagues, and that this book will offer further ways of exploring how we can work with displaced persons.

REFERENCES

Albanese, F. (2024). Anatomy of a Genocide – Report of the Special Rapporteur on the situation of human rights in the Palestinian territory occupied since 1967 to Human Rights Council. United Nations. www.un.org/unispal/document/anatomy-of-a-genocide-report-of-the-special-rapporteur-on-the-situation-of-human-rights-in-the-palestinian-territory-occupied-since-1967-to-human-rights-council-advance-unedited-version-a-hrc-55.

Waldschmidt, A., Karačić, A., Sturm, A., & Dins, T. (2015). 'Nothing about us without us' disability rights activism in European countries: A comparative analysis. *Moving the Social*, 53, 103–138. https://doi.org/10.13154/mts.53.2015.103-138.

CHAPTER 1

A Critical Review of the Literature on Using Music and Music Therapy with Displaced Persons

EMMA MACLEAN

INTRODUCTION

This critical review provides an overview of literature published between 2014 and 2024 on music therapy and music with displaced persons, including asylum seekers and refugees. The term 'displaced persons' recognizes the transitional nature of having to leave one's home due to political disruptions including war. It includes 'asylum seekers' who may be temporarily seeking refuge and those who have been granted refugee status.

The search[1] identified two systematic reviews. The first, by Henderson *et al.* (2017), reviews research exploring the role of music participation for positive health and well-being outcomes with migrant populations. In contrast, Bernard and Dvorak (2023) review research on the use of music to address trauma with refugees. Research papers identified by this critical review showed a continuum of outcomes from more medically informed models of 'treating' trauma to contextual and ecological perspectives.

Beck and Messel *et al.* (2018) and Beck and Meyer *et al.* (2021), in their randomized control trial, demonstrate that attending between 12 and 20

---

1   The literature was searched in the EBSCO database using the terms 'music' OR 'music therapy' AND 'displaced person' OR 'refugee' OR 'asylum seeker'. Papers published before 2014 and dissertations that have not been peer reviewed for publication were excluded. The literature included had all been published in the English language, which may mean that some important papers written in other languages were also excluded.

trauma-focused Music and Imagery (tr-MI) sessions is not inferior to treatment as usual in mental health care with displaced persons. Heynen *et al.* (2022), in a mixed methods process evaluation, demonstrate the benefits of a Dutch programme, Safe & Sound, in decreasing negative affect in refugee children while also building social connectedness and a safe environment in which teachers' abilities to respond to children's needs were developed. Ahonen and Mongillo Desideri (2014) use phenomenological and narrative methods to generate increased understanding of how music facilitated sharing difficult emotions during resettlement of female refugees in Canada. Skinner (2022) uses ethnographical approaches to get closer to the experiences of three young men living in the Occupied West Bank, detailing affordances of rap to express difficult emotions within masculine and authoritarian environments. Using phenomenological microanalysis, Jin (2016) brings out themes from interviews with music therapists and music facilitators about their experiences of facilitating groups with displaced persons in Australia. Chantah *et al.* (2024) use an online survey to compare experiences of displaced musicians and non-musicians in Germany, demonstrating the benefits of group music-making for acculturation. Gever *et al.* (2022), through evaluation surveys, demonstrate some positive impacts of social media-based arts therapies to support the re-integration of Nigerians to their home country following evacuation from Ukraine during the war.

The search also identified case studies and case study research illustrating what happens in music therapy, psychotherapy incorporating music, or music-based projects. These include Enge and Stige's (2022) study of refugee children's experiences of music therapy in Norway, Coombes' (2018) experiences of building a new project to use music therapy with families in Wales, and Carnevali *et al.*'s (2024) reflections on incorporating psychotherapy using music with adolescents in Italy. From community music perspectives, Kenny (2022) writes about facilitator experiences of music-based projects in asylum-seeker accommodation centres in Ireland, while De Quadros and Vu (2017) explore experiences within choral and music projects across Sweden.

Other papers propose or evaluate theoretical models. Mallon and Hoog Antink (2021) present the COVER model of music therapy: **CO**ntext-sensitive classification model for music therapeutic inter**VE**ntions with **R**efugees. Marsh (2017) builds on research with refugees in Australia and cross-cultural play in other countries to present a model for music and play. Coombes and Tombs-Katz (2017) and Parker *et al.* (2020) evaluate skill-sharing projects which aim to build music therapy and music resources with displaced persons in international communities.

Finally, perspectives, comments, and opinions invite readers to consider the potentials of music therapy with displaced persons (Krüger & Diaz, 2023), increase reflexivity around international development practices (Bolger & Skewes McFerran, 2020), and avoid the traps of what Comte (2016) terms *neocolonialism*.

THEMES

The review generated two main themes. First is the focus on music-based 'interventions' that can 'treat' trauma and associated 'symptoms'. The quotation marks emphasize the positivist lens used by research studies in healthcare settings, including psychiatric units (Beck *et al.*, 2018, 2021), in relation to reducing the impact of trauma. In contrast to this, broader themes appear to shape decision-making in music and music therapy projects in relation to ongoing social transformations and increased cultural connections. These will be explored in more detail throughout the chapter to illustrate a growing continuum of practices and practitioners working through and in music and music therapy with displaced persons.

Trauma and post-traumatic stress disorder in healthcare settings

Recognizing the adverse experiences of living in and escaping zones of conflict, much of the published literature on music and music therapy focuses on alleviating symptoms of trauma (Beck & Meyer *et al.*, 2021; Bernard & Dvorak, 2023; Enge & Stige, 2022; Gever *et al.*, 2022; Heynen *et al.*, 2022). These authors recognize that displaced persons can be more likely than the average population to seek support from mental health or psychiatric services (Beck & Messel *et al.*, 2018; Beck & Meyer *et al.*, 2021).

Beck and Messel *et al.* (2018) and Beck and Meyer *et al.* (2021) evidenced that tr-MI can support a reduction in avoidance, better quality of sleep with fewer nightmares, and an increase in social interaction. Their findings suggest that building within a therapeutic relationship can increase a person's ability to regulate emotions and change an emotional state outside therapy sessions. The research also found that attrition rates were much lower for music therapy, with the use of receptive music within a therapeutic relationship appearing to provide increased motivation to continue attending psychological therapy.

Bernard and Dvorak (2023) note that approaches to using music to address trauma are mainly measured using psychological outcomes and demonstrate changes such as improvement in coping strategies, well-being, sleep, and decreased trauma. Such studies reflect increased use of self-report measures to demonstrate effectiveness of interventions within health and social care settings. Beck and Meyer *et al.* (2021) use the Harvard Trauma Questionnaire (Mollica *et al.*, 1992) and Gever *et al.* (2022) utilize the International Trauma Questionnaire (Cloitre, 2018). These questionnaires capture the extent to which problems or deficits created by traumatic experiences remain present, such as having recurring nightmares, being 'super-alert', feeling worthless or like a failure, and avoiding situations and/or interactions.

Tick-box responses can be a quick and easy-to-administer way of demonstrating change over time but have been criticized for individualizing distress based on diagnostic criteria (Puras, 2020). Recent shifts within the music therapy profession towards anti-oppressive practice (Baines, 2013), decolonization (The Colonialism and Music Therapy Interlocutors (CAMTI) Collective, 2022), and cultural humility (Edwards, 2022) invite practitioners to challenge power dynamics within medical models. Building on human-rights-based approaches, Comte (2016) suggests that an over-emphasis on a trauma narrative with therapists taking on an expert role could dehumanize practice and fail to recognize experiences of displaced persons having been powerless and in fear. For Comte (2016), music therapists trained within the milieu of Western philosophies can over-emphasize the homogeneity of a refugee population. She warns against assumptions that a displaced person's trauma narrative should be privileged over cultural identity and acculturation.

Medical models, as Comte (2016) points out, triumph absence of disease as well-being; however, more community-based models may look towards spirituality, transformations, acculturation, and integration and alternative methods or tools for research and evaluation. Ahonen and Mongrillo Desideri (2014) take a broader phenomenological approach, analysing content of sessions and interviewing participants at the end of the project to narrate what happened in music therapy with displaced women aged 30–60 in Canada. Their findings recognize the complexities of working with displaced persons who may have experienced multiple losses, including loss of loved ones, security, finances, health, hobbies, and the landscape and traditions of their country of origin. They demonstrate the transformational potential of the narration of trauma in groups. Such experiences can create spaces for what might not have been heard, enabling participants to build new identities as survivors. Chantah *et al.* (2020) show that actively making music in groups supports acculturation using the Riverside Stress Acculturation Inventory (Miller *et al.*, 2011) and Frankfurt Acculturation Scale (Bongard *et al.*, 2020). Parker *et al.* (2020) reflect on the challenges presented by the growth of neoliberalism, including the need for financial accountability, monitoring, and evaluation. They suggest that rather than measuring change within the individual, action-learning methodologies can support ongoing active social change within communities.

Trauma and post-traumatic stress disorder in educational contexts

Within school settings the impact of post-traumatic distress on mental health and well-being is often observed in challenging 'behaviours' such as increased aggression, anxiety, and concerns for safety (Heynen *et al.*, 2022) or pupils struggling in academic or social areas (Enge & Stige, 2022). Using a visual analogue scale, Heynen *et al.* (2022) demonstrate that music therapy reduces negative affect while also demonstrating broader impact on the wider learning environment through a classroom climate questionnaire.

Developmental trauma can be complex and systemic and can include exposure to traumatic events alongside potential neglect from distressed or absent caregivers. Children who have experienced multiple adversities can often become easily dysregulated and need to experience co-regulation or a regulating social environment. Enge and Stige (2022) demonstrate that affect regulation within a musical relationship can be an important part of working with displaced children with developmental trauma, while Coombes (2018) touches on the importance of attachment theory. It may be that increasing focus on the availability of main caregivers may provide another lens to evaluate relational models which support family units and communities, rather than individuals.

Trauma-informed practice and establishing trust through musical connections

Through the lens of trauma-informed practice, the therapeutic relationship is essential to facilitate trust and ensure that the displaced person attending is heard and validated. Building a secure therapeutic alliance can increase epistemic trust and improve social integration for persons who often have tendencies, due to the experiences of trauma, to avoid social connections. Bernard and Dvorak (2023) note that establishing trust between the therapist and person attending requires time. The importance of psychodynamic knowledge becomes increasingly apparent as frameworks and boundaries are created through reliable and predictable timing of sessions. Enge and Stige (2022) and Coombes (2018) advocate for the use of repeated songs or activities to provide safe predictable environments and enable increasing moments of attunement. Marsh (2017) notes that the predictability afforded by musical structures can be important for children who are negotiating social uncertainty, enabling them to 'connect with others, draw comfort, express emotion and develop self-esteem, identity and resilience' (p.70). Beck and Messel *et al.* (2018) also highlight the importance of careful decision-making when choosing music. They advocate that, to begin with, receptive music experiences should promote stabilization (phase one) before more explorative profiles, in which the music chosen aims to stimulate connections with the trauma experiences and emotional containment (phases two to four).

In their paper about incorporating music in psychotherapy, Carnevali *et al.* (2024) echo that music is intersubjective. For them, engaging in music can enable emotional journeys and transformations. Their choice to use rap music reflects assumptions that this style empowers agency and resistance of authoritarianism. In their project, collaborative working between psychoanalysts and a professional rapper aims to build a stable container in the community. Here, psychoeducation becomes an important element, with 'arrival' and 'host' participants learning together about tolerance, racism, and discrimination, leading to a co-created educational performance for the whole community. Skinner (2022) also identifies power in the use of rap music, particularly for young men. She suggests that this style can build connections, kinship, and community with other males. For her, this can enable agency, and spaces for participants to make their own decisions and express anger in a safer and often more contained manner.

Language appropriation and transitional identities

With language acquisition also comes a recognition that new arrivals may be interested in building a new identity and letting go of what they have had to persevere before flight from their home country (De Quadros & Vu, 2017). Musical games can bring together multiple identities in complementing the cultural heritage of displaced persons with Western repertoire (Parker *et al.*, 2020). De Quadros and Vu (2017) identify that choir leaders or music educators may choose songs often equated with the early years, which offer simple language in repeated phrases to assist refugees with language acquisition. Similarly, Heynen *et al.* (2022) advocate for music as a non-verbal method of communicating difficult emotions while also heralding the importance of participants learning Dutch through musical activities.

Working in groups and building social capital

In their position paper, Krüger and Diaz (2023) write that groups support the building of connections with others who have had similar experiences. For Heynen *et al.* (2022), preventative group-work approaches build strengths and emotional resilience, while also providing a space for therapists to notice when someone is struggling and may benefit from more individualized support. Enge and Stige (2022) advocate that community music therapy approaches (CoMT) can offer continuity and stability for children who need safety, nurture, and a sense of mastery. They propose that by bringing together knowledge of trauma-informed ways of working, and resource-oriented and educational approaches, music therapists can nurture refugee children who are not successfully integrating with others, providing opportunities in one-to-one and small groups to build increased readiness to engage with others.

Building a shared repertoire together can strengthen trust while also forming an important part of integration and becoming part of a community of practice. Parker *et al.* (2020) suggest that the building blocks of inclusion – *sharing* and *co-operating* – are promoted when hosting and displaced citizens actively engage together in making music. They advocate for music's ability to create connections and nurture interactions between participants, while also building on Small's (1998) concept of *musicking* as a political act, which happens within a field of action connecting persons and building social capital. Enge and Stige (2022) show that engagement with popular and well-known music can support refugees to integrate within pop music, which for young people can also become cultural capital.

Ahonen and Mongillo Desideri (2014) outline ways that music psychotherapy can incorporate integrated approaches, including Guided Imagery in Music, to bring participants together to share difficult emotions including loss, fear, anxiety, pain, and guilt. For them, group experiences afford different perspectives which encourage acceptance and hope. Jin (2016) identifies that sharing musical identities and learning how someone from a different culture 'musicks' can contribute to humanizing practices. However, she also advises therapists to engage with self-care to avoid vicarious trauma and burnout highlighting the complexities and multiple layers within such work.

Supporting ongoing social transformations and increased cultural connections

Through the lens of participatory music projects (Henderson *et al.*, 2017) the focus appears to shift towards cultural maintenance and integration, inclusiveness, and acceptance. Community connections and acculturation gain importance (Chantah *et al.*, 2024; De Quadros & Vu, 2017) and decision-making focuses on how music can create environments and spaces to build new relationships, and welcome and integrate displaced persons.

In examining how Swedish choral directors and musical educators seek to include refugees through creating a hospitable community music environment, De Quadros and Vu (2017) focus on the community and social and political contexts within which each project takes place. Recognizing that Sweden was, until recently, mostly homogenous as a country and that not everyone has welcomed the recent rapid influx of refugees, the musical relationship becomes about integration, community establishment, empowerment, and humanity. Music creates spaces that extend beyond tolerance. Participants actively engage with one another, notice each other's humanness, and build relationships. Coffee, cake, and socialization (*fika* in Sweden) after the singing becomes an important part of such community music groups, providing another way to learn about identities, with participants sharing different foods. Heynen *et al.* (2022) similarly contextualize their project within a wider political response to hosting refugees in the Netherlands through additional support aimed at assisting teachers to integrate new and possibly temporary arrivals.

Integration and acculturation

The World Health Organization (2021) in its guidance for person-centred and human rights-based community mental health services emphasizes the importance of building meaningful connections with local communities to support mental well-being. De Quadros and Vu (2017) argue that established musical community choirs in Sweden provide a different way of actively welcoming and integrating new arrivals. Group singing builds connections in playful and creative ways that can ripple out into other community activities. Nevertheless, they also recognize that selecting songs can bring challenges. Leaders may want to use songs to build a new 'home' while recognizing other 'homes' which may have different languages, rhythms, and tempos. In contrast, Marsh (2017) suggests that as forced and voluntary migrants, children often experience and internalize more than one cultural identity. Her experiences are that safe musical spaces can facilitate ways of sharing and exploring multiple or fluid identities.

While acculturation can sometimes mean assimilating to new host culture, Chantah *et al.* (2024) show through their survey-based research that participation in community music groups can orient participants to the host country without loss of culture of origin. However, the literature suggests that it may not always be easy to engage participants. Kenny (2022) noted many challenges in promoting group singing with asylum seekers in Ireland, including high turnover and mental health challenges. The most successful Song Seeking projects were able to capitalize on participants' interests and enable leaders to emerge from within the group, facilitating increased motivation for others to attend. Kenny recognizes the risks of 'othering' in community-based projects while also noticing how bearing witness in bigger performances can enable empowerment and agency. However, De Quadros and Vu (2017) question to what extent Western approaches of performativity and group dynamics in organized choirs can make refugees feel 'at home', if the country of origin has very different cultures of group singing.

Professionalization of music therapy in many Westernized countries has celebrated improvisation as a fundamental aspect (Sutton, 2020). However, Comte (2016) criticizes music therapists for assuming improvised music can transcend cultural barriers and create meaningful dialogues between host and participant. She suggests that to facilitate anti-oppressive practices, culturally informed musical vocabularies need to be shared through careful listening and shared playing.

Enge and Stige (2022) and Heynen *et al.* (2022) argue that building a shareable musical repertoire can support a sense of belonging and create connections with the wider school community. For them, it appears to be the playful and improvisational nature which is co-created within such flexible repertoires that facilitates integration and acculturation. This reflects Marsh's (2017) suggestions that within agreed frameworks, creative collaboration can build moments within which children, whose opportunities for agency have been limited, feel empowered. Henderson *et al.* (2016) similarly conclude in their systematic review that participatory music projects can build a cultural platform within which displaced persons can make sense of their lives, including ongoing social transitions.

Cultural responsiveness and cultural humility

Bernard and Dvorak (2023) write that music therapists must approach differences with cultural sensitivity (consciousness and understanding), humility (respect and openness to learn), and responsiveness (integrating cultural factors into practice).

Beck and Meyer *et al.* (2021), in their quantitative research with displaced persons, demonstrate responsiveness in their approach to implementing tr-MI. This approach traditionally incorporates the use of playlists to guide the participant through different therapeutic phases, including stabilization and exploration. In their research protocol Beck and Messel *et al.* (2018) recognize that practitioners need to be aware when Western music typically used in listening profiles is not meaningful. To overcome this barrier, preparatory steps include establishing an intercultural meeting in which practitioners use available resources, including the knowledge of translators, to find appropriate pieces of music from the person attending's country of birth.

However, it may be that cultural sensitivity requires more than careful repertoire choices. De Quadros and Vu (2017) ask whether hierarchical power relations in choirs can, in contrast to supporting inclusion, emphasize the distance between cultures. While they note spontaneous examples of individual refugees sharing songs from their homelands with other members of Swedish choirs in an *ad hoc* manner, they also recognize that songs in the home languages of displaced choir members were not included in the repertoire. Edwards (2022) advises on the importance of ambiguity and discomfort when we approach projects with humility. Cultural identity linked to dynamic interactions between the different groups of which we are all members must be dynamic and ongoing.

Music therapists working with displaced persons will often begin as outsiders within marginalized communities. Coombes (2018) describes her 'outsider' research visits that she makes to South Wales communities where asylum seekers have been housed. Recognizing her sense of feeling lost helps to deepen her emotional resonance with the work through careful working through of the countertransference. She recognizes a sense of fragmentation which the mothers may be experiencing and could be impacting on their ability to form healthy attachment styles with their children. Staying with difficult moments with curiosity and interest appears here to reflect cultural humility. Psychodynamic theory may offer a way for music therapists and music practitioners to digest, contain, and work with difficult emotions in a more manageable form. Coombes' (2018) example suggests that the mothers notice, not the expertise of the therapist, but the eagerness to listen, to learn about them, and create spaces to share experiences.

Where sharing is a strength of work with displaced persons, holding diverse groups from multiple cultures can be seen as a limitation. Heynen *et al.* (2022) notice that a common factor for displaced persons is that they have lost their social network. This can be a stressor for developing what the medical profession term mental health 'disorders' and requiring increased access to health professionals and interventions. Here, individual work may be more suitable, with Beck and Messel *et al.* (2018) noting that their study includes displaced persons from Iraq, Afghanistan, Syria, and Iran seeking psychiatric support in Denmark. Many authors herald the importance of being heard by another person. Both in individual work and in groups a process of generative listening can offer new and different ways to create something together. Building a song or recording together (Heynen *et al.*, 2022) or working towards a concert (Kenny, 2022) can provide an artefact which represents a new, supportive relationship or community.

Stepped approaches

Krüger and Diaz (2023), Enge and Stige (2022), and Parker *et al.* (2020) advocate for music therapy as an intervention that can help displaced children and young persons to experience emotional regulation in small social activities with the hope of strengthening coping strategies for wider engagement in community music-making and everyday life. Increasing ability to negotiate how to participate in small social activities and building a shared repertoire is thought to help with ongoing transformations.

Two articles propose named models or approaches, which build on moving through different stages. Mallon and Hoog Antink (2021) propose their COVER model for working in refugee reception centres and follow-on camps in Hamburg in three stages. In this model, enabling early intervention focuses on sharing music and being heard in large open groups, not in a psychiatric setting but where displaced persons are based. Being witnessed by others seems more appropriate when the future holds ongoing uncertainties. The first stage thus enables the displaced person still in transition to be simply seen and heard. Naming this 'Listen to me', practitioners are encouraged to notice the mixed feelings that are heard, including sadness, hopelessness, and frustration alongside hope and expectations. In the next stage, 'Listen to each other', used in follow-on camps, increased importance is placed on facilitating social connections with those who have had similar experiences. The final stage, 'Listen to yourself', follows when there is increased stability in the host country and the displaced person is more ready to engage in-depth one-to-one therapeutic approaches to look at self, resources, and needs.

Heynen *et al.* (2022) offer a similar model for school settings in their Safe & Sound intervention. In this, offering classroom-based preventative group work enables all displaced children to be heard and make music, while highlighting those who are struggling and may benefit from more tailored individual interventions. One could argue that there are similarities between this stepped approach and trauma-informed ways of working that recognize the need for safety and stabilization before focusing on, and accepting, traumatic experiences and being able to move forwards into the here and now (Beck & Messel *et al.*, 2018; Beck & Meyer *et al.*, 2021).

Skill sharing and empowering ongoing wider ripples

Within the broader global context, music therapists and musicians often choose to travel to share their skills with the aim of empowering local project leaders, teachers, and others to work with people with disabilities and/or persons who have been displaced. Parker *et al.* (2020) demonstrate through their ethnographic study that skill-sharing projects can resource environments and support local project leaders to build spaces which have the potential not just to be therapeutic, but to empower ongoing social change. In Palestinian refugee camps in Lebanon, they overcame many barriers, including limited spaces, limited resources, and low levels of musical education, to build safe and welcoming environments for large groups of children to engage in musical activities. Coombes and Tombs-Katz (2017) evaluate similar exchanges in the Occupied Palestine Territories curated by Music as Therapy International (MasT), with a focus on sustainability. They focus on what motivates trainers to attend six-week training programmes and to what extent they can continue to embed skills in ongoing developments. Bolger and Skewes McFerran (2020) suggest that 'visitor' practitioners should engage in dialogues around practical and ethical issues which enable or create barriers to maximizing sustainability. When done well, Parker *et al.* (2020) notice many benefits for the host country. Training young adults as music leaders to work with younger members of the displaced community can build increased self-confidence, agency, and sustainability, and reduce the impact of risk factors, such as domestic violence and drug and alcohol abuse, which can lead to young people joining armed groups.

FINAL THOUGHTS

The literature suggests a continuum from psychotherapy treatment models (Ahonen & Mongillo Desideri, 2014; Carnevali *et al.*, 2024) to more community music therapy models (Enge & Stige, 2022) and music as a facilitator of community integration. In the latter, the role of music and musicking facilitates play (Jin, 2016; Marsh, 2017; Parker *et al.*, 2020), inspires creativity, and creates spaces in which participants can share traumatic experiences. The literature suggests that psychodynamic theory may add strength and understanding which enables the practitioner to process, contain, and be present with difficult emotions from traumatic experiences, which, as Jin (2016) expresses, can support the music therapist, or practitioner, to avoid vicarious trauma and burnout.

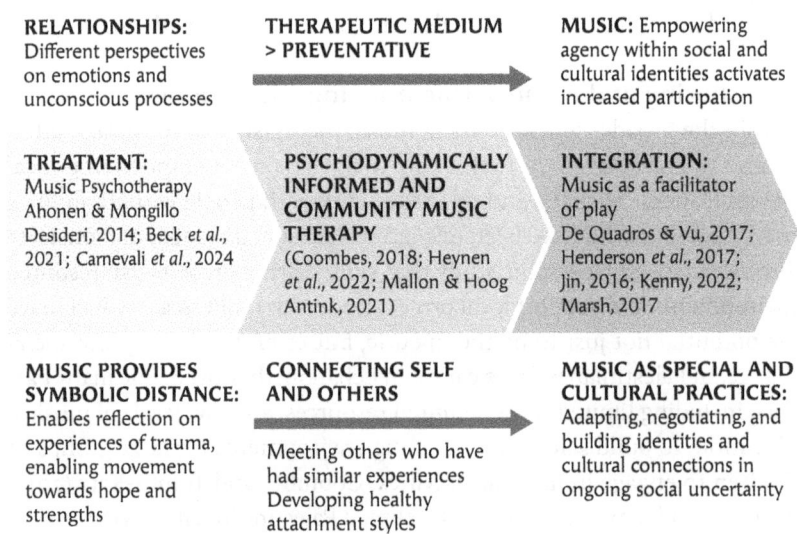

RELATIONSHIPS: Different perspectives on emotions and unconscious processes

THERAPEUTIC MEDIUM > PREVENTATIVE

MUSIC: Empowering agency within social and cultural identities activates increased participation

TREATMENT: Music Psychotherapy Ahonen & Mongillo Desideri, 2014; Beck *et al.*, 2021; Carnevali *et al.*, 2024

PSYCHODYNAMICALLY INFORMED AND COMMUNITY MUSIC THERAPY (Coombes, 2018; Heynen *et al.*, 2022; Mallon & Hoog Antink, 2021)

INTEGRATION: Music as a facilitator of play De Quadros & Vu, 2017; Henderson *et al.*, 2017; Jin, 2016; Kenny, 2022; Marsh, 2017

MUSIC PROVIDES SYMBOLIC DISTANCE: Enables reflection on experiences of trauma, enabling movement towards hope and strengths

CONNECTING SELF AND OTHERS

Meeting others who have had similar experiences Developing healthy attachment styles

MUSIC AS SPECIAL AND CULTURAL PRACTICES: Adapting, negotiating, and building identities and cultural connections in ongoing social uncertainty

Figure 1.1: Approaches underpinning music therapy and music projects with displaced persons

Approaches and facilitator training

While this review only included papers written in the English language, it is evident that there is a breadth of music and music therapy approaches being used with displaced persons. This spectrum of course exists within a global context where there are many different levels of professionalization, and varying recognition of qualifications required to use the title 'music therapist'. It is important to recognize that there are also different levels of training in different countries, for example a Bachelor's degree in the Netherlands (Heynen *et al.*, 2022) in contrast with a Master's level training in the UK and Australia. It is often in the countries where musical training is under-resourced that skill-sharing projects flourish (Coombes & Tombs-Katz, 2017; Parker *et al.*, 2020), but the literature suggests that practitioners should continue to consider practical and ethical implications to build towards sustainable models of global education.

Building bridges

Krüger and Diaz (2023) are not alone in asking how we might build bridges between the uses of music in everyday life and music therapy as treatment for those in need of acute help and support. With ongoing technological advances there may also be increasing opportunities to promote and share the arts therapies via social media (Gever *et al.*, 2022). However, we must continue to create spaces for displaced persons to be heard, to share decision-making, and to co-create projects, models, and approaches that bring benefits and ongoing transformations for individuals and communities.

REFERENCES

Ahonen, H. & Mongillo Desideri, A. (2014). Heroines' journey – emerging story by refugee women during group analytic music therapy. *Voices: A World Forum for Music Therapy*, 14(1). https://doi.org/10.15845/voices.v14i1.686.

Baines, S. (2013). Music therapy as an anti-oppressive practice. *The Arts in Psychotherapy*, 40(1), 1–5. https://doi.org/10.1016/j.aip.2012.09.003.

Beck, B., Messel, C., Lund Meyer, S., Oluf Cordtz, T., *et al.* (2018). Feasibility of trauma-focused Guided Imagery and Music with adult refugees diagnosed with PTSD: A pilot study. *Nordic Journal of Music Therapy*, 27(1), 67–86. https://doi.org/10.1080/08098131.2017.1286368.

Beck, B., Meyer, S., Simonsen, E., Søgaard, U., *et al.* (2021). Music therapy was noninferior to verbal standard treatment of traumatized refugees in mental health care: Results from a randomized clinical trial. *European Journal of Psychotraumatology*, 12(1). https://doi.org/10.1080/20008198.2021.1930960.

Bernard, G. & Dvorak, A. (2023). Using music to address trauma with refugees: A systematic review and recommendation. *Music Therapy Perspectives*, 41(1), 30–43. https://doi.org/10.1093/mtp/miac013.

Bolger, L. & Skewes McFerran, K. (2020). Current practices and considerations for international development music therapy: A world federation of music therapy scoping project. *Voices: A World Forum for Music Therapy*. https://doi.org/10.15845/voices. v20i1.2951.

Bongard, S., Etzler, S., & Frankenberg, E. (2020). *Frankfurter Akkulturationsskala* [Frankfurt Acculturation Scale]. Göttingen: Hogrefe Publishing.

Carnevali, C., Ravaioli, L., & Vandi, G. (2024). Adolescence, migration, music and psychoanalytic tools into play. *British Journal of Psychotherapy*, 40(2), 195–212. https://doi.org/10.1111/bjp.12887.

Chantah, J., Frankenberg, E., Kasanda, Z., & Bongard, S. (2024). Music-making facilitates acculturation and reduces acculturative stress: Evidence from a survey of migrants living in Germany. *Psychology of Music*, 1–16. https://doi.org/10.1177/03057356241243333.

Cloitre, M., Shevlin, M., Brewin, C. R., Bisson, J. I., *et al.* (2018). The International Trauma Questionnaire: Development of a self-report measure of ICD-11 PTSD and Complex PTSD. *Acta Psychiatrica Scandinavica*, 138(6), 536–546. doi: 10.1111/acps.12956.

Comte, R. (2016). Neo-colonialism in music therapy: A critical interpretive synthesis of the literature concerning music therapy practice with refugees. *Voices: A World Forum for Music Therapy*, 16(3). https://doi.org/10.15845/voices.v16i3.865.

Coombes, E. (2018). We all came from somewhere. *Voices: A World Forum for Music Therapy*, 18(1). https://doi.org/10.15845/voices.v18i1.915.

Coombes, E. & Tombs-Katz, M. (2017). Interactive therapeutic music skill-sharing in the West Bank: An evaluation report of project Beit Sahour. *Approaches: An Interdisciplinary Journal of Music Therapy*, 9(1), 67–79.

De Quadros, A. & Vu, K. T. (2017). At home, song, and *fika* – portraits of Swedish choral initiatives amidst the refugee crisis. *International Journal of Inclusive Education*, 21(11), 1113–1127. https://doi.org/10.1080/13603116.2017.1350319.

Edwards, J. (2022). Cultural Humility in Music Therapy Practice. In L. E. Beer & J. C. Birnbaum (eds) *Trauma Informed Music Therapy Theory and Practice* (pp.28–36). London: Routledge.

Enge, K. E. A. & Stige, B. (2022). Musical pathways to the peer community: A collective case study of refugee children's use of music therapy. *Nordic Journal of Music Therapy*, 31(1), 7–24. https://doi.org/10.1080/08098131.2021.1891130.

Gever, V., Onosahwo Iyendo, T., Obiugo-Muoch, U., Kayode Okunade, J. *et al.* (2022). Comparing the effect of social media-based drama, music and art therapies on reduction in post-traumatic symptoms among Nigerian refugees of Russia's invasion of Ukraine. *Journal of Pediatric Nursing: Nursing Care of Children and Families.* https://doi.org/10.1016/j.pedn.2022.11.018.

Henderson, S., Cain, M., Istvandity, L., & Lakhani, A. (2017). The role of music participation in positive health and wellbeing outcomes for migrant populations: A systematic review. *Psychology of Music*, 45(4), 459–478. https://doi.org/10.1177/0305735616665910.

Heynen, E., Bruls, V., van Goor, S., Pat-El, R., Schoot, T., & van Hooren, S. (2022). A music therapy intervention for refugee children and adolescents in schools: A process evaluation using a mixed method design. *Children*, 9(10), 1434. doi: 10.3390/children9101434.

Jin, S. (2016). Giving and gaining: Experiences of three music facilitators on working and musicking with asylum seekers in Australia. *Australian Journal of Music Therapy*, 27, 13–27.

Kenny, A. (2022). Music facilitator experiences of working in asylum seeker centres: Complexities, dilemmas and opportunities. *International Journal of Music Education*, 40(4), 542–553.

Krüger, V. & Diaz, E. (2023). The potential to meet the needs of refugees and other migrants through music therapy. *The Lancet Regional Health – Europe*, 29, 100637.

Mallon, T. & Hoog Antink, M. (2021). The sound of lost homes – introducing the COVER model – theoretical framework and practical insight into music therapy with refugees and asylum seekers. *Voices: A World Forum for Music Therapy*, 21(2). https://doi.org/10.15845/voices.v21i2.3124.

Marsh, K. (2017). Creating bridges: Music, play and well-being in the lives of refugee and immigrant children and young people. *Music Education Research*, 19(1), 60–73. https://doi.org/10.1080/14613808.2016.1189525.

Miller, M. J., Kim, J., & Benet-Martínez, V. (2011). Validating the riverside acculturation stress inventory with Asian Americans. *Psychological Assessment*, 23(2), 300–310. https://doi.org/10.1037/a0021589.

Mollica, R. F., Caspi-Yarvin, Y., Bollini, P., Truong, T., Tor, S., & Lavelle, J. (1992). The Harvard Trauma Questionnaire. Validating a cross-cultural instrument for measuring torture, trauma, and posttraumatic stress disorder in Indochinese refugees. *The Journal of Nervous and Mental Disease*, 180(2), 111–116. doi: 10.1097/00005053-199202000-00008.

Parker, D., Gentili, D., Brown, H., & Balducci, A. (2020). Adjusting the pitch: An ethnographic exploration of action learning in an international music exchange project. *Voices: A World Forum for Music Therapy*, 21(2). https://doi.org/10.15845/voices.v21i2.3075.

Puras, D. (2020). *Report of the Special Rapporteur on the right of everyone to the enjoyment of the highest attainable standard of physical and mental health*. United Nations General Assembly. https://undocs.org/A/HRC/44/48.

Skinner, C. (2022). 'There was something inside of me I needed to let out': Occupied masculinities, emotional expression and rap music in a Palestinian refugee camp. *Men and Masculinities*, 25(2), 292–309.

Small, C. (1998). *Musicking: The Meanings of Performing and Listening*. Lebanon, NH: University Press of New England.

Sutton, J. (2020). Improvisation. Our controversial discussions. *Nordic Journal of Music Therapy*, 29(2), 97–111.

The Colonialism and Music Therapy Interlocutors (CAMTI) Collective. (2022). *Colonialism and Music Therapy*. Dallas, TX: Barcelona Publishers.

World Health Organization. (2021). *Guidance on community mental health services: Promoting person-centred and rights-based approaches*. Geneva: World Health Organization. www.who.int/publications/i/item/9789240025707.

TRAVERSING TRAUMA

CHAPTER 2

Impact of Trauma on Displaced Persons

Integrating a Neuroscience Perspective

GENE-ANN BEHRENS

As conflicts increase across the world, so do the number of displaced persons – those needing to flee to another country or another area of their country to seek safety (United Nations High Commission for Refugees, 2024). Families experience loss of life, become separated from each other, or struggle to find food and shelter as they escape – often with no end to the conflicts. These extremely complex and chronic stressors impose levels of trauma beyond what is described by traditional definitions (Azab, 2024). Therefore, it often is unrealistic to consider approaches that focus on getting well and resolving trauma, especially during their early years of resettlement. Instead, to better meet the extreme needs of displaced persons, I propose that practitioners working in treatment sessions, communities, or shelters integrate information from a neuroscience perspective into the psychosocial approach they employ (Clark, 2020; Luke *et al.*, 2019; Shaffer, 2016). The integration and application of neuroscience concepts provide insights into new or modified methods for working with persons who are displaced and for monitoring the practitioner's nervous system and that of the persons with whom they work.

However, many practitioners may find relevant neuroscience articles challenging to read due to their technical language and limited discussions of therapeutic applications. To aid in reading the literature, many online journals now provide summaries of recent studies in layperson's terms. For example, many authors who write for open-access, online magazines publish short reviews of research studies in layperson's terms soon after the studies are published. Others write books that serve as a review of the many topics and concepts related to neurocounselling. Becoming immersed in neuroscience literature can help practitioners shift from focusing on wellness and trauma resolution to goals that increase neuroplasticity, vagal tone, resiliency, and a sense of personal safety or calm. From a psychosocial perspective, those neural goals would help empower persons within their next resettlement, increase their sense of control and tolerance, and enable them to develop trusting relationships and learn coping skills.

Bringing neuroscience into any field of practice is not about replacing but rather integrating the concepts with the practitioner's current psychosocial perspective (Luke *et al.*, 2019). This integration of neuroscience brings hope to individuals dealing with trauma, demystifies the symptoms of a person's experience, and decreases the guilt and blame they often feel (Greenberg, 2021; van der Kolk, 2015). In fact, because each person's nervous system is a product of their past encounters, practitioners can potentially help the persons with whom they work learn to better regulate by providing positive experiences that change the structure of their nervous system.

The authors contributing to this book represent a variety of practitioners who conduct sessions in agencies or work within communities, settlements, or camps with persons who are displaced. These dedicated practitioners describe a variety of supportive experiences that have positively helped these individuals – and I also would add, positively impacted the nervous systems of those persons. I am a music therapist and retired professor with a keen interest in neuroscience for more than 16 years. These concepts have guided my trauma work and the more than 90 trauma-related workshops I have presented. I believe, as does Russell-Chapin (2016), that neuroscience is the final frontier of discovery in healthcare. I hope this chapter will help all who serve persons who are displaced to consider integrating neuroscience concepts into their work.

Following a brief overview of the nervous system and the impact of trauma on a child's developing brain, I will describe four neural concepts and how they and related strategies can be applied to trauma work; those concepts are neuroplasticity, vagal tone, resiliency, and a sense of personal safety or calm. As I am a music therapist, I will use the terms strategies and experiences to refer to any level of work in any type of setting with children or adults, whom I will refer to as clients. In addition, most of my example experiences will focus on the use of music interactions.

MICRO AND MACRO VIEWS OF
THE NERVOUS SYSTEM

An understanding of these four neural concepts may be aided by an initial review of a micro and macro perspective of the nervous system (NS). Learning to monitor one's NS and the nervous systems of clients is an important skill for all practitioners. Neurotypical clients who possess a level of abstract thinking can benefit from learning certain concepts and skills to monitor their own nervous systems. Some of my clients as young as eight to ten years old were able to grasp and use the concepts. The NS is like a barometer, a way to measure and read slight changes in how someone may react and respond throughout the day, providing feedback that can help develop self-regulation. Therefore, having a basic understanding of a balanced, flexible, regulated NS versus one that is dysregulated further enhances a practitioner's observation and interpretation of clients' music and non-music responses and symptoms.

A micro review of the NS begins at the level of the neuron or nerve cell (see Figure 2.1). Each neuron has five parts that can be impacted by trauma (National Institute of Neurological Disorders and Stroke, 2023) – the first four are a *cell body*, the central part of a neuron; an *axon*, a nerve fibre that carries messages, sent as electrical impulses, away from the cell body; *dendrites*, nerve fibres that receive and send the messages to the nerve cell body; and a *myelin sheath*, a fatty substance that wraps around the axon and protects it while also enhancing the speed of sending messages.

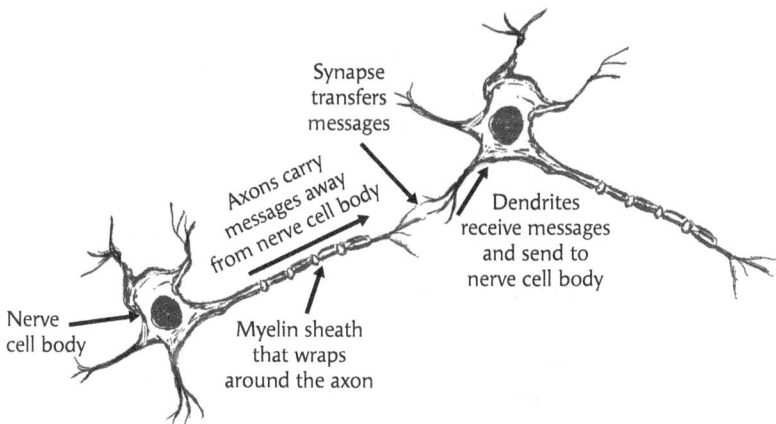

Figure 2.1: *Parts of a neuron*

The *synapse* is the fifth key part of the neuron and is the space between the end of an axon and the beginning of a dendrite that connects one neuron to the next. While newborns have about 86 billion neurons, most of those are not connected by synapses at birth (Azevedo *et al.*, 2009). Infants are born with only about 50,000 synaptic connections or 2500 connections per neuron. However, from birth to around age three, the growth of synaptic connections accelerates to the rate of one million per second. By age three, a child has approximately 100 trillion neural connections or about 15,000 for each neuron (Cover Three, 2024), and by adulthood, individuals have about 600 trillion or 7000 connections per neuron (Wanner, 2018). Trauma impacts the brain by dysregulating these synaptic connections and destroying neurons.

Turning to a more macro view of the NS, Figure 2.2 outlines the structure of the three nervous systems that have evolved to help individuals deal with stress. Starting at the top, the NS is divided into two portions, the *central NS*, made up of the brain and brainstem, and the *peripheral NS*, which consists of the *somatic* and *autonomic NS* (Cherry, 2022). The *somatic NS* deals with voluntary sensory and motor functions of the body, and the *autonomic NS* regulates involuntary functions such as respiration and heart rate.

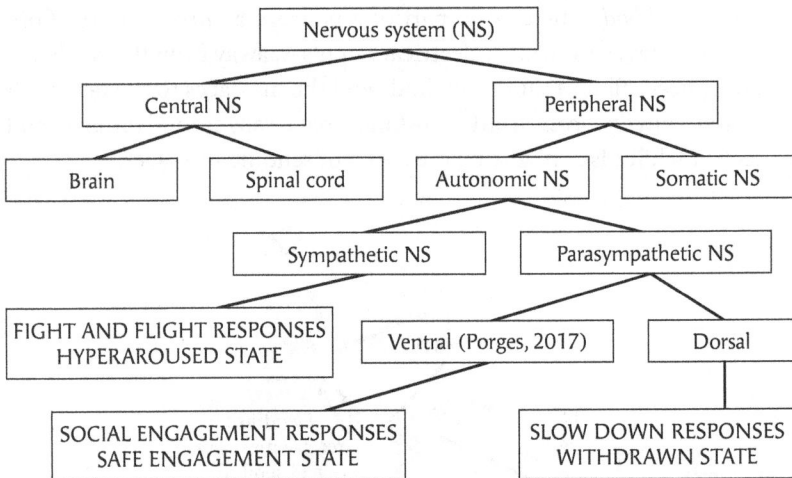

Figure 2.2: Structure of the nervous system

For many years, the autonomic NS was assumed to include only two tracts that evolved to protect persons dealing with stress (Dana, 2018). The sympathetic or hyperaroused NS is the second oldest from an evolutionary perspective, is partially myelinated, and responds to interruptions or threats by increasing a person's involuntary body functions such as heart and respiration rates. If threats continue or are interpreted as extremely significant, certain body functions may begin to slow down as the dorsal or withdrawn parasympathetic NS, the oldest and unmyelinated system, begins to respond to further protect the person.

However, in 1994, Porges (2017) identified a third NS tract, the *ventral parasympathetic* or *safe-engaged NS*. It is the newest and completely myelinated NS that activates when a person is feeling safe and focused. The ventral NS supports a person when focusing and learning a new task, problem-solving, or socially interacting. The three NSs often are depicted along the steps of a ladder (Dana, 2018) which symbolizes how a person would move in and out of their ventral, sympathetic, and dorsal nervous systems (see Figure 2.3).

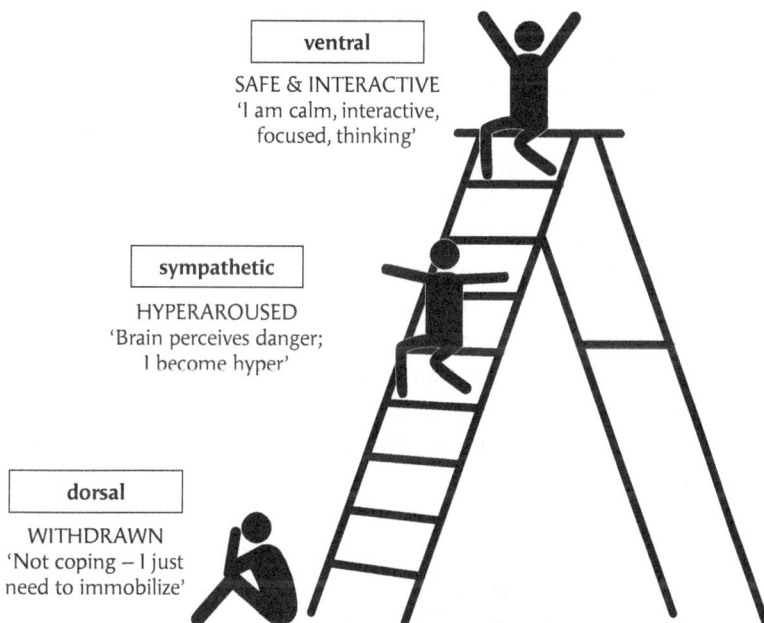

ventral

SAFE & INTERACTIVE
'I am calm, interactive,
focused, thinking'

sympathetic

HYPERAROUSED
'Brain perceives danger;
I become hyper'

dorsal

WITHDRAWN
'Not coping – I just
need to immobilize'

Figure 2.3: Moving in and out of the ventral, sympathetic, and dorsal nervous systems

A closer look at the parasympathetic NS highlights an important nerve that makes up a large portion of the system, the *vagal nerve* – cranial nerve X, also known as the longest nerve in the body (Porges, 2023). Both the ventral and dorsal portions of the vagal nerve originate in the brainstem with the dorsal or withdrawn NS portion extending down into a person's digestive system. The pathways that extend up into the individual's voice box, face, eyes, and middle ear include the ventral or safe-engaged NS. Activation of the ventral vagal nerve is one immediate way to calm activity in the brain and body.

These three tracts or nervous systems (sympathetic, dorsal, and ventral) respond to internal and external stimuli – safe, interruptive, or threatening

– that individuals face throughout each day. When a person is calm, focused, and socially connected, their ventral or safe-engaged NS is activated. One set of neurochemicals signals the protected, more efficient, and myelinated vagal nerve to stay active, acting as a vagal brake to support the person in their ventral vagal NS while keeping their heart rate slow (Porges, 2023). Essentially, the vagal brake inhibits the release of another set of neuro-chemicals from three organs that respond to stress, the hypothalamic-pi-tuitary-adrenal (HPA) axis, which in turn signals the release of the vagal brake, the activation of the sympathetic NS, and an increase in heart rate. The vagal brake does not go on and off like a car hand brake but relaxes and re-engages based on signals from both sets of neurochemicals. The stronger and more flexible a person's vagal brake, the more balanced and flexible the person's NS, which in turn helps the person better regulate their responses to internal and external stimuli, especially when under stress.

During each day, individuals are confronted with internal or external stimuli that often act as *interruptions* or *threats*, increasing a person's invol-untary responses such as heart rate (Dana, 2018). These interruptions or threats activate the sympathetic NS and range from minor events, such as a phone ringing, to major threats, for example learning a friend was hurt in a car accident. The level of perceived threat is individualized and based on a person's past encounters – each person's NS is a product of their past experiences (Greenberg, 2021; van der Kolk, 2015). What follows is an over-view of how a person with a balanced, flexible NS versus someone whose NS is dysregulated would respond to an interruption. Only major details in this very complex process are discussed.

REGULATED VERSUS DYSREGULATED RESPONSES TO INTERRUPTIONS OR THREATS

Once an internal or external disturbance is perceived and categorized gen-erally in the thalamus, the brain of a person with a balanced, flexible NS responds via a fast and a slow sequence of neural chemicals and connections among areas of the brain (Porges, 2017; van der Kolk, 2015). The amyg-dala, which processes the valence (the pleasantness or unpleasantness) and intensity (strength or energy) of emotions, is a key brain area along the fast sequence that ends with the HPA axis and the release of cortisol and other neurochemicals. These neurochemicals in turn activate the relaxation of the vagal brake, which begins to increase a person's heart rate as they move into their sympathetic NS. The fast sequence of neural connections takes only a nanosecond as the person's NS is briefly hijacked. However, soon the slower processing of the prefrontal cortex begins to send messages of calm and reassurance as the person processes ways to cope. If the individual's NS is balanced and flexible and the incoming information is complete and organized for processing, the person can apply coping strategies that calm the amygdala, interrupt the release of cortisol, and re-engage the vagal brake as the person moves back into their social-engaged NS.

However, unresolved trauma leads to the dysregulation of many of these functions and connections in the brain, which causes threats to generalize and elevates mild interruptions into major threats (van der Kolk, 2015). For example, a person fleeing from a country steeped in a series of conflicts may respond to a door slamming or a person yelling with the same sympathetic response as when a bomb exploded. Often not all the information involved in a threatening experience is even perceived and then those pieces of information remain fragmented in the thalamus and later the hippocampus (van der Kolk, 2015). This sense of uncertainty elevates an already vigilant level of anxiety as the person seeks to make sense of an experience.

Therefore, a person with a dysregulated, inflexible NS will respond with heightened emotions that the amygdala interprets as part of the fast-track sequence. Due to the experience of highly intense and unpleasant emotions, the amygdala releases high levels of norepinephrine and other neurochemicals that in turn activate the HPA axis, which releases high levels of cortisol and other corticosteroids. As a result, the vagal brake relaxes and moves a person into their hyperactive sympathetic NS (Dana, 2018; Porges, 2017; van der Kolk, 2015).

Unfortunately, individuals who are displaced will repeatedly experience chronic stressors, and with each stressor, cortisol will be released into the body, including the brain. This constant release of cortisol will result in high levels of the neurochemical and the constant relaxation of the vagal brake – the person essentially becomes stuck in their hyperactive sympathetic NS. Meanwhile, their prefrontal cortex, also dysregulated, is trying to process the incomplete, disorganized information sent along the slow track from the thalamus. As a result, incorrect messages of extreme threat are sent to the amygdala from the prefrontal cortex. Even if coping skills could be identified, their use often is too late to have an impact on an extremely hyperaroused amygdala. Therefore, the person remains stuck in their hyperactive sympathetic NS or may even begin to withdraw as they move into their dorsal NS.

CHRONIC TRAUMA AND TOXIC LEVELS OF CORTISOL
With an understanding of how a nervous system that is balanced and flexible versus one that is inflexible and dysregulated responds to stress, we

should not find it surprising that constant, chronic levels of stress can result in the build-up of toxic levels of cortisol and other neurochemicals in the brain (Bremner, 2006; van der Kolk, 2015). Each time a stressful response occurs, cortisol and other neurochemicals are released. The long-term, constant release of cortisol and other neurochemicals becomes toxic in the brain, which begins to inhibit the development of synaptic connections and reduce a person's ability to focus and engage in higher-order processing. Eventually, due to the toxic levels, neurons die and areas in the brain, especially the hippocampus (memory), begin to shrink. When the shrinkage is long-term, the damage cannot be reversed (Lupien *et al.*, 2018).

If the constant levels of stress and release of cortisol are addressed, the process of neurogenesis can begin to regrow neurons. Neurogenesis, the regrowth of neurons, is a rather recent discovery in the brain (Jones *et al.*, 2022). Previously, neurologists believed that the number of neurons at birth is what a person has for life except those lost due to injury or illness. However, recent research confirms that neurons do regrow but only in limited areas of the brain – the hippocampus (memory), amygdala (emotions), and hypothalamus (hormone regulation) (Roeder *et al.*, 2022; Sharif *et al.*, 2021). While the loss of neurons activates the process of neurogenesis, it also is enhanced by aerobic exercise, a healthy diet, and the learning of new tasks such as learning to play a new rhythm instrument or tell a story – experiences often only available to displaced persons with the support of dedicated practitioners.

IMPACT OF TRAUMA ON THREE NEURAL DEVELOPMENTAL CONCEPTS

Children are further impacted by trauma due to key developmental changes that are inhibited – growth that takes place from birth to age three and continues until around the age of 30 (van Blooijs *et al.*, 2023). Furthermore, neural researchers now conclude that the adult brain also continues to grow new neurons and synaptic connections long after the age of 30 (Gregory, 2024). Therefore, while early experiences are important in initially shaping a person's NS, supportive future experiences can have a positive impact in eventually helping calm and regulate a dysregulated NS. Three developmental concepts provide additional insight into the impact of trauma on a child's brain and into the selection of strategies or experiences.

Concept one: Brain development

The brain develops from the inside out but, more importantly, from the bottom up (Perry, 2000). Perry and others discuss four areas of the brain that begin developing sequentially a few weeks after conception. The brainstem, which controls many autonomic functions needed for survival, develops first and is fairly well established by birth. The midbrain, which regulates other autonomic responses but primarily controls sensory and motor responses, also starts to develop prenatally and then continues after birth as the infant begins to explore their environment.

The limbic and then the cortex areas are last to develop, with the limbic system in place by around age 10–13 and the cortex not until a person is over 30 (Jones, 2019; van Blooijs *et al.*, 2023). As previously stated, the limbic system, involving the amygdala, not only evaluates and regulates the valence and intensity of emotional perceptions and responses but also has a role in developing relationships, trust, and the ability to deal with stress (Haas *et al.*, 2015). The cortex area of the brain is key to the development of higher-level processing such as concrete and abstract thinking, problem-solving, and decision-making skills. The cortex, specifically the medial prefrontal cortex and insula, also supports emotional regulation, the development of relationships, and the assessment and management of risks such as trusting others (Haas *et al.*, 2015).

Concept two: Maturational changes

Three types of maturational changes take place in the brain: progressive changes from birth to around age 30; continued neural growth and changes that occur as an adult; and growth spurts occurring at specific ages or milestones that need positive experiences for support (Power & Schlaggar, 2017; Tierney & Nelson, 2009). Most important are the maturational milestones that need rich, stimulating experiences at critical ages to support the neural growth that occurs. Some of these milestones involve: the increase in synaptic connections due to the growth and lengthening of dendritic branches; pruning, the reduction of synapses not used, to create efficiency; and the myelination of axons (Khanal & Hotulainen, 2021; Tierney & Nelson, 2009).

Concept three: Repetition and synaptic change

Changes in the brain related to development and learning occur most often due to repetition. As Hebb's Theory (1949) is often paraphrased, 'Neurons that fire together get wired together.' That is, responses that are repeated and form neural pathways of connected synapses in the brain shape a person's NS and behaviour. Perry *et al.* (1995) discuss a similar concept, the use-dependency theory, that the brain develops according to how it is used.

Impact of trauma on development

Applying these three developmental concepts, it is apparent why children, adolescents, and young adults are impulsive and do not have the emotional and higher-level processing to make the best decisions – but they can develop self-regulation as they age. However, those children, adolescents, and young adults who live in situations of extreme conflict and with the unpredictability of displacement get stuck in those reactive developmental stages due to the impact of trauma. The lack of supportive life experiences inhibits the development of their limbic and higher-order processing. When conflicts and displacements are ongoing, generations of children will grow up rehearsing hypervigilant, reactive behaviours that result in either hyperactive or withdrawn response patterns. In addition, adults experiencing similar constant trauma often regress to their reactive response patterns.

Because of these reactive responses, practitioners debate the use of a bottom-up (the perception and integration of sensory input to process information) versus a top-down (the use of higher-order processing to integrate new information with past information) approach to the use of strategies or experiences. Some practitioners begin with experiences that support somatic or bottom-up processing to help clients reconnect and learn to cope with their dysregulated feelings and sensory responses (Grabbe & Miller-Karas, 2018). Other practitioners discuss the importance of combining bottom-up with top-down processing to support the integration and regulation of sensory, physiological, emotional, and cognitive responses (van der Kolk, 2015). Creative arts therapies – such as music, movement, dance, and visual arts – provide safe mediums for integrating bottom-up and top-down responses (Shafir *et al.*, 2020). Clients working within these therapies can slowly move from non-verbal to verbal expressions, and gradually perceive, analyse, and integrate sensory, emotional, and thought responses.

FOUR NEURAL FOCUSES THAT SUPPORT TRAUMA WORK

With an overview of a micro and macro perspective of the NS and how trauma impacts the structure and function of the brain, here are four neural concepts that practitioners can integrate when working with displaced persons.

Neuroplasticity

Neuroplasticity is the ability of synaptic connections in the brain to develop and reorganize based on a person's experiences and responses – basically, the ability of the brain to rewire itself (Gamma, 2023). Researchers have identified two types of neuroplasticity: structural plasticity – when the brain is injured and neural connections are assigned to another part of the brain; and functional plasticity – when neural connections in the brain change due to experiences (Gamma, 2023).

Researchers suggest every thought or response of a person creates a synaptic connection, and those that get organized and repeated will form strong pathways (Kaczmarek, 2020). Due to the importance of synaptic connections, specific approaches for increasing neuroplasticity have been developed, for example 'self-directed neuroplasticity' by Bosman (2021) or 'intentional neuroplasticity' by Desautels (2023). However, given the inherent negative bias of brains (Cacioppo *et al.*, 2014) and the chronic stress levels of persons who are displaced, tasks that require higher-level processing and lead to neuroplasticity will be challenging. Therefore, methods for slowly changing the neuroplasticity of persons who are displaced may be an invaluable focus.

Music and other creative experiences can be designed to inherently calm and support synaptic growth (Speranza *et al.*, 2022). A part of many music-making interactions is the inherent repetition of synchronized playing that is built into most ensemble rehearsals – key to neuroplasticity. Research also suggests that strong, predictable beat patterns provide some of the most effective cues to increase neuroplasticity and synchronize interactive playing (Fukuie *et al.*, 2022; Grahn & Brett, 2007; MacKinnon, 2012).

Neuroplasticity also is enhanced through social connections (Kok & Friedrikson, 2010) and smiling, as discussed by Giang (2015) in a research summary. For example, group singing was more effective than solo singing in releasing oxytocin, which in turn impacts neuroplasticity (Froemke & Young, 2021; Good & Russo, 2022).

I have found that the use of Lummi sticks, 10–11-inch sticks cut out of PVC or wooden dowels and used in various tapping and passing tasks, is a music experience that involves several strategies for increasing synaptic connections. Using this experience in various countries, I have found that it easily adapts to any size circle of people or can be performed in pairs. The tapping and passing patterns involve making social connections, trusting oneself and others, repetition, learning new motor movements, synchronization, and imitation.

Most music therapists also often use call-and-response music experiences and the strategy of reciprocal interactions. Call-and-response experiences can be imitative (playing the same music pattern as the leader) or performed as question-answer responses (playing a music response that is reflective of the leader). The important component of reciprocity is the back-and-forth exchange of interactions (Dana, 2018), which increases neuroplasticity (Kok *et al.*, 2013). In addition, other benefits occur: (a) the activation of the mirror neuron network (a neural network involved in imitation, empathy, and language) (Bonini *et al.*, 2022; Schmidt *et al.*, 2021) and (b) the release of oxytocin (a hormone that within these experiences results in feelings of trust and calm) (Rauchbauer *et al.*, 2019). Research also suggests that if the rehearsal of music interactions increases connections within the corpus callosum (the connective nerve fibres between the right and left hemispheres) repeated reciprocal music interactions also can impact the development of those pathways (Schlaug, 2015). Neuroplasticity also is influenced by vagal tone, the next neural concept (Porges, 2023).

Vagal tone

Vagal tone refers to the level of activity in the vagal nerve or the strength of the signal sent from the brain to the body (Porges, 2023). High vagal tone suggests a flexible vagal brake, a metaphor for the neurochemicals that keep the heart rate and body calm and help the person feel more grounded, present, and engaged. Higher vagal tone also promotes clearer thinking and problem-solving. Heart rate variability (HRV), the amount of time between heartbeats, is an indirect measure of vagal tone (Porges, 2023). Several research studies focus on methods for increasing vagal tone, HRV, and the strength and flexibility of the vagal brake as strategies for reducing stress and trauma (Lamb *et al.*, 2017).

Deep breathing is one of the quickest ways to activate the vagal nerve and increase vagal tone (Allen *et al.*, 2023; Balban *et al.*, 2023). However, deep breathing can be difficult for clients to correctly perform without a cue to stimulate the movement of the diaphragm. Of the several different methods for deep breathing, cyclic sighing was found to result in significantly higher levels of relaxation than box and meditative breathing (Balban *et al.*, 2023). The technique of cyclic sighing involves slowly inhaling through the nose, then taking in an additional short inhale of air again through the nose, and exhaling even more slowly through the mouth.

Various music experiences also can be used to increase vagal tone. Singing and humming are two in-the-moment coping strategies that quickly activate the vagal nerve if they are perceived by the client as safe (Cleveland Clinic, 2022). Because the ventral vagus is connected to the vocal cords, throat, and middle ear, the vibrations from singing or humming stimulate the vagal nerve. Meditation or relaxation to music could be used to begin or end community music rehearsals. Breaks during ensemble rehearsals also could involve short isometric pressure and release exercises (Groß & Kohlmann, 2021) – another in-the-moment coping skill.

Higher vagal tone also enables a person to feel empowered to recover from stressors, which involves resiliency, the third neural concept.

Resiliency

Many practitioners refer to any level of stress recovery as resilience. From a neuroscience perspective, resiliency is the NS's ability to adapt to stressors as solutions are found and then return to a level of balance in the NS (Dana, 2018). Increasing resiliency not only aids a person's ability to deal with stress but also improves one's tolerance for engaging with persons who have differing views, taking risks, and recovering from mistakes (Harrod *et al.*, 2023; Johnson *et al.*, 2017; Pinna & Edwards, 2020).

Resiliency often is selected as a psychosocial goal for persons dealing with trauma. Individuals who are displaced continually need to adapt and adjust to the unpredictability of ongoing conflicts or the norms and diversity of several settings before their final destination. Integrating a neuroscience perspective provides additional direction when developing experiences that slowly rehearse and strengthen the synaptic pathways that support resiliency. Coping strategies, problem-solving skills, and cognitive reframing require higher-level processing that may need to be relearned.

Music experiences provide many opportunities to rehearse these coping skills or to slowly develop effective responses for tolerating change. Group music-making experiences can involve warm-ups that randomly adjust changes in tempo or dynamics and require clients to tolerate the fluctuations and adjust their performances to play with the group (Fancourt *et al.*, 2016). Practitioners can further help clients rehearse coping strategies by slowly challenging them with songs that they dislike or instruments that are new.

To best begin establishing resiliency, vagal tone, and neuroplasticity, clients must feel some level of a sense of personal safety or calm – the last neural concept.

Sense of personal safety or calm

A sense of personal safety or calm involves both an internal physiological state and a subjective feeling (Porges, 2022). The internal physiological state of safety or calm is regulated by the autonomic NS – that is, this sense comes from the brain. The feeling of safety or calm is the subjective interpretation of the internal autonomic response. A sense of safety is what leads to trust and the development of relationships. When a person's brain is calm, high alpha waves (around 13 Hz) fire, which puts the person in a state of 'relaxed alertness'.[1] The person is fully present and feels a sense of safety within their ventral NS, manages energy more efficiently, has a broader and longer attention span, is more other-focused and compassionate, can think more 'outside the box', and remains open to developing relationships and trust.

However, when the person is experiencing chronic high stress or trauma, high beta waves take over (18–30 Hz) in the brain, and high levels of neurochemicals are released that dampen synaptic connections. The person tends to feel unsafe within their sympathetic NS, is hypervigilant, reactive, and has racing thoughts, struggles to think positively and smile, is less focused and creative, and is mistrustful. If even a brief sense of calm in the brain is not experienced, it will be difficult for the person to socially connect and practise in-the-moment coping skills.

Co-regulation

To help persons begin to experience a sense of calm, practitioners can employ co-regulation, a strategy that occurs when the dysregulated NS of a client reads and imitates the calm, balanced, and regulated NS of a practitioner (Bornstein & Esposito, 2023). Research indicates that co-regulation is both biological, involving the mirror neuron network and hormones, and behavioural, engaging affective and cognitive responses.

Because humans tend to be wired to be social, the 'I smile-you smile' response of co-regulation also is a natural response (Lieberman, 2013). However, co-regulation must be developed before a person can self-regulate (Dana, 2018). In supportive early environments, infants learn to co-regulate when reinforced by the loving interactions of a caretaker (Lobo & Lunkenheimer, 2020). Yet, these early experiences are often non-existent for children who have lost their caretaker/s in a conflict or become challenging for caretakers who are themselves traumatized and regressed in their ability to self-regulate. Therefore, co-regulation becomes an important strategy to employ to help persons who are displaced begin to experience a sense of calm. By rehearsing those neural connections over and over, their higher-level processing will begin to form pathways that potentially can support self-regulation.

To effectively use this strategy, practitioners must monitor not only the nervous systems of their clients but also their own NS to maintain a sense of calm despite the situation or setting (Dana, 2018). Their NS in essence provides an anchor for persons who are displaced. Practitioners

---

1   New research by Mendoza-Halliday *et al.* (2024) suggests that neurons are arranged in six layers, each with their own level of electrical activity. Generally, the fast gamma waves are in the outer layers, and the slower alpha and beta waves are deep within the brain. When 'actively alert', the alpha waves would regulate the faster outer waves.

will experience their personal stressors, threats associated with the setting, and the interruptions that occur from moment to moment – all activators that could potentially send them into their sympathetic NS. Therefore, the situations also will require practitioners to quickly employ in-the-moment coping skills to return to their ventral, safe-engaged NS.

Besides being a co-regulator for clients, most creative arts therapists have the use of their art medium as a second, supporting co-regulator. As a music therapist, I use a variety of music components, instruments, and experiences to help clients co-regulate. Researchers suggest that music experiences that involve reciprocal interactions and strong predictable beat patterns provide some of the most effective cues to increase neuroplasticity and synchronize interactive rhythmic firing in the brain (Fukuie *et al.*, 2022; Grahn & Brett, 2007; MacKinnon, 2012), thus supporting a sense of calm, safety, and empowerment. Practitioners also can consider preferences, opportunities to make decisions, and what is perceived as safe by the client as they design experiences – for example, the selection of instruments, songs, chord sequences, tempos, sound levels, movement patterns, seating arrangements, types of experiences, and so forth.

When working in Bethlehem in the Occupied Palestinian Territories, my choice of instruments was key to helping the children co-regulate. The first night I worked with a group of children in a community where several fathers had recently been killed. I quickly learned that a frame drum further activated their initially high level of hyperactive and dysregulated NS – their NSs were hijacked and unable to slow down. After much pondering, I began the next session with rhythm sticks, which provided interesting limits and co-regulation such that their fast, aggressive playing quickly calmed. The transformation in their playing was so dramatic that even the children talked about how empowered they felt to play with the group.

Challenging clients

Even though supporting a sense of safety is a major focus when working with persons dealing with stress and trauma, at some point it also is important to help clients progress by introducing new elements – the process of *challenging clients*. Many practitioners look for consistent performance while others use intuition to decide when best to challenge. Neural science again may provide guidance and support by helping clients progress while returning to a sense of calm and safety (Dana, 2018). My thought process for challenging clients became more purposeful as I learned to monitor the NS of myself and my clients. I also learned to not challenge a client with a new element until some level of safety first was established with the client. If safety is not established first and the client is challenged, any change, no matter how small, will act as an interruption or threat to a highly traumatized client's NS. Their NS will be hijacked, and no insight, learning, or progress will be possible. Establishing some level of safety helps the client engage with the challenge using an NS that is calmer and slightly more flexible, also helping them bounce back from the interruption. Once a change has been introduced, the cycle of monitoring and interacting with the client begins again.

CONCLUDING THOUGHTS

Neuroplasticity, vagal tone, resiliency, and a personal sense of safety and calm are four intricately connected neural concepts that provide insights into the responses and possible strategies and experiences for persons who are displaced. Neuroplasticity and vagal tone have a reciprocal relationship such that increases in one positively impact the other – which in turn fosters the development and flexibility of resiliency. As a result, persons who are displaced are better able to deal with the constant interruptions and threats that impact their lives. As they develop an ability to co-regulate and tolerate the diversity within their new communities, persons who are displaced become empowered to self-regulate and socially engage in activities for the greater good of the groups they join. Although discussed last, some level of safety and calm is the critical initial building block that supports the other three neural concepts and the development of trust and relationships.

Practitioners can benefit by integrating an understanding of these four as well as other neuroscience concepts and related strategies into their existing perspectives and methods for working with persons who are displaced. As practitioners better understand the nervous system, they can become more focused and purposeful in how they work with persons who are displaced and how they take care of themselves – learning to monitor their nervous system as well as their clients' NS will be critical. In addition, the methods and neuroscience concepts shared with clients may help demystify their symptoms and provide hope that change can occur as they begin to feel empowered to regulate their thoughts, responses, and feelings. I believe that the neurotherapist Russell-Chapin (2016) was correct when he stated in an interview:

> I really do think the brain is the final frontier, and we're at this point where every day, we learn something new [about the nervous system]. If we as a profession want to go forward, we've got to go forward with the future, and this is where the future is. ... The more I know [about the brain], the better counsellor I'm going to be.

REFERENCES

Allen, M., Varga, S., & Heck, D. H. (2023). Respiratory rhythms of the predictive mind. *Psychological Review*, 130(4), 1066–1080. https://doi.org/10.1037/rev0000391.

Azab, l. (2024, 22 February). The trauma experienced in Gaza is beyond PTSD – Guest essay. *The New York Times*. www.nytimes.com/2024/02/22/opinion/gaza-palestinians-mental-health.html.

Azevedo, F. A., Carvalho, L. R., Grinberg, L. T., Farfel, J. M., *et al.* (2009). Equal numbers of neuronal and nonneuronal cells make the human brain an isometrically scaled-up primate brain. *The Journal of Comparative Neurology*, 513(5), 532–541. https://doi.org/10.1002/cne.21974.

Balban, M. Y., Neri, E., Kogon, M. M., Weed, L., *et al.* (2023). Brief structured respiration practices enhance mood and reduce physiological arousal. *Cell Reports. Medicine*, 4(1), 100895. https://doi.org/10.1016/j.xcrm.2022.100895.

Bonini, L., Rotunno, C., Arcuri, E., & Gallese, V. (2022). Mirror neurons 30 years later: Implications and applications. *Trends in Cognitive Sciences*, 26(9), 767–781. https://doi.org/10.1016/j.tics.2022.06.003.

Bornstein, M. H. & Esposito, G. (2023). Coregulation: A multilevel approach via biology and behavior. *Children (Basel, Switzerland)*, 10(8), 1323. https://doi.org/10.3390/children10081323.

Bosman, M. (2021, 18 August). *Self-directed neuroplasticity: Change your life by changing your focus*. Strategic Leadership Institute. www.stratleader.net/sli-blog/self-directed-neuroplasticity.

Bremner, J. D. (2006). Traumatic stress: Effects on the brain. *Dialogues in Clinical Neuroscience*, 8(4), 445–461. https://doi.org/10.31887/DCNS.2006.8.4/jbremner.

Cacioppo, J. T., Cacioppo, S., & Gollan, J. K. (2014). The negativity bias: Conceptualization, quantification, and individual differences. *The Behavioral and Brain Sciences*, 37(3), 309–310. https://doi.org/10.1017/S0140525X13002537.

Cherry, K. (2022, 7 September). *How the peripheral nervous system works*. Verywellmind. www.verywellmind.com/what-is-the-peripheral-nervous-system-2795465.

Clark, S. (2020). *Neurocounseling and the Counseling Profession: Integrating Neuroscience into the Practice of Counseling* (Publication No. 410) [Master's thesis, Minnesota State University Moorhead]. Red: A Repository of Digital Collections. https://red.mnstate.edu/thesis/410.

Cleveland Clinic. (2022, 10 March). *Five ways to stimulate your vagus nerve*. Cleveland Clinic – Health Essentials. https://health.clevelandclinic.org/vagus-nerve-stimulation.

Cover Three. (2024). Kid's brain development. Cover Three. https://coverthree.com/blogs/brain-health/kids-brain-development#:~:text=Research%20shows%20that%20they'll,has%20about%20I%2C000%20trillion%20synapses.

Dana, D. (2018). *The Polyvagal Theory in Therapy: Engaging the Rhythm of Regulation*. New York, NY: W. W. Norton & Company.

Desautels, L. (2023, 23 January). *The power of reframing to 'rewire' students' brains*. Edutopia. www.edutopia.org/article/reframing-rewire-student-brains.

Fancourt, D., Perkins, R., Ascenso, S., Carvalho, L. A., Steptoe, A., & Williamon, A. (2016). Effects of group drumming interventions on anxiety, depression, social resilience and inflammatory immune response among mental health service users. *PloS One*, 11(3), e0151136. https://doi.org/10.1371/journal.pone.0151136.

Froemke, R. C. & Young, L. J. (2021). Oxytocin, neural plasticity, and social behavior. *Annual Review of Neuroscience*, 44, 359–381. https://doi.org/10.1146/annurev-neuro-102320-102847.

Fukuie, T., Suwabe, K., Kawase, S., Shimizu, T., *et al.* (2022). Groove rhythm stimulates prefrontal cortex function in groove enjoyers. *Scientific Reports*, 12(1), 7377. https://doi.org/10.1038/s41598-022-11324-3.

Gamma, E. (2023, 17 August). Brain plasticity (neuroplasticity): How experience changes the brain. *SimplyPsychology-Psychology-Biopsychology*. www.simplypsychology.org/brain-plasticity.html.

Giang, V. (2015, 28 January). *How smiling changes your brain*. FastCompany. www.fastcompany.com/3041438/how-smiling-changes-your-brain.

Good, A. & Russo, F. A. (2022). Changes in mood, oxytocin, and cortisol following group and individual singing: A pilot study. *Psychology of Music*, 50(4), 1340–1347. https://doi.org/10.1177/03057356211042668.

Grabbe, L. & Miller-Karas, E. (2018). The Trauma Resiliency Model: A 'bottom-up' intervention for trauma psychotherapy. *Journal of the American Psychiatric Nurses Association*, 24(1), 76–84. https://doi.org/10.1177/1078390317745133.

Grahn, J. A. & Brett, M. (2007). Rhythm and beat perception in motor areas of the brain. *Journal of Cognitive Neuroscience*, 19(5), 893–906. https://doi.org/10.1162/jocn.2007.19.5.893.

Greenberg, M. (2021, 30 June). Understanding the trauma brain: Neuroplasticity provides hope if you suffer from trauma or PTSD. *Psychology Today*. www.psychologytoday.com/us/blog/the-mindful-self-express/202106/understanding-the-trauma-brain.

Gregory, S. Y. (2024, 12 April). *The power of neuroplasticity: How your brain adapts and grows as you age*. Mayo Clinic Press-Healthy Aging. https://mcpress.mayoclinic.org/healthy-aging/the-power-of-neuroplasticity-how-your-brain-adapts-and-grows-as-you-age/#:~:text=Though%20the%20number%20of%20neurons,View%20Healthy%20Aging.

Groß, D. & Kohlmann, C. W. (2021). Increasing heart rate variability through progressive muscle relaxation and breathing: A 77-day pilot study with daily ambulatory assessment. *International Journal of Environmental Research and Public Health*, 18(21), 11357. https://doi.org/10.3390/ijerph182111357.

Haas, B. W., Ishak, A., Anderson, I. W., & Filkowski, M. M. (2015). The tendency to trust is reflected in human brain structure. *NeuroImage*, 107, 175–181. https://doi.org/10.1016/j.neuroimage.2014.11.060.

Harrod, E. G., Shrira, I., Martin, J. D., & Niedenthal, P. M. (2023). Living in ancestrally diverse states of the United States is associated with greater vagal tone. *Frontiers in Psychology*, 13, 1068456. https://doi.org/10.3389/fpsyg.2022.1068456.

Hebb, D. O. (1949). *The Organization of Behavior: A Neuropsychological Theory*. New York, NY: John Wiley and Sons.

Johnson, J., Panagioti, M., Bass, J., Ramsey, L., & Harrison, R. (2017). Resilience to emotional distress in response to failure, error or mistakes: A systematic review. *Clinical Psychology Review*, 52, 19–42. https://doi.org/10.1016/j.cpr.2016.11.007.

Jones, K. L., Zhou, M., & Jhaveri, D. J. (2022). Dissecting the role of adult hippocampal neurogenesis towards resilience versus susceptibility to stress-related mood disorders. *NPJ Science of Learning*, 7(1), 16. https://doi.org/10.1038/s41539-022-00133-y.

Jones, P. B. (2019, March). *The influence of the environment on the developing brain: A perspective from adult mental illness*. [Video]. YouTube. www.youtube.com/watch?v=kDAkSLGzaUo.

Kaczmarek, B. (2020). Current views on neuroplasticity: What is new and what is old? *Acta Neuropsychologica*, 18(1), 1–14. https://doi.org/10.5604/01.3001.0013.8808.

Khanal, P. & Hotulainen, P. (2021). Dendritic spine initiation in brain development, learning and diseases and impact of bar-domain proteins. *Cells*, 10(9), 2392. https://doi.org/10.3390/cells10092392.

Kok, B. E., Coffey, K. A., Cohn, M. A., Catalino, L. I., *et al.* (2013). How positive emotions build physical health: Perceived positive social connections account for the upward spiral between positive emotions and vagal tone. *Psychological Science*, 24(7), 1123–1132.

Kok, B. E. & Fredrickson, B. L. (2010). Upward spirals of the heart: Autonomic flexibility, as indexed by vagal tone, reciprocally and prospectively predicts positive emotions and social connectedness. *Biological Psychology*, 85(3), 432–436. https://doi.org/10.1016/j.biopsycho.2010.09.005.

Lamb, D. G., Porges, E. C., Lewis, G. F., & Williamson, J. B. (2017). Non-invasive vagal nerve stimulation effects on hyperarousal and autonomic state in patients with post-traumatic stress disorder and history of mild traumatic brain injury: Preliminary evidence. *Frontiers in Medicine*, 4, 124. https://doi.org/10.3389/fmed.2017.00124.

Lieberman, M. (2013). *Social: Why Our Brains are Wired to Connect*. New York, NY: Crown Publishers.

Lobo, F. M. & Lunkenheimer, E. (2020). Understanding the parent-child coregulation patterns shaping child self-regulation. *Developmental Psychology*, 56(6), 1121–1134. https://doi.org/10.1037/dev0000926.

Luke, C., Miller, R., & McAuliffe, G. (2019). Neuro-informed mental health counseling: A person-first perspective. *Journal of Mental Health Counseling*, 41(1), 65–79. https://doi.org/10.17744/mehc.41.1.06.

Lupien, S. J., Juster, R. P., Raymond, C., & Marin, M. F. (2018). The effects of chronic stress on the human brain: From neurotoxicity, to vulnerability, to opportunity. *Frontiers in Neuroendocrinology*, 49, 91–105. https://doi.org/10.1016/j.yfrne.2018.02.001.

MacKinnon, L. (2012). The Neurosequential Model of Therapeutics: An interview with Bruce Perry. *The Australian and New Zealand Journal of Family Therapy*, 33(3), 210–218. https://doi.org/10.1017/aft.2012.26.

Mendoza-Halliday, D., Major, A. J., Lee, N., Lichtenfeld, M. J., *et al.* (2024). A ubiquitous spectrolaminar motif of local field potential power across the primate cortex. *Nature Neuroscience*, 27(3), 547–560. https://doi.org/10.1038/s41593-023-01554-7.

National Institute of Neurological Disorders and Stroke. (2023, November). *Know Your Brain – The Basics*. Publication No. 23-NS-3440a. U.S. Department of Health and Human Services Public Health Service. https://catalog.ninds.nih.gov/sites/default/files/publications/know-your-brain-brian-basics.pdf.

Perry, B. D. (2000). The Neuroarcheology of Childhood Maltreatment: The Neurodevelopmental Costs of Adverse Childhood Events. In B. Geffner (ed.), *The Cost of Child Maltreatment: Who Pays? We All Do*. San Diego, CA: Family Violence and Sexual Assault Institute.

Perry, B. D., Pollard, R. A., Blakley, T. L., Baker, W. L., & Vigilante, D. (1995). Childhood trauma, the neurobiology of adaptation, and 'use-dependent' development of the brain: How 'states' become 'traits.' *Infant Mental Health Journal*, 16(4), 271–291. <271::AID-IMHJ2280160404>3.0.CO;2-B.

Pinna, T. & Edwards, D. J. (2020). A systematic review of associations between interoception, vagal tone, and emotional regulation: Potential applications for mental health, wellbeing, psychological flexibility, and chronic conditions. *Frontiers in Psychology*, 11, 1792. https://doi.org/10.3389/fpsyg.2020.01792.

Porges, S. W. (2017). *The Pocket Guide to the Polyvagal Theory: The Transformative Power of Feeling Safe*. New York, NY: W. W. Norton.

Porges, S. W. (2022). Polyvagal Theory: A science of safety. *Frontiers in Integrative Neuroscience*, 16, 871227. https://doi.org/10.3389/fnint.2022.871227.

Porges, S. W. (2023). The vagal paradox: A polyvagal solution. *Comprehensive Psychoneuroendocrinology*, 16, 100200. https://doi.org/10.1016/j.cpnec.2023.100200.

Power, J. D. & Schlaggar, B. L. (2017). Neural plasticity across the lifespan. *Wiley Interdisciplinary Reviews. Developmental Biology*, 6(1). https://doi.org/10.1002/wdev.216.

Rauchbauer, B., Nazarian, B., Bourhis, M., Ochs, M., Prévot, L., & Chaminade, T. (2019). Brain activity during reciprocal social interaction investigated using conversational robots as control condition. *Philosophical Transactions of the Royal Society B*, 374, 20180033. http://dx.doi.org/10.1098/rstb.2018.0033.

Roeder, S. S., Burkardt, P., Rost, F., Rode, J., *et al.* (2022). Evidence for postnatal neurogenesis in the human amygdala. *Communications Biology*, 5, 366. https://doi.org/10.1038/s42003-022-03299-8.

Russell-Chapin, L. A. (2016). Integrating neurocounseling into the counseling profession: An introduction. *Journal of Mental Health Counseling*, 38(2), 93–102.

Schlaug, G. (2015). Musicians and music making as a model for the study of brain plasticity. *Progress in Brain Research*, 217, 37–55. https://doi.org/10.1016/bs.pbr.2014.11.020.

Schmidt, S. N. L., Hass, J., Kirsch, P., & Mier, D. (2021). The human mirror neuron system—A common neural basis for social cognition? *Psychophysiology*, 58(e13781), 1–6.

Shaffer, J. (2016). Neuroplasticity and clinical practice: Building brain power for health. *Frontiers in Psychology*, 7, 1118. https://doi.org/10.3389/fpsyg.2016.01118.

Shafir, T., Orkibi, H., Baker, F. A., Gussak, D., & Kaimal, G. (2020). Editorial: The state of the art in creative arts therapies. *Frontiers in Psychology*, 11, 68. https://doi.org/10.3389/fpsyg.2016.01118.

Sharif, A., Fitzsimons, C. P., & Lucassen, P. J. (2021). Neurogenesis in the adult hypothalamus: A distinct form of structural plasticity involved in metabolic and circadian regulation, with potential relevance for human pathophysiology. *Handbook of Clinical Neurology*, 179, 125–140. https://doi.org/10.3389/fpsyg.2020.00068.

Speranza, L., Pulcrano, S., Perrone-Capano, C., di Porzio, U., & Volpicelli, F. (2022). Music affects functional brain connectivity and is effective in the treatment of neurological disorders. *Reviews in the Neurosciences*, 33(7), 789–801. https://doi.org/10.1515/revneuro-2021-0135.

Tierney, A. L. & Nelson, C. A. (2009). Brain development and the role of experience in the early years. *Zero to Three*, 30(2), 9–13.

United Nations High Commissioner for Refugees. (2024). *Global trends: Forced displacement in 2023*. www.unhcr.org/uk/global-trends.

van Blooijs, D., van den Boom, M. A., van der Aar, J. F., Huiskamp, G. M., *et al.* (2023). Developmental trajectory of transmission speed in the human brain. *Nature Neuroscience*, 26(4), 537–541. https://doi.org/10.1038/s41593-023-01272-0.

van der Kolk, B. (2015). *The Body Keeps the Score*. New York, NY: Penguin Random House.

Wanner, M. (2018, 11 December). 600 trillion synapses and Alzheimers disease. *The Jackson Library*. www.jax.org/news-and-insights/jax-blog/2018/december/600-trillion-synapses-and-alzheimers-disease#.

CHAPTER 3

Homecoming

*Resettlement and Acculturation Processes in
Music and Imagery Therapy for Female Refugees
Suffering from Post-Traumatic Stress Disorder*

BOLETTE D. BECK

INTRODUCTION

The process of uprooting and resettling in a new country or part of the world can be challenging, especially for asylum seekers and refugees who have had to flee from dangerous and intolerable life circumstances. The ongoing migration stressors related to resettlement in a new country can also create barriers to integration and acculturation.

In a research project involving a pilot study and a randomized clinical trial, a group of music therapists with Guided Imagery and Music certification investigated whether the trauma-informed Music and Imagery approach could decrease trauma symptoms and dissociation and increase well-being, sleep quality, and safe attachment in adult refugees (Beck *et al.*, 2017, 2018, 2021). The clinical goals were to help the participants access inner resources, stabilize the nervous system, process traumatic memories, and finally gain hope and energy to build a new life.

This chapter will focus on the concept of homecoming in the acculturation process, how shared music listening can create a relational healing space, and how processes of imagery and embodiment can bridge and integrate different inner and outer places. Three women with flight experience will be given a voice through case vignettes and this will be reflected on with a feminist and intercultural lens.

BACKGROUND

People with flight experiences have often experienced war, persecution, torture, rape, violence, and other horrible traumatic incidents that can potentially profoundly change one's feeling of being safe and trustful in the world. In some cases, the reactions to these experiences fall into the category of post-traumatic stress disorder (PTSD), which has a highly varying prevalence among refugees as seen in the literature, probably because of the high degree of complexity in the population. A systematic review by Fazel *et al.* (2005) found that 9% of persons with flight experience developed PTSD, with symptoms of hypervigilance, intrusion (flashbacks and nightmares), and avoidance (as outlined in the *International Classification of Diseases, ICD-11*, World Health Organization, 2019a).

When working with people with flight experience, it also becomes clear that the diagnosis of complex PTSD is relevant too. *ICD-11* describes the symptoms as 'severe and pervasive problems in affect regulation such as heightened emotional reactivity to minor stressors, violent outbursts, reckless or self-destructive behaviour, dissociative symptoms when under stress, and emotional numbing, particularly the inability to experience pleasure or positive emotions' (World Health Organization, 2019b). Furthermore, feelings of worthlessness, shame, guilt, failure, and difficulties sustaining relationships and closeness to others impair daily functioning in family, social, and work settings.

Creating a new home

Acculturation and resettling in a new country with relative safety can greatly relieve people who have fled from war or other dangerous circumstances. However, having shelter or a place to stay does not necessarily give a feeling of being at home. The concept of home is complex and includes both material and immaterial elements. Kim and Smets found that Syrian refugees' home practices in Amsterdam combined sociality and materiality, where 'a sense of home can develop in a way that includes people's multiple identities. Thus, we see that leisure activities, consumption practices, homing practices and housing designs all impact residents' identities' (Kim & Smets, 2020, p.621). In an interview study with resettled persons in New Zealand, the authors concluded that feelings of homeliness depend on dynamic multisensory stimuli:

> ...people can feel at home in unfamiliar places when they experience vibes or sensory stimuli that provoke memories or positive associations for them or they can lose a feeling of homeliness and belonging as new sensory stimuli occur through relocation and resettlement, or through the transplanting

of others' practices into their environment, provoking unfamiliarity. (Kale *et al.*, 2019, p.7)

Boccagni (2018) stated that migrants' experience of the home reflects both temporality and spatiality and that migrants find a sense of home related to their country of origin, their previous life experiences (there and then), and their actual place of living (here and now).

Thinking about psychologically living in both the past and the present as a form of transit, one can imagine how difficult it is for the body to relax and feel safe. Creating an attachment to places, people, institutions, and natural surroundings can be felt as meaningless. This estrangement adds to the stress of being away from the well-known environment, country of origin, culture, family, work, nature, and climate ingrained in a human's body from early childhood. When one's place is temporal and maybe sensed as 'out of place', it can potentially add to dissociative symptoms often accompanying PTSD, such as feeling 'unreal', out of the body, or as if life is passing by (van der Hart *et al.*, 2006). There could be an interaction between feeling out of place and out of synchronization with time, as trauma victims can be mentally and bodily 'locked in the past' by the intensity of unprocessed traumatic incidents, and, so to speak, also 'locked to the places' where the trauma took place, which are not the places of living in the present life. According to van der Hart *et al.* (2006), the creators of the structural dissociation theory, 'presentification' is one of the goals of therapy for people with traumatic dissociation.

Music as a home

Music is an art form played out in time, and a musical experience can be a way to catch up with the here and now, arriving in the present time and place. According to the literature on music therapy with people with flight experience, music can create positive moments of care and positive emotions, provide a connection with oneself and others, and serve as a cultural meeting point (Abdulbaki & Berger, 2020; Coombes, 2018; Lenette & Sunderland, 2017; Mallon & Hoog Antink, 2021). In a review of literature on arts therapies for homesickness, the arts and music were found to be 'not only a container that offers a temporary home' but also 'a bridge that gently guides refugees to a stepwise integration in the host country' (Dieterich-Hartwell & Koch, 2017, p.1).

Listening to calm, well-known, or predictable music can bring a sense of being enveloped, contained, or held (Bonny, 2002), and music can remind of memories, places, and persons and give access to uplifting emotions such as longing, love, gratitude, or joy as well as feelings of sadness and grief

(Juslin, 2019; Koelsch, 2014). It is also well known that music can regulate arousal and influence the autonomic nervous system (Ho & Loo, 2023), and a large body of studies has demonstrated that music listening can decrease the experience of both physical and psychological pain (Martin-Saveedra et al., 2018).

According to Stephen Porges' polyvagal theory, a human being constantly scans the environment for signs of danger, a process called 'neuroception' (Porges, 2022). In calm and predictive surroundings, the brain can go into rest and restoration (parasympathetic activation). Sound/hearing is one of the primary sensory pathways to neuroception. Porges has suggested that support from other humans can have a regulating effect through face-to-face contact and communication through speech and vocal sounds. As the middle area of our hearing spectrum corresponds to the human voice, human speaking, humming, and singing can have a potential calming effect as they affect the tone of the vagus nerve (Porges, 2022). The prosocial and regulative affordances of calming music in the middle of the hearing spectrum can be one of the healing mechanisms in music therapy listening practices that help people to feel at home and safe on a bodily level.

A MUSIC THERAPY RESEARCH PROJECT

In an outpatient specialized psychiatric transcultural clinic for refugees diagnosed with post-traumatic stress disorder, a Danish team of music therapists adopted the Music and Imagery method, adhering to trauma treatment and intercultural meetings. A pilot project with 16 adults was carried out (Beck et al., 2017). Following that, a randomized clinical trial (RCT) took place with 75 participants who were randomized to music and imagery or standard verbal trauma psychotherapy (Beck et al., 2018, 2021). The results showed that the music therapy intervention significantly improved trauma symptoms, sleep quality, quality of life, and Global Assessment of Functioning (GAF) score in the pilot study, and in the RCT, music therapy was non-inferior to the active control regarding change of trauma symptoms. In the RCT, there was a 40% dropout in verbal psychotherapy. In contrast, only 5% dropped out of music therapy, and the changes in dissociation and quality of life were more significant in the music therapy group.

Trauma-focused music and imagery in a transcultural setting

The Music and Imagery (MI) method conceptualizes music as a stimulus for inner exploration and transformation, a supportive container, and a driver of multimodal imagery experiences that can act as metaphors for personal change (Bonny, 2002; Grocke, 2022) in modern psychodynamic music therapeutic understanding (Pedersen *et al.*, 2022). The structure of a Music and Imagery session contains a pre-music discussion, music choice, the therapist's induction (relaxation/focus), two to ten minutes of music and imagery (listening without dialogue), processing, and verbal integration (Grocke & Moe, 2015). In tune with the original ideas of Judith Herman (1997) and international guidelines for trauma treatment, a phased treatment with three phases was applied: finding inner resources and a sense of safety; mourning and negotiating traumatic memories (trauma exposure); reconnection and future orientation. Not all patients go to the third or even the second phase, as the after-effect of severe traumatization heavily burdens the body and mind. In the study, we identified a phase between the first and the second specific for music therapy, where the participants seemed to use the music to contain and process contrasting emotions – a prerequisite for trauma processing (Beck *et al.*, 2017). Another part of the trauma-informed adaptation of MI was to form a supportive therapeutic relationship carefully and use music listening in co-regulative processes with an awareness of the 'window of tolerance' of the client and their capacity for trauma exposure. Normally, music listening takes place with closed eyes in a slightly altered state of consciousness. However, as people with PTSD have a dysregulated nervous system, it is safer to listen with open eyes to prevent overwhelming contact with traumatic memories in the early phase of therapy, where the focus is on trust and safety and learning to use music to calm down the nervous system. When they enter the mourning and exposure phase, some clients have developed the capacity to close their eyes and work on more altered levels of consciousness, with reimagination of traumatic episodes or complex emotions. As an induction to the music listening, the therapist guides the client to pay attention to their breathing and relax the body or experience muscular strength if this is acceptable. In some cases, the clients cannot bear to focus on the body, and they can choose to focus on visual imagery (such as a safe place in nature or a memory of a loved one) or a concept (such as calmness or freedom).

Choosing music in an intercultural setting

When choosing music in an intercultural setting, the cultural sensitivity of the therapist is crucial. The client is the expert in their own culture and musical preferences, and their reactions to music in the moment-to-moment experience of music are unique, personal, and validated by the therapist. Attention and support from the therapist are provided with cultural humility (Edwards, 2022) with a listening and learning approach.

In the studies, the participants received a list of therapist-chosen music pieces at the beginning of music therapy, including seven instrumental pieces with a low tempo and calm atmosphere, in different genres such as light classical, easy listening, meditative, and Middle Eastern new age style (Beck, 2018). These so-called 'supportive' pieces (Bemman *et al.*, 2023) helped the therapist assess the client's musical preferences. During the first sessions, the therapist and client carried out a shared search for music, and the client was asked to bring their music to the session. If the client needed help finding music from their original country or culture, the therapist tried to find suitable pieces with the translator's help. When the therapist chose the music, 10–20 seconds of two different pieces were often played to give the client the choice, and the volume was always checked out with the client before the listening began. The client also had the power to stop the music at any point. During the pilot study, we found that around 25% asked for music from their own (non-Western) music culture (Beck *et al.*, 2017). Music served as a holding structure in the later phases of therapy, mirroring the sadness or loss in traumatic episodes, containing emotions, and mourning, and empowering the clients. An imagined 'renegotiation' of a traumatic incident could occur with the music's support, enabling the client to feel a sense of mastery instead of powerlessness (Levine, 2010; Beck, 2019).

Through the post-therapy interviews of the pilot study (Beck *et al.*, 2017), we understood that sharing music could be intimate, supportive, and touching, and it could bring contact with both negative and positive feelings and an intercultural meeting beyond words.

Woman-to-woman encounters – an epoché

As background for telling the stories of three women with refugee experience and how they worked with their resettling process and sense of space and home in their music therapies, I will disseminate my position, background, and understanding of power balances and cultural negotiations.

As a white, cisgendered, middle-aged female from a Scandinavian country holding a part-time position at a university, I have the privilege of having been born in a time and place with economic freedom for women and fantastic opportunities, seen in a historical perspective, compared to many of the people who arrive in the transcultural clinic. However, as a daughter, a sister, a mother, and a wife, I see patterns from former generations of women still repeating themselves, and realize that there still is a long way to go towards women's inner and outer liberation. At age 15, I joined the feminist movement and began a lifelong journey of solidarity for women worldwide, indigenous people, and people of colour. During seven years of marriage with my late husband from Africa, I realized how much racism there is in my culture below the surface, and I started to grow in consciousness and carve it out of myself. I think that authentic intercultural sensitivity must be trained, it is not just there automatically. Travelling and living closely with a person from another culture has, I hope, enabled me to spot power imbalances better and be aware of prejudices and postcolonial and patriarchal structures.

After completing music therapy and ethnology education and entering Guided Imagery and Music training and trauma therapy training, I began to work as a therapist with people with flight experiences in 2001, with a wish to give these people care and respect in contrast to the hostile political tone towards refugees and immigrants that started to spread in Denmark and other European countries.

When meeting female clients from different cultures, I open myself to what I do not know about their reality. I manage the power imbalance in the developing therapeutic relationship by being transparent about not sharing my own story verbally, even though it is present in the relationship as a resonance. I have experienced that women from Arabic cultures often enjoy the company of other women, and the presence of a female translator, together with the therapist and client, has sometimes worked as a small community of care for the clients. Working with trauma is a big responsibility and needs a sensitive approach, managing countertransference well. I intend to give my clients the safety and power to feel and decide what they need from the therapy. The music choices rely on the client's preferences and needs.

I am aware of the patriarchal structures of a psychiatric hospital, diagnostic systems, medication, research traditions, and so on, that can counteract the attempts to provide safety, agency, compassion, and empowerment. However, after the experience of carrying out treatment in a local citizen cafe setting for refugees, I think that an outpatient clinic, when run in a good way, can be an interdisciplinary support structure for the therapist and client and be beneficial for the space of intercultural learning.

When working on the topic of home and space, looking at my cases, I realized that the female clients worked with this focus rather than the male clients. I tried to understand what it was like to live as a female in a Muslim world and how these women found support in their religion. I also have a faith. I understand prayer. So, working with people from other parts of the world becomes something more than a psycho-therapeutically staged treatment; it also becomes a felt experience of mutual suffering, love, and faith – and hopefully, for them, the power of being listened to and supported by another woman, and held by the music as a mothering comfort.

VIGNETTES

Three vignettes from the MI research projects will be shared. The first is a composite vignette made of elements from different therapies. The second and third were discussed and included with consent from the participants (the women chose their own pseudonyms). The cases are selected because they all, in different ways, related to the relationship to one's place of living and how music and imagery influenced their difficulties of getting a home and feeling at home.

Vignette 1: The sorrow of a mother

Hanna, a 49-year-old woman from Syria, married with six children, was reunited with her husband after two years alone in Syria with the children during the war. Her husband was unable to work due to PTSD. In the first music therapy sessions, Hanna told how she had changed after the war; before, she was lively and creative, but now she felt dead inside. She held much sorrow that she tried not to show to her children. Hanna had been very attached to her deceased mother, who had taught her to cry when things were hard, but now she could not cry; it was as if her heart was a black stone. Being a mother herself kept her going, but she could not receive something for herself and let go of her tension and sorrow – she feared that if she began to do that, she would lose control and be unable to be there for her children.

In this case, it was only possible to work with the introduction of positive resources bit by bit to help her begin to regulate herself. We listened to a song that she chose, with dance music from her youth that reminded her of herself before the war. I taught her how to relax her body to soft music ('Dawn', by Skovgaard). Hearing how much she worked in her home from early morning to bedtime, I asked her to try to take small breaks during her days, which she began to do.

Hanna identified an unbearable number of traumatic experiences, deaths, and losses in Syria. I asked her how she managed to keep up during this time, and she said that she prayed daily. We talked about the power of prayer, and about fate and meaning, and she recognized a feeling of gratitude due to the children's survival. We listened to a music piece focusing on gratitude ('Magic', by Enya). It was a very precious moment as we happened to find a resource to hold on to when working with the traumatic experience of being exposed to the war without being able to protect herself and the children.

During the time of therapy, the family lived in an apartment with the children. There was mould in the apartment, which affected the health of the family. After many months of complaints, the family got re-hosted temporarily while the first apartment was cleaned. The new place, however, was even worse, and she nearly gave up. I asked her to visualize a good house for the family. She listened to 'Gabriel's Oboe' (by Morricone) while she thought about the dream house on ground level with a small garden, and how she would have a party in the garden one day. The imagery changed her mood for a short while. Her ability to dream and imagine helped her to sustain the waiting.

In the final session, Hanna and I agreed that she needed to have more treatment, and that in a few years, when her children are older, she will come back to music therapy and do her crying.

Comment on vignette 1

For me as a music therapist, the story of Hanna was overwhelming at times; there was much to contain, and there was not immediately any way out. In such cases, it is essential not to give in to hopelessness.

The vignette demonstrates how fear from past trauma related to the loss of a safe living place weaves into and colours the perception of the present situation and how former coping mechanisms from the traumatic situations are still active. Hanna kept her family together and alive, and although she came into therapy and asked for help, she was not yet capable of allowing herself to do the mourning that she needed, nor to relax and let go. Nevertheless, the therapy helped her share her story and not feel so alone with her sorrow, and she told how important it was to come and have these small moments of relief for herself with someone she trusted. The music also helped her relax and get tiny moments of rest.

Regarding the home theme, the case illustrates how poor housing conditions can add to the physical and psychological strain in a refugee family. The vignette also illustrates that post-traumatic stress can be very complex when there has been a long and continued period of strain and exposure to death and how the deep freeze and shock in the nervous system can be tough to release when continued difficult life circumstances add to the feeling of an ongoing threat.

Vignette 2: Feeling safe at home alone

Nasima was a 38-year-old woman from Afghanistan who came to therapy with post-traumatic stress following losses and ongoing exposure to threats and war since childhood. Nasima needed a translator, and the same female translator was present in all therapy sessions.

Nasima remembered how bombs were falling in her neighbourhood throughout her childhood and how her father was captured and imprisoned by intruding soldiers. She had a recurrent nightmare of a huge stone falling down from the sky. As her husband felt increasingly politically threatened, they fled to Europe with their four children. They lived in an apartment; the two children at home were thriving. Nasima had a job in a kitchen ('work trial'), which she unfortunately lost halfway through therapy due to inflammation in her shoulder caused by overworking.

In therapy, Nasima worked with her sense of home in several ways. Nasima realized that as a younger woman in her country of origin, she did not have a space for herself at home. She used to be surrounded by people, so now, in her new home in Denmark, she had difficulties adjusting to being alone. In the first phase of therapy, we worked with body awareness, and breathing to music to help her to relax. We used music such as Enya's 'A Day Without Rain' for music breathing (according to the method developed by Körlin, 2010). Working with inner resources, she imagined sitting at the table and having a family dinner in her flat in Denmark, where everybody shared a meal and had a cosy feeling. An Afghan instrumental flute piece ('Khudo Buad Yoret' by Ahmad Zahir, played in E-minor by Jahed Jahede) became her 'safe music place' used at home every day.

Entering the second therapy phase, she confronted traumatic memories. Nasima worked with her nightmares related to experiences of bombing and being insecure at home and with her anxiety about being alone in the flat. She conveyed that she sometimes vaguely saw a shadow of an unknown male in her home, making her very anxious. Nasima did not know who or what it was – and we discussed whether it could be a 'jinni'.[1] We agreed on using a powerful music piece called 'Eld Gjaldr' by Ragnarop (a folk music group from Finland) with open eyes. During the music, she entered a bodily posture where she took more place and seemed bigger and broader. Listening to the piece a second time, she started to push away the shadow in her imagery. After the music listening, she drew the shadow on a piece of paper, and when asked about what she would like to do with it, she got anxious. I suggested that she dared to tear it apart, which she did, and threw it in the bin. These actions gave her a sense of power over the fear connected to the shadow, and she got a livelier expression on her face and expressed both laughter and tears. She did not see the shadow in her home again after that session. In another session, while listening to music, I guided her to imagine that she placed her burdening memories and thoughts on leaves that flew down a river. She used this exercise a lot at home to help her get rid of worrying. During the ending sessions, she felt safe enough

---

1   A jinni can be described as an invisible or barely visible spirit that can possess people or show up in the surroundings, being the reason of diseases. Jinnis are connected with fear, and it can be difficult to get an exact description, but I have had a number of clients describing it as a dark shadow.

to uncover what she thought was the main reason behind her stress and anxiety: that her mother-in-law had abused her physically with beatings and had also been verbally insulting and dominating on a daily basis for years. Nasima had additional therapy after the end of this therapy course to be able to work with this.

After the therapy had ended, Nasima spoke in an interview:

Nasima: Before, if I sat alone in my home, it was as if the ceiling came very close to my head, and I could not breathe, but this has changed. I can sit alone without having these feelings. Before, when I was alone at night (because my husband worked nightshifts), I could not sleep in my own bed before my husband came home. I often slept in my children's rooms, where I felt safe. Now I can sleep alone, but the light must be on. Sometimes when I close my eyes, I can be a little scared, as if somebody stands at my feet, but then I get up and look around, and then I can lie down and sleep.

Interviewer: You have become braver?

Nasima: Yes, before I did not dare to look around. Before, I could not sit alone and eat; I sat either at the window or with my eyes on the door. Now, I can sit and eat in my kitchen in peace without being afraid and having that anxiety in my body.

Comment on vignette 2

The vignette describes how the cultural differences between Nasima's life in Afghanistan and Denmark were processed and how her sense of having a space and a home was different then and now. She mourned the loss of her country and family but also enjoyed her new freedom and independence – the imagery of family dinners connected past and present.

The therapy revealed how her childhood experiences of insecurity during attacks and bombings had created a foundation for her current anxiety, and how the ongoing physical abuse had affected her sense of safety. Working with the anxiety did not entirely remove her fear, but she could begin to manage in a better way, even though the loss of her job did make her more isolated.

I want to add some comments to Nasima's experience of seeing a shadow. In some Arabic cultures, the concept of a 'jinni' is seen as a mythic being mentioned in both pre-Islamic and Islamic religions as an invisible spirit that can cause harm and illness (Encyclopaedia Britannica, n.d.). It is mentioned in the Koran and described as a fire spirit, that can be both good and evil. According to a survey study carried out in a transcultural psychiatric clinic, 43% of the sample of 119 Muslim participants saw their psychiatric symptoms as connected to a jinni (Lim *et al.*, 2018), and many patients declined to participate in the survey because of a fear of stigmatization or metaphysical repercussions. It is essential to be sensitive to this matter. While in Western psychology seeing a shadow could be interpreted as a dissociated experience or a hallucination caused by fear, meeting the client in their world, and working with the phenomena as a lived experience, serves as cultural humility, as presented above. By providing support and resources, one can stay open to what the client needs to do to cope with their experience, realizing the spiritual connotations of the issue.

Vignette 3: Fighting for her house

Cinderella, a 48-year-old woman, married with three children, fled from Iraq with her husband. She had experienced war incidents, but the therapy soon focused on her childhood, where issues of insecurity and abuse came to the surface. Her grandmother raised Cinderella, whereas her twin sister stayed home with their mother because her mother could not cope with two babies on top of the other children. Cinderella thus suffered an upbringing where she served her grandmother and aunt; she never had any new clothes or toys, and she experienced plenty of physical abuse. From age eight to the end of the high school, she worked in the family fabrics store without any salary, and she had to cook for herself. She did not have time to play. As a young woman, she met a well-educated and kind man and married him. They had three children together. Because her husband worked as a translator for the Danish army in Iraq, he and the family were threatened, and they fled to Denmark.

In the therapy, Cinderella listened to meditative pieces such as Secret Garden's 'Song to a Secret Garden' and 'Ode to Simplicity' to sense her body and relax. She presented a music preference for both Arabic and Native American music. She asked me to find music with drumming, songs such as 'Woman's Dance' and 'Dance of the North' by Shenandoah and recordings of traditional music. While listening to the music, she remembered episodes from her childhood, and she imagined embracing her younger self, giving herself nourishment and love. As she had a very low self-confidence, a cousin managed to touch her and abuse her sexually during several family gatherings. She imagined standing up for herself and rejecting her cousin.

Cinderella had been working in several different 'work trial' places, and she spoke Danish language at a basic level, so we worked without a translator. Her husband worked in the health sector. Well into the therapy, her husband became mentally unstable and finally left their home to live by himself. Cinderella was very unhappy about that but supported her husband in his process. She now had to manage life with the children on her own.

The house owner asked her to move out because the apartment was in her husband's name. She felt unsafe about the neighbours, too. She tried to find a new apartment she could afford but without success.

In a therapy session, she focused on her feelings about the threat to her living situation while listening to a native American chant, 'Lyolay Aleloya', from the album *Sacred Spirit*, and to Carlos Nakai's 'Earth Spirit'. The music helped her to feel empowered. From this position, she got the idea to talk to the house owner, negotiate, and get her own contract. Some days later, she went to the office and got an unlimited contract. To celebrate and support her victory and pride in the following session, we got up and moved to a piece of music ('Palladio' by Karl Jenkins) that gave her a feeling of moving forward. Towards the end of therapy, she remembered that she had always dreamed about getting an education to have a job of her own, which I heartily supported.

When we met three years later, she had not managed to get an education, but had a so-called 'flex' job nine hours a week that she was very happy about. Her three children did well, and she had been contacted by and had formed a close relationship with the daughter of her twin sister in Iraq. She was unfortunately again in a situation of homelessness and lack of finances.

Comment on vignette 3

This case vignette, like vignette 2, sheds light on how childhood trauma, abuse, and war trauma can be intertwined. This woman's childhood home was never safe, but she had an optimistic outlook and worked hard in her therapy. As a music therapist, one often expects that people from a specific country want to listen to music from their original culture. Cinderella acknowledged that she identified with the oppression of the people of the American First Nations and found comfort in the sorrow and pride in their voices due to her marginalization in her original family.

According to her living situation, she did not expect to be a lone mother and never took responsibility for practical issues or the economy. The music therapy became a container for the family crisis and her empowerment process, which led to her saving their living place and safety in a 'heroic deed'. The drumming and singing music reminded her on a bodily level of her power, the power of resistance. This had implications for her self-worth, as she saw herself in a new light. Future planning indicates the third phase of trauma work, where the time lock of trauma starts to lift off, the trauma memory can be placed in the past, and the future and social connections appear more clearly. Only when accessing this phase did Cinderella reveal that she was well-connected on social media and often acted as an online advisor to other people.

DISCUSSION AND ENDING

Conquering fear, suffering profound tragedy, and overcoming childhood trauma were some of the themes in these three vignettes from trauma-informed music and imagery therapy. Despite the complexity and differences of the three stories, they had the theme of homecoming in common: homecoming to the body and the inner world and homecoming and family life in new surroundings. Music had many roles: building a therapeutic alliance, facilitating imagery, holding emotions, assisting mind-body connection and arousal regulation, empowering, and much more.

Homecoming to the self and the body is significant when it comes to traumatization, as trauma, according to van der Hart *et al.* (2006), is often accompanied by a phobia towards feeling and sensing oneself and the body where the fearful re-traumatization takes place repeatedly, every day. Music and imagery bring structure, holding, 'presentification', focus, and safety, and especially those who learned to use music in a new way daily saw a considerable improvement in their symptoms and state. For the music to be a helping agent for processes of homecoming in therapy, the therapist must make informed choices of music according to musical parameters such as a low tempo, a simple structure, instrumental music, a warm sound, repetitions, and clear melody lines. For this work I was specifically informed by the Music Taxonomy by Wärja and Bonde (2014) and basic receptive music theory (Grocke & Skewes-McFerran, 2021). However, it can be very difficult to identify music pieces that are stable rhythmically or that do not include singing in music from Arabic countries, as much of this music is very percussive and includes alternating singing and instrumental passages. I also find that it is important to know that slow music often has a connotation of sadness in these cultures. An attitude of sensitivity and curiosity to music from the client's culture is very important. It is an art to find 'good enough pieces' from the repertoire and preferred styles of the client, that can be used for imagination and regulation, such as the Afghan flute piece in vignette 2. Furthermore, I find it very important to not have prejudices about what might work for a specific client, such as believing that it is necessary to look for music from their country of origin: some clients identify with music from other parts of the world, some clients have a need to avoid music from their culture as it might act as a trauma trigger, and some clients might have a big interest in, for example, classical Western music.

Carrying out music therapy in many cases contains some elements of social justice. Sometimes it is necessary to help with practical issues and needs related to basic daily living. Cooperation between therapeutic teams and regional administration is part of the work, and network meetings are often part of a therapeutic course, as a client needs to feel safe and protected to be able to work with trauma. I have experienced several cases of poor housing and poor economy that have taken up much energy and time in the therapies. From a humanitarian point of view, it seems counterintuitive to grant expensive therapy hours working to mend psychological reactions on subjects that are so fundamental: refugees should have decent housing so that they do not need to fight even more for their safety and survival than they already do.

Finally, addressing the theme of gender, I do think that due to the gender roles that are still present in most of the world, it is often the women who carry the responsibility for the children and the home and who use their energy on the family before they heal themselves. In this chapter, the focus has been on the women and mothers, but men and fathers also need treatment. Careful support for the children is also very important, as it is often the whole family who suffers.

Taking care of home and family is carried by tremendous love. I want to honour the ongoing strength, love, and care for children, homes, and families that women and men carry out. Coming home to ourselves is both an individual journey and a journey of mutuality, community, and care.

REFERENCES

Abdulbaki, H. & Berger, J. (2020). Using culture-specific music therapy to manage the therapy deficit of post-traumatic stress disorder and associated mental health conditions in Syrian refugee host environments. *Approaches: An Interdisciplinary Journal of Music Therapy*, 12(2). https://approaches.gr/wp-content/uploads/2020/12/4-Approaches-12-2-2020-a20190530-abdulbaki.pdf.

Beck, B., Messell, C., Meyer, S., Cordtz, T., *et al.* (2017). Feasibility of trauma-focused Guided Imagery and Music with adult refugees diagnosed with PTSD – a pilot study. *Nordic Journal of Music Therapy*, 27(1), 67–86. http://dx.doi.org/10.1080/08098131.2 017.1286368.

Beck, B. D. (2018). Music therapy with refugees. In S. L. Jacobsen, I. N. Petersen, & L. O. Bonde (eds), *A comprehensive guide to music therapy* (pp. 342–352). London: Jessica Kingsley Publishers.

Beck, B. D., Lund, S. T., Søgaard, U., Simonsen, E., *et al.* (2018). Music therapy versus treatment as usual: Protocol of a randomized non-inferiority study with traumatized refugees diagnosed with posttraumatic stress disorder (PTSD). *Trials*, 19, 301. https://doi.org/10.1186/s13063-018-2662-z.

Beck, B. D. (2019). Sacred moments in Guided Imagery and Music. *Approaches: An Interdisciplinary Journal of Music Therapy*, 11(1). https://doi.org/10.56883/aijmt.2019.230.

Beck, B. D., Meyer, S. L., Simonsen, E., Søgaard, U., *et al.* (2021). Music therapy was non-inferior to verbal standard treatment of traumatized refugees in mental health care: Results from a randomized clinical trial. *European Journal of Psychotraumatology*, (12)1. https://doi.org/10.1080/20008198.2021.1930960.

Bemman, B., Bertelsen, L. R., Wärja, M., & Bonde, L. O. (2023). Inter-rater agreement in classifying music according to a Guided Imagery and Music taxonomy. *Journal of Music Therapy*, 60(3), 282–313. https://doi.org/10.1093/jmt/thad014.

Boccagni, P. (2018). At the Roots of Home, Away From It: Meanings, Places and Values of Home through the Biographic Narratives of Immigrant Care Workers in Italy. In K. Davis, H. Ghorashi, & P. Smets (eds) *Contested Belonging: Spaces, Practices, Biographies* (pp.313–332). Leeds: Emerald Publishing.

Bonny, H. (2002). *Music and Consciousness. The Evolution of Guided Imagery and Music.* Gilsum, NH: Barcelona Publishers.

Coombes, E. (2018). We all came from somewhere. *Voices,* 18(1). https://voices.no/index.php/voices/article/view/2539/2310.

Dieterich-Hartwell, R. & Koch, S. C. (2017). Creative arts therapies as temporary home for refugees: Insights from literature and practice. *Behavioral Science (Basel),* 7(4), 69. doi: 10.3390/bs7040069.

Edwards, J. (2022). Cultural Humility in Music Therapy Practice. In L. E. Beer & J. C. Birnbaum (eds) *Trauma-Informed Music Therapy* (Chapter 3). London: Routledge.

Encyclopaedia Britannica. (n.d.) Jinni. www.britannica.com/topic/jinni.

Fazel, M., Wheeler, J., & Danesh, J. (2005). Prevalence of serious mental disorder in 7000 refugees resettled in Western countries: A systematic review. *Lancet London England,* 365, 1309–1314.

Grocke, D. (ed.). (2022). *The Bonny Method of Guided Imagery and Music and Beyond* (second edition). Gilsum, NH: Barcelona Publishers.

Grocke, D. & Moe, T. (2015). *Guided Imagery & Music (GIM) and Music Imagery Methods for Individual and Group Therapy.* London: Jessica Kingsley Publishers.

Grocke, D. & Skewes-McFerran, K. (2021). *Receptive Music Therapy* (second edition). London: Jessica Kingsley Publishers.

Herman, J. (1997). *Trauma and Recovery: The Aftermath of Violence – From Domestic Abuse to Political Terror.* New York, NY: Basic Books.

Ho, H. Y. & Loo, F. Y. (2023). A theoretical paradigm proposal of music arousal and emotional valence interrelations with tempo, preference, familiarity, and presence of lyrics. *New Ideas in Psychology,* 71. https://doi.org/10.1016/j.newideapsych.2023.101033.

Juslin, P. (2019). *Musical Emotions Explained.* Oxford: Oxford University Press.

Kale, A., Stupples, P., & Kindon, S. (2019). Feeling at home: A multisensory analysis of former refugee and host society residents' integration in Wellington, Aotearoa New Zealand. *Emotion, Space and Society,* 33, 1–8. https://doi.org/10.1016/j.emospa.2019.100615.

Kim, K. & Smets, P. (2020). Home experiences and homemaking practices of single Syrian refugees in an innovative housing project in Amsterdam. *Current Sociology,* 68(5), 607–627. https://doi.org/10.1177/0011392120927744.

Koelsch, S. (2014). Brain correlates of music-evoked emotions. *Nature Reviews Neuroscience,* 15, 170–180. https://doi.org/10.1038/nrn3666.

Körlin, D. (2010). *Music Listening, Imagery and Creativity in Psychiatry.* Saarbrücken: Lambert.

Lenette, C. & Sunderland, N. (2017). 'Will there be music for us?' Mapping the health and well-being potential of participatory music practice with asylum seekers and refugees across contexts of conflict and refuge. *Arts & Health: International Journal for Research, Policy & Practice,* 8(1), 32–49. https://doi.org/10.1080/17533015.2014.961943.

Levine, P. (2010). *In an Unspoken Voice: How the Body Releases Trauma and Restores Goodness.* Berkeley, CA: North Atlantic Books.

Lim, A., Hoek, H. W., Ghane, S., Deen, M., & Blom, J. D. (2018). The attribution of mental health problems to Jinn: An explorative study in a transcultural psychiatric outpatient clinic. *Frontiers of Psychiatry,* 28(9), 89. doi: 10.3389/fpsyt.2018.00089.

Mallon, T. & Hoog Antink, M. (2021). The sound of lost homes – Introducing the COVER Model – theoretical framework and practical insight into music therapy with refugees and asylum seekers. *Voices,* 21(2). https://voices.no/index.php/voices/article/view/3124/3260.

Martin-Saavedra, J. S., Vergara-Mendez, L. D., & Talero-Gutiérrez, C. (2018). Music is an effective intervention for the management of pain: An umbrella review. *Complementary Therapies in Clinical Practice*, 32, 103–114. https://doi.org/10.1016/j.ctcp.2018.06.003.

Pedersen, I. N., Lindvang, C., & Beck, B. D. (2022). *Resonant Learning in Music Therapy. A Training Model to Tune the Therapist.* London: Jessica Kingsley Publishers.

Porges, S. W. (2022). Polyvagal theory: A science of safety. *Frontiers in Integrative Neuroscience*, 16. doi: 10.3389/fnint.2022.871227.

van der Hart, O., Nijenhuis, E. R. S., & Steele, K. (2006). *The Haunted Self: Structural Dissociation and the Treatment of Chronic Traumatization.* New York, NY: W. W. Norton & Co.

Wärja, M. & Bonde, L. O. (2014). Music as co-therapist: Towards a taxonomy of music in therapeutic music and imagery work. *Music and Medicine*, 6(2), 16–27. https://doi.org/10.47513/mmd.v6i2.175.

World Health Organization. (2019a). *International Classification of Diseases (ICD-11).* https://icd.who.int/en.

World Health Organization. (2019b). *Complex Post-Traumatic Stress Disorder.* https://icd.who.int/browse11/l-m/en#/http://id.who.int/icd/entity/585833559.

CHAPTER 4

Sounds of Pain and Hope

*Storytelling with Music – Narrative Music Psychotherapy
Through the Lens of Trauma and Recovery*

HEIDI AHONEN

INTRODUCTION

This chapter looks through the lens of refugees as survivors of trauma and my explorations into building a model I have named Narrative Music Psychotherapy with individuals and groups. The rationale for using this method is explored, and practical ideas suitable for different phases of the therapy process are introduced. Developing this technique was a long process and continuum of the Group Analytical Music Therapy I developed previously. My training at Harvard University Medical School's Global Trauma Recovery Certificate programme taught me the importance of clients' stories and narrative approaches. I currently practise in Ontario, Canada, in my small private practice, but have also conducted workshops and training with volunteers in the Middle East and refugee camps.

Telling one's story, finding and acknowledging the truth, and having it validated and believed by others are essential elements of refugee trauma recovery, as is regaining one's dignity after terrorism, mass violence, torture, and other purposely planned brutality. Humiliation and cultural destruction are often the very goals and instruments of the perpetrators of these acts and are closely linked to how many refugees think the world sees them, turning them into a powerless person. According to Mollica (2006a, pp.70–71), 'Perpetrators intentionally try to get the tellers of the trauma story to doubt their sanity. Because of this, survivors, in turn, doubt a listener's ability to believe in the truthfulness of their experience.' The storyteller-listener relationship is the core of the compassionate, sensitive, and empathetic therapeutic relationship; as Mollica (2006a, p.47) says, 'the storyteller is the teacher, and the listener is the student'. As Mollica states, every trauma story needs witnessing to be therapeutic.

Schauer *et al.* (2011) introduce the importance of autobiographical memories. Refugees with post-traumatic stress disorder (PTSD) have a substantial distortion in their autobiographical memory and chronological order of lifetime periods, including their beginnings and endings. The traumatic event may feel timeless; it is not represented as a general event or positioned in a lifetime period. Although intense recollections of the event, including sensory details, may remain (i.e. the smell of blood, loud sounds, pictures of soldiers in uniforms, and the kinaesthetic sensation of feeling cold), it may be impossible to verbalize the details consistently and chronologically. Because trauma memory is fragmented, this disturbs the cortical inhibitory control of the fear response, and as a result, the person cannot differentiate between past and present threats. Physically and mentally, they may be out of touch with their here-and-now feelings but, at the same time, react with the same panic reaction they did during the original trauma. It is as if the trauma event is still going on. Not being able to share the trauma memories may lead to social isolation, numbness, depression, flashbacks, and nightmares.

Trauma-focused psychotherapists (Chu, 2011; Courtois & Ford, 2014; Levine, 2015; Mollica, 2006a, 2011; Schauer *et al.*, 2011; van der Kolk, 2015) advocate safety and stabilization in therapy, followed by processing the trauma story. Narrative Music Psychotherapy, a model I developed for my refugee clients' individual and group work, combines the general ideas of exposure therapy with Mollica's (2006b) trauma-storytelling elements and Group Analytic Music Therapy (Ahonen-Eerikainen, 2007), Herman's (1997) three trauma recovery phases, and Klein and Schermer's (2000) healing factors of the trauma group (Ahonen, 2014, 2018, 2019a).

With Narrative Music Psychotherapy interventions that utilize improvisation, therapeutic music listening, and songwriting, the role of music is to provide a safe symbolic distance, allowing transitional objects and transforming images to arise. Music enhances both externalization and internalization processes that will enable clients to externalize their pain, despair, and confusion and to internalize hope, the first step for recovery. In these sessions, trauma storytelling is used. According to different Group Analytic Music Therapy levels, such as projection (Ahonen, 2016; Ahonen-Eerikainen, 2007), the client may experience, for example, the following: 'This (external) music sounds as my (inner) feelings feel.' 'This (external) music sounds like me (inside).' 'This song tells my refugee journey...' 'This is how my fear sounds...' Music may also activate the transference level

(Ahonen, 2016; Ahonen-Eerikainen, 2007): 'This is the atmosphere of my flashback or nightmare...' 'This music tells about my home country...' The role of music can serve as a therapeutic self-representation, enabling the client to reflect different parts of themselves and their experiences: 'This music represents me, my family, my feelings, my future fears, my dreams...'

The ultimate purpose of therapy is to diminish shame and isolation, and facilitate sharing, validation, and the witnessing of difficult experiences. It can also provide emotional support and empathy, enhance coping, self-healing, and personal post-traumatic growth, and instil trust and hope. While many traumatizing experiences cannot be 'cured' and erased from memories, they no longer need to define who the person is for the rest of their lives, nor determine their destiny. Despite the trauma experience, it is possible for them to view themselves, others, the world, and the future from a healthier perspective.

Why use trauma storytelling in therapy?

Trauma storytelling is a powerful way to overcome the impacts of trauma and fear. Telling the story again, step by step, in every detail, in chronological order, while simultaneously processing the related emotions, allows the brain to organize the fragmented memory and store it properly in the right area of the brain. It enables the reconstruction of the episode's chronological, explicit, declarative, and autobiographical representation. It also allows the brain to regulate the original fear activation and gain control over disturbing images. It will enable learning to activate sensory and emotional memory without fear. It will guide in distinguishing between past and current dangers (Schauer *et al.*, 2011). According to Mollica (2006a), 'all trauma stories are personal and historical accounts by ordinary people who want to heal themselves while also teaching others about survival and healing' (p.48). As therapists, we should always have a phenomenological perspective on the stories we hear. We should encourage the storyteller to share their subjective, lived experience and their insights into the meaning of their experiences. Mollica (2006b) tells us that 'the refugee trauma story is their narrative told in their own words about the traumatic life events they have experienced and the impact of these events on their social, physical, and emotional well-being' (p.21). Using this lens, we can say that finding trauma's personal and cultural meaning is essential to healing, where 'self–healing occurs at the psychological level when the mind is able to construct a new meaning out of violence' (Mollica, 2006b, p.97). According to Viktor Frankl (1985), 'in some ways suffering ceases to be suffering at the moment it finds a meaning, ... we may also find meaning in life even when confronted with a hopeless situation when facing a fate that cannot be changed' (p.135).

The trauma stories shared during therapeutic discussions are also survivor stories, where the victims become survivors.

Why use music with refugees who have experienced trauma?

Memories and emotions can be triggered by music listening and improvisation (Brown et al., 2004; Juslin et al., 2015; Koelsch, 2014). According to Frühholz et al. (2014), the part of the brain called the amygdala is specifically involved in the initial decoding of the emotional value of music. The hippocampus processes more complex vocal and musical emotions, providing memory-based and contextual associations. Because trauma memories are stored as sensations, similar sensations can trigger associated memories.

A strong rationale for using music as a tool of trauma psychotherapy is the fact that body memories include the nervous system that communicates the somatic trauma memories between the brain and all other parts of the body. It seems that music can access implicit, unconscious (body) memory more easily than words; with music, it is possible to experience these trauma memories without the explicit (conscious, cognitive) memory that is often needed to verbalize or make sense of it (Rothschild, 2000).

Many hormonal effects attached to music have a direct implication on which music therapy interventions to choose. Refugees who have PTSD live with elevated amounts of the stress hormone cortisol, which can result in measurable changes to their brain structures, such as the size of the amygdala and hippocampus. The fact that music decreases the amount of cortisol is a strong rationale for using it as a therapy tool (Helsing et al., 2016). When working with refugees from various cultural backgrounds, knowing what type of music they feel uplifting is crucial. According to research, only person-preferred uplifting music activates areas in the limbic system, releasing endorphins that naturally increase our body's threshold for pain, battle depression, increase our overall immunity system, and affect our emotions (Gangrade, 2012).

Another rationale for using music with refugees who have experienced trauma is that music releases serotonin and, therefore, counteracts depression (Evers & Suhr, 2000). Music has also been shown to increase levels of melatonin and, at the same time, decrease insomnia, a typical symptom of PTSD (Kumar et al., 1999). Many studies also claim that music releases dopamine; dopamine explains the spurts of pleasant memories while listening to the music we enjoy as well as supporting bonding with others. It also describes the pleasure we feel during an anticipated chord resolution and the peak experiences we often have during music (Salimpoor & Zatorre, 2013). Dopamine may also explain some of the cathartic events often experienced during improvisation. Listening, singing, and playing music together releases oxytocin that helps us to feel belonging and connectivity, restoring trust in each other (Ahonen, 2018; Chanda & Levitin, 2013).

THERAPEUTIC PHASES AND SESSION STRUCTURE OF NARRATIVE MUSIC PSYCHOTHERAPY

A typical Narrative Music Psychotherapy process includes various therapeutic phases that I analyse through the lens of Herman's (1997) three trauma recovery phases, Klein and Schermer's (2000) healing factors of the trauma group, and Mollica's (2006a) trauma-storytelling elements (Ahonen, 2014, 2018, 2019a). The seven dynamic phases of a typical therapeutic process are as follows:

1. Establishing grounding, stabilization, safety, and empowerment.

2. Telling and witnessing the trauma/survivor story.

3. Experiencing and expressing trauma/survivor story related emotions.

4. Processing and grieving the trauma and its consequences.

5. Restructuring the assumptive world that was damaged during the trauma; finding new meanings.

6. Restoring trust and the sense of reality.

7. Reconnecting and reintegrating the personality so that the trauma no longer defines it; launching future dreams.

A typical Narrative Music Psychotherapy individual session (1.5 hours) follows the structure of:

1. Relaxation/grounding.

2. Storytelling and processing with music, art, discussion.

3. Relaxation/grounding.

For individual sessions, the room is arranged with two chairs and a selection of instruments and art materials. The instruments include various styles of drums, rainsticks, chimes, singing bowls, flutes, and instruments from the participants' cultural origins. The art materials include markers, crayons, stickers, clues, colourful paper, colourful yarn, and clay.

A typical group session (2 hours 15 minutes) is as follows:

1. Stabilization: relaxation/grounding exercise.

2. Psychoeducational content and discussion.

3. Break.

4. Stabilization: relaxation/grounding exercise.

5. Processing: music and art interventions.

6. Sharing through therapeutic discussion and improvisation.

7. Stabilization: relaxing/grounding (closing) exercise.

For group sessions, the chairs and tables are in a circle. Each client receives a handout including material on the session's psychoeducational topic.

Stabilization: grounding and relaxation

Every session must start with stabilization and grounding; these are aspects of trauma work that must be held in mind by the therapist throughout the process. Before embarking on the storytelling, the therapist should reflect on whether safety is necessary for a particular content, technique, next phase of processing, or particular emotions. Moving gracefully backwards and forwards between the different therapy process phases and reinforcing the safety, stability, and grounding should never be seen as a failure but rather a sign of a safe and ethical work environment. The goal is to empower the trauma survivor so that their symptoms no longer rule their lives.

During the first session, I spend significant time regulating breathing, ensuring that the clients master the technique. The goal is to choose a breathing exercise to incorporate before, during, and after the session or whenever needed – during and outside the therapy. I use short, concrete, deep belly breathing and progressive relaxation exercises. I explain that we can consciously regulate our breathing, gain control over disturbing images/flashbacks, and calm our bodies and minds.

Choosing the right type of music to enhance body relaxation is essential. The tempo should be steady and slow with a melody line that includes repetition and nothing surprising. The harmonic structure should be familiar. Breathing and body relaxation exercises can also be administered by me playing flute, singing bowls, rainsticks, or singing, humming, or drumming together. I may incorporate culturally appropriate music with a slow tempo, asking clients to make sounds while they exhale. There may be guided, deep abdominal breathing exercises during slow, structured music listening or drumming – safe, comforting, and empowering images would be used as induction. I may ask clients to bring their own music (song, melody, rhythm) that makes them feel safe, comfortable, relaxed, calm, grounded, energized, strong, and empowered.

The grounding exercises allow clients to experience making conscious choices about something that can be controlled during a flashback. I ask clients to drop their feet on the ground and change their posture to feel more grounded. I may ask them to change their position and become aware of the sensations. Grounding exercises could involve drumming or playing together, singing a particular theme song that the client or group has adopted or written themselves, or using a grounding image during music listening. I also teach clients to use music outside sessions to prevent and overcome their flashbacks and triggers. For example, what song or melody could they sing or hum when triggered by disturbing memories? What song, melody, or rhythm reminds them that they are safe or makes them feel grounded or strong?

All exercises involving physical sensations aim to help the clients become aware of the real sensations they have, thus helping them focus on these and allowing flashbacks to fade. Musical sound discrimination activities during improvisation or music listening help connect with the here and now. If disturbing images or flashbacks are present during music listening, I may ask the client to focus on the music and describe the different instruments they hear. During improvisation, I ask them to consciously make different rhythmical patterns or play softly and very slowly.

As a grounding intervention, I often invite the clients to imagine their safe, relaxing favorite place or thing during rhythmically and melodically steady music. This could be something they perceive as pleasant or lovely from their past or an imaginary place, a place in nature, a favourite food, or a memory of them doing something they enjoy doing, such as cooking, gardening, dancing. I will ask the clients to describe it to themselves in detail, write it down, or draw a picture of it. What is there, what colours do they see, what sounds do they hear, are there smells or tastes they experience? What do they do? How do they feel? If an intrusive thought or image arises, I encourage them to remember this favourite place. This image can also be used at the beginning of the session as a way of providing emotional grounding, something that is as essential as physical grounding.

The closing exercise to the session often incorporates the grounding or relaxation exercises described earlier. Sometimes, I have objects that I ask clients to choose, reflect on, and take home with them – for example, stones with words such as peace, love, trust, and hope, postcards with an encouraging message, colourful leaves with motivational words, short poetry, or verses of wisdom. Closing with a song or a particular drumming exercise may become a specific ritual with some groups. Whatever the intervention, the aim is to ensure that the client leaves the room fully grounded.

Psychoeducation

The psychoeducational section usually takes 30 minutes at the beginning of each group session. The chosen topics aim to help the clients gain an understanding of their trauma symptoms and see them as normal reactions for any refugees. The topics vary depending on the needs and, for example, whether or not the clients have already resettled in a new country. At the beginning of every session, I will explain that the session aims to show what the researchers have found from other refugees' experiences, encourage clients to reflect on their experiences, and highlight that they are the experts who can teach me about refugee experiences and recovery. In every session, I also acknowledge resilience and self-healing and that the clients are authors of a survivor's story.

Processing: Storytelling with music

Silenced because of feelings of humiliation, many refugees never share their trauma experiences nor seek help for their trauma symptoms (Van der Veer, 1998). Narrative Music Psychotherapy techniques aim to provide clients with a safe space to process their emotions. When working with refugees who have experienced trauma, it is essential to understand that an intellectual insight, such as acknowledging and understanding the trauma, is only the first yet important step before the actual trauma processing. The painful emotions must also be expressed and processed. Trauma reconstruction, as well as the construction of autobiographical knowledge about the traumatized event, is sometimes challenging; anger, shame, and guilt are difficult to process, so it is often easier to avoid these. During the groups, the therapeutic, free-flowing group discussion after musical interventions follows the principles of Group Analytic Music Therapy (Ahonen, 2007). Every group member's voice is essential, and their experiences are validated. At the beginning of every session, I clearly state that it is up to the clients to choose how much they feel comfortable sharing in this context. These discussions also occur in individual sessions between therapist and client.

It is usual for any trauma survivor to avoid recalling the trauma-related emotions such as shame, humiliation, and helplessness and protect themselves from pain and re-traumatization. Although Narrative Music Psychotherapy involves telling trauma stories, the first rule is to respect the defences and not to force any trauma memories. The client must feel safe to feel unsafe – to experience 'I am safe even though I may not feel safe'. The defences are there for a reason. Without inner resources to cope with difficult memories, a cathartic recollection of traumatic events and re-experiencing the associated emotions would not be therapeutic; it would be re-traumatizing. Sometimes, trauma stories should be told in brief segments. At the Harvard University clinic specializing in global refugee trauma, they have a saying: 'A little bit, a lot over a long period' (Mollica, 2006a, p.124).

USING NARRATIVE MUSIC PSYCHOTHERAPY INTERVENTIONS WITH GROUPS AND INDIVIDUALS
I have set out below some examples of interventions in this method.

My refugee journey
I often ask the refugee client(s) to draw their refugee journey on a map. They frequently remember the exact date and time when the horrible things started to happen. They may describe long periods during which things got gradually worse. I also ask them to reflect on their identities: who were they before the event, and who are they now? Musical processing may include referential, titled improvisations representing specific parts of the journey, life before the trauma events, or certain emotions. Sometimes songwriting about this journey may be used.

If I were a tree...
This is a typical intervention where I share pictures of trees growing in different, sometimes challenging environments. I usually start with the following induction: *'Close your eyes...but you can open them if you wish. Sitting in your chair, feel the ground beneath your feet and toes. Lift your feet above the ground and stomp so that you feel grounded. You are grounded! Feel your back on the chair. You can move your shoulders, stretch your hands, and feel that you control your movement. Focus on breathing. Inhale through your nose. Exhale through your mouth. Allow yourself to breathe deeper than usual so you feel it everywhere in your body while you are very grounded, your feet on the floor. When the music begins, allow yourself to imagine that you are a tree... Allow yourself to see that tree: How big is it; how tall? How is the ground around it? Roots? Trunk? Branches? Leaves, fruits, birds/animals? Weather, past storms? Where in your tree do you see what it has experienced? How does your tree demonstrate its resilience, its ability to bounce back? Is there post-traumatic growth visible in your tree – growth after the traumatizing episode? How does your tree reach towards the light? Always remember that having a difficult experience is not the only thing that defines who you are. You have your history, unique personality, strengths, gifts, and talents. You are much more. Your tree is beautiful.'*

After clients have selected their trees, they are encouraged to add any details to make them even more representative of their life experiences. I then encourage them to reflect on the tree, having a dialogue with it. I may give them a handout with questions:

- What kind of ground does the tree have? Is it stable/changing/flat/bumpy? What is underground? Rocks/soft soil/spring…? Where does it get its nutrition? How is it connected with water? Did it grow in challenging surroundings without water or nutrition?

- What roots impact the tree? Family/cultural/ethnic/religious roots…? Do they bring nutrition or something toxic? How can the tree celebrate its origins?

- What kind of trunk does the tree have? How tall/sturdy? How does the trunk feel? Any visible scars? What are the tree's inner strengths, gifts, talents, core values?

- What kind of branches does the tree have? Delicate/solid/weak/long/short?

- What type of leaves does the tree have? Is there new growth/flowers/seeds/fruits? How are they used, and by whom? What are its hopes/dreams/wishes/goals/aspirations, its legacy for others or the world?

- What kind of weather, climate, atmosphere is around the tree? Is it sunny/warm/cold/freezing/dry/cloudy/rainy/stormy/a hurricane/a tornado…? Is there light around, and how does the tree reach for it? Has the tree experienced storms in the past? If so, how did it cope? How does the tree protect itself?

- Is the tree alone or surrounded by other trees or plants? What is the support system and its relationships? Any birds/other animals living in the tree? Does the tree provide shelter/food?

- How does the tree take care of itself every day, when it is scared/sad/angry/feels injustice/helplessness/loneliness/despair?

- From where does the tree draw hope?

- If the tree could speak, what would it say?

- If the tree were to teach other trees about their experiences and learning, what would it teach?

I then ask them to give their tree a title. If this takes place within a group, there are Group Analytic Music Therapy improvisations following this, one group member being the leader and others supporting and reflecting on that person's improvisation. The improvisations may be about the entire tree or one detail or reflection. I ask: 'If a composer were to make music about the tree, how would it sound?', 'How does the feeling/experience of the tree sound?' There could also be an improvisation about the forest that includes all the group's trees, or there could be individual or joint songwriting. This intervention can also be adapted for individual therapy during which the client improvises their tree reflections with the therapist.

Chronological life journey: Sounds of pain and hope

This is a technique I use with refugees over several sessions in individual therapy; it can be adapted for the group setting. I combine Schauer *et al.*'s (2011) Narrative Exposure Therapy with music interventions such as referential improvisation, therapeutic music listening, songwriting, and creative art techniques. The client chooses a piece of yarn and places it on a large piece of paper to represent their life journey, past and present. I ask them to leave some yarn to represent the future and then write their birth date at the beginning. They then place flower stickers or sparkly, colourful 'diamonds' onto the yarn to represent positive and happy moments in their life. After this, the different events are discussed in detail. I usually write down the story, and the titles and descriptions of the events are added to the paper. Emotions are acknowledged and perhaps coloured into the paper. Referential improvisations are made to express the feelings, thoughts, images, and so on related to the different events. There could also be a songwriting process: 'What kind of good memories do you have stored in your heart?' If a song is written, we may start the following sessions with this song.

The next phase of the intervention is to add stones to the paper. Sometimes, I ask the client to explore a nature-based environment outside sessions and collect stones of different sizes and colours. They are to represent the difficult times of their life, particularly bad or traumatizing events. Several stones can be piled together to represent difficult episodes. The discussion addresses each stone separately. The clients give a general title to each episode and then discuss more details. The processing of the stones takes several sessions. Each episode is processed in detail, and the story is told chronologically, starting with what happened right before the traumatic event, what happened during it, and what happened right after it. I write it all down and ask for clarification about the details, such as where they were, who else was there, and what they were doing. I ask about each sensation separately: Do they remember hearing anything? If so, what kind of sound exactly? What did they see, colours, shapes, and so on? Any kinaesthetic sensations? Anything they smelled or tasted? These are important to recall in understanding the possible triggers for their flashbacks. I particularly ask about emotions: how they felt then versus how they feel now when they look at these stones and think about the event. The feelings can be coloured into the paper, and a referential improvisation may occur in the middle of the verbal processing. I also ask about the thought processes during the event, before, and after.

Referential improvisations may incorporate the empty chair technique. This is where a client imagines a specific person or aspect of themselves in the chair and communicates with them. It aims to enhance emotional expression and a dialogue with the other people present (or not present) during the episode. Another typical intervention includes writing a letter to oneself showing empathy and care. The letter can then be improvised, or a song can be written about it. After all the stones have been processed, there is usually a discussion about the entire life journey, different turning points, transition phases, gateways to other experiences, and before-after events that changed everything. Improvisations will often be made in those moments. Sometimes, I encourage clients to analyse the different patterns, relationships, or roles that keep repeating in their journey or their typical ways of using defence mechanisms. Discussions about the overall meaning of life often occur.

My future...

Towards the end of the individual and group therapy process, I utilize interventions that help clients process their future in the new country. There could be a referential improvisation on their future hopes, wishes, dreams, or fears, or guided music listening, including imagining their life in the future, for example, as if seeing it in a magical crystal ball. There could be songwriting about the advice they would like to give or what they would like to teach others based on their refugee experience.

KEEPING THE THERAPY SAFE

When working with refugee clients who have experienced trauma, it is essential to ensure safe use of music (Ahonen, 2019b). The therapist should never purposefully bring music that would trigger the client's trauma memory as they may not be ready to process it. The following rules help keep the therapeutic music listening, including Guided Imagery and Music (GIM), clinical improvisation, and songwriting interventions safe.

At the beginning of the musical intervention

- Explain the structure of the intervention (i.e. length of the music listening) or what happens during improvisation (i.e. the client starts, and the therapist/other clients join to support right afterwards).

- Do not ask clients to lie down during music listening as this could evoke triggering memories.

- Ask clients to keep their eyes open.

- Ask clients to write, draw, paint, or work with clay during listening.

- The relaxation before music listening should be short – one to two minutes.

- Avoid using a hypnotic vocal tone; keep your voice natural.

Induction image

- Have a clear focus before music listening/improvisation.

- Use grounding, safe, comforting, familiar, empowering induction images (i.e. client's safe place/chosen colour).

- Avoid floating images (i.e. flying/swimming).

- Never initiate trauma-related topics.

- Support emotional expression and trauma processing when it is initiated by the client.

- Suggest positive memories, inner resources, topics that support coping/ego strengths.

- Start with a phrase: 'Allow the music to bring you a sense of safety, any help, or resources needed...'

Music selection

- Have a clear justification for the music choice and how you are using it.

- Understand the neurological and psychological impact of musical elements.

- Use short listening pieces – between 4 and 12 minutes.

- If utilizing GIM, combine short pieces from different programmes to support and structure the client's imagery.

- Only use music that provides a structured, secure, reliable container; music that your client feels is supportive, safe, and comforting.

- Use music with a predictable melody, consonant harmony, reliable rhythm. The tempo should be neither too fast nor too slow.

- Use rhythmic music to promote breathing and grounding.

- Avoid 'timeless' new-age music as well as music with surprises, dissonance, atonality, less predictable harmonic structure.

- Use music from the client's cultural origin.

- Use meaningful and inspirational songs.

- NEVER use music that evokes and triggers trauma reactions.

Guided music listening

- Be highly directive and 'travel' with the client, utilizing active dialogue during music listening and checking in with the client often.

- Ask detailed questions during the process, and provide supportive suggestions.

- Offer validation, reinforcement, encouragement, and concrete problem-solving options.

- During flashbacks and recalling of disturbing images, suggest comforting or empowering images, and provide structure to the images so that the client can handle them better. Help them to find positive resources needed to restore a sense of control and empowerment.

- Incorporate stabilization, grounding, and relaxation when needed, even in the middle of the musical intervention (i.e. ask them to count the instruments they hear).

- Notice dissociation and intervene as needed.

Improvising with the client

- Be willing to support, hold, and contain even the most chaotic sounds.

- Be ready to provide a safe structure, rhythm, harmony, resolution of tension, and grounding when needed.

- Know when to intervene. It may be therapeutic to express chaos and all the related emotions, but it may also be too much or too early for the client.

- Do not let your client slip into overwhelming trauma material without even being aware of it.

CONCLUDING THOUGHTS

How do we sit with a suffering person and carry their burden without becoming traumatized ourselves? How do we protect ourselves without stopping listening? These are questions I often explore in the various trauma workshops I conduct and while reflecting on my own emotions after working with refugees. When listening to clients' trauma stories, as a therapist, it is crucial to know that the stories we listen to may also transform us. When we improvise with our clients and hear and feel their pain and hope, we are empathetically attuned to their disconnection, helplessness, and disempowerment. Music takes us into their dark and insecure world when we witness their experiences and write their songs. When our music sounds like their feelings, it also contains their grief, sorrow, anger, and horror. It can be difficult to stop the pain and suffering the storyteller transfers to us.

While remaining empathetic and open, and therefore vulnerable, and when we must respond with therapeutic interventions while having to control our reactions such as our horror and sense of injustice, we may not be able to always protect our core self. As therapists, we must acknowledge the possibility of vicarious traumatization that may take place when we are listening and containing refugee stories (Ahonen, 2014, 2018).

Self-care when working in this way is crucial. We must help ourselves first, understanding how to ground and stabilize our own bodies and emotions, or our containers will overflow from carrying other people's material. To keep the people we serve safe, we must also remain safe and acknowledge the sound of our pain and hope. That is the safe and effective use of self in therapy.

Narrative Music Psychotherapy is a method I developed for refugee clients who have experienced trauma. I wanted to understand and appreciate their subjective experiences and the meaning of those experiences for them. I wanted to give a voice to those who had been and continued to be silenced. The key to this method is to keep it safe for all – the client and the therapist – and to know why, when, and how to use music safely.

REFERENCES

Ahonen, H. (2014). Music as a Cure of Soul: Helping Helpers with Vicarious Trauma or Burn Out to Empty their Containers. In T. O'Connor, K. Lund, & P. Berensden (eds) *Spirituality and Psychotherapy: Cure of the Soul* (pp.139–151). Waterloo, Ontario: WLU Press.

Ahonen, H. (2016). Adult Trauma Work in Music Therapy. In J. Edwards (ed.) *The Oxford Handbook of Music Therapy* (pp.268–288). Oxford: Oxford University Press.

Ahonen, H. (2018). Music medicine's influence on music psychotherapy practice with traumatized individuals. *Music & Medicine*, 10(1), 26–38.

Ahonen, H. (2019a). Processing Refugee Journey and Promoting Self-Healing with Music and Art. In L. Willingham (ed.) *Community Music: Walking the Boundaries, Bridging the Gaps*. Waterloo, Ontario: WLU Press.

Ahonen, H. (2019b). Putting the Lights to the Room. Guided Imagery and Music (GIM) with Trauma Survivors. In D. Grocke (ed.) *Guided Imagery and Music: The Bonny Method and Beyond* (second edition, pp.149–186). Gilsum, NH: Barcelona Publishers.

Ahonen-Eerikainen, H. (2007). *Group Analytic Music Therapy*. Gilsum, NH: Barcelona Publishers.

Brown, S., Martinez, M. J., & Parsons, L. M. (2004). Passive music listening spontaneously engages limbic and paralimbic systems. *NeuroReport*, 15, 2033–2037.

Chanda, M. L. & Levitin, D. J. (2013). The neurochemistry of music. *Trends in Cognitive Sciences*, 17(4), 179–193.

Chu, J. B. (2011). *Rebuilding Shattered Lives: Treating Complex PTSD and Dissociative Disorders*. Hoboken, NJ: Wiley.

Courtois, C. A. & Ford, J. D. (2014). *Treating Complex Traumatic Stress Disorders. Scientific Foundations and Therapeutic Models*. New York, NY: Guilford Press.

Evers, S. & Suhr, B. (2000). Changes of the neurotransmitter serotonin but not of hormones during short time music perception. *European Archives of Psychiatry & Clinical Neuroscience*, 250(3), 144–147.

Frankl, V. E. (1985). *Man's Search for Meaning*. London, New York, NY: Pocket Books.

Fruhholz, S., Trost, W., & Grandjean, D. (2014). The role of the medial temporal limbic system in processing emotions in voice and music. *Progress in Neurobiology*, 123, 1–17.

Gangrade, A. (2012). The effect of music on the production of neurotransmitters, hormones, cytokines, and peptides: A review. *Music & Medicine*, 4(1), 40–43.

Helsing, M., Västfjäll, D., Bjälkebring, P., Juslin, P. N., & Hartig, T. (2016). An experimental field study of the effects of listening to self-selected music on emotions, stress, and cortisol levels. *Music & Medicine*, 8(4), 187–198.

Herman, J. (1997). *Trauma and Recovery: The Aftermath of Violence – From Domestic Abuse to Political Terror*. New York, NY: Basic Books.

Juslin, P. N., Barradas, G., & Eerola, T. (2015). From sound to significance: Exploring the mechanisms underlying emotional reactions to music. *American Journal of Psychology*, 128(3), 281–304.

Klein, R. & Schermer, V. (2000). *Group Psychotherapy for Psychological Trauma*. New York, NY: Guilford Press.

Koelsch, S. (2014). Brain correlates of music-evoked emotions. *Nature Reviews*, 15(3), 170–180.

Kumar, A. M., Tims, F., Cruess, D. G., Mintzer, M. J., *et al.* (1999). Music therapy increases serum melatonin levels in patients with Alzheimer's disease. *Alternative Therapies in Health and Medicine*, 5(6), 49–57.

Levine, P. A. (2015). *Trauma and Memory. Brain and Body in a Search for the Living Past*. Berkeley, CA: North Atlantic Books.

Mollica, R. F. (2006a). *Healing Invisible Wounds. Paths to Hope and Recovery in a Violent World*. Nashville, TN: Vanderbilt University Press.

Mollica, R. F. (2006b). *Trauma Story Assessment and Therapy: Therapist Journal for Field and Clinic*. Cambridge, MA: The Harvard Program in Refugee Trauma. Harvard Medical School.

Mollica, R. F. (2011). *Global Mental Health: Trauma and Recovery. A Companion Guide for Field and Clinical Care of Traumatized People Worldwide.* Cambridge, MA: The Harvard Program in Refugee Trauma. Harvard Medical School.

Rothschild, B. (2000). *The Body Remembers: The Psychophysiology of Trauma and Trauma Treatment.* New York, NY: W. W. Norton & Co.

Salimpoor, V.N. & Zatorre, R.J. (2013). Neural interactions that give rise to musical pleasure. *Psychology of Aesthetics, Creativity, and the Arts,* 7(1), 62–75.

Schauer, M., Neuner, F., & Elbert, T. (2011). *Narrative Exposure Therapy. A Short-Term Treatment for Traumatic Stress Disorder.* Göttingen: Hogrefe Publishing.

Van der Veer, G. (1998). *Counselling and Therapy with Refugees and Victims of Trauma. Psychological Problems of Victims of War, Torture and Repression.* Chichester: Wiley.

van der Kolk, B. (2015). *The Body Keeps the Score: Brain, Mind, and Body in the Healing of Trauma.* New York, NY: Penguin Books.

CHAPTER 5

Safe & Sound

A Music Therapy Intervention for Refugee and Asylum Seeker Children

SANDER VAN GOOR AND EVELYN HEYNEN

INTRODUCTION

At this present moment, worldwide there are more refugees than ever before, seeking safety and protection. They are fleeing their countries due to war, violence, and persecution. A significant proportion of them are children and young people. They primarily need safety. Additionally, they must be provided with basic needs such as food, water, shelter, medical care, and psychosocial support. Once these are addressed, children need perspective, often gained through education. This chapter will specifically focus on the group of displaced children and adolescents which includes refugees, migrants and those with an asylum-seeking background[1] in the Netherlands.

A specific music therapy intervention called Safe & Sound, developed by Sander van Goor in 2015,[2] is a preventive intervention that utilizes music therapy in a cultural and trauma-sensitive way. The goal of the intervention is to support the well-being of children and adolescents growing up in challenging circumstances, like refugee children. We identify two types of prevention: selective prevention and indicated prevention (GGZ standaarden, 2024). Selective prevention targets the whole group, including children with or without trauma-related problems. For children who don't show any symptoms, Safe & Sound aims to strengthen the connection between the children and their surroundings and thus enhance resilience and self-control. The purpose of the intervention is to mitigate the risk of psychosocial problems resulting from stressful or traumatic events (Heynen *et al.*, 2022).

---

1   In this chapter we will describe this group as 'refugees'.
2   www.safeandsoundfoundation.com

Indicated prevention is aimed at individuals who show symptoms but have not received a diagnosis of a disorder (GGZ standaarden, 2024). In these situations, Safe & Sound strives to prevent these early symptoms from developing into a disorder. Many young refugees have encountered adverse and traumatic situations in their countries of origin, during their journey to Europe, and in their search for a secure new home. Stripped of their social support networks, they grapple with the uncertainties surrounding their future, confronting the cumulative stress associated with forced migration. This challenging journey has demonstrated a significant correlation with stress and mental health disorders, including post-traumatic stress disorder, depression, anxiety, and substance use disorders (Blackmore *et al.*, 2020; Crepet *et al.*, 2017; Idemudia *et al.*, 2013; Solberg *et al.*, 2020). When left untreated, these conditions have the potential to become chronic and undermine overall functioning (Bogic *et al.*, 2015; Center for Substance Abuse Treatment, 2014; Thomason & Marusak, 2017).

Non-verbal relational interventions, such as music therapy, have been shown to promote positive psychosocial development in children, diminishing stress and enhancing their resilience (Tiems, 2016). The universal nature of music can bridge linguistic and cultural gaps (Wiess & Bensimon, 2020). Since 2015, Safe & Sound has consistently been facilitated in primary and secondary schools for refugee children in the Netherlands. These specific schools, called 'schools for newcomers', and their programmes ensure that children and youth from a refugee background attend initially to acquire proficiency in Dutch. After this language-learning phase, they are able to proceed to mainstream educational institutions.

In educational settings, stress and instability are frequently recognized in refugee children, manifested through factors such as limited social relationships and less positive integration and participation (Heynen *et al.*, 2022). This contributes to a higher likelihood of school drop-out in comparison to non-refugee children. Refugee children exhibit increased instances of concentration difficulties, more aggressive incidents, anxiety, and a heightened concern for personal safety and safety of others (Blackmore *et al.*, 2020; Heynen *et al.*, 2022; Yayan *et al.*, 2020). These behavioural challenges have been observed to impact classroom climate and the dynamics between children and teachers (Beld *et al.*, 2019). There was thus an urgent need for effective programmes to prevent these issues. At the same time, considerable resilience was observed in the children. Their enthusiasm to attend school underscores the significance of educational institutions in their lives. Schools provide a daily structure and, for many, are the first or the only place to engage in activities in their new home country. Children and young people want to feel that they belong, that they are part of something greater, and can contribute to their well-being (Vandamme, 2019). A consistent environment can help children navigate and comprehend their life experiences (van Oudheusden, 2023). School can be a safe place where they receive beneficial support from adults and peers (Horeweg, 2017). They can make new friends, play together, and, despite all the difficult experiences and their consequences, just be children again.

After the implementation of the Safe & Sound intervention in different schools in the Netherlands in 2019 and 2020, research was conducted to investigate the effects of the intervention on refugee children (Heynen *et al.*, 2022). The results of the process evaluation indicated that the intervention Safe & Sound strengthens the development of social connectedness, resulting in a 'sense of belonging', which refers to the psychological feeling of belonging or being connected to a social group or a community (Heynen *et al.*, 2022). This can be interpreted as an early stage of resilience (Marley & Mauki, 2019).

INTERVENTION DESCRIPTION: SAFE & SOUND

The intervention Safe & Sound includes two key elements: a group-based part, and potentially an individual intervention. The group sessions are regularly embedded in the educational programme of all participating schools (Heynen *et al.*, 2022). This means that every child at the participating school will attend Safe & Sound group sessions during the whole school year. The group sessions contribute to how music therapy can foster a positive learning environment, enhance social connections, and cultivate a sense of belonging among the children. As the intervention works in co-creation with teachers, parents, and other caregivers, any trauma-related issues some children may face can actively be identified in an early stage during group sessions. It is important to identify these problems as early as possible (GGZ standaarden, 2024). Those children who require individualized support can be directed towards individual Safe & Sound music therapy sessions (Heynen *et al.*, 2022). The children who will get individual sessions still attend the group sessions.

Benefits of group and individual sessions

Group sessions are held year-round for all children, with individual sessions arranged as required and lasting between 5 and 15 individual sessions. The music therapist oversees both, enabling effective monitoring of the progress of children in individual sessions during group sessions. It also makes it easier for the child to attend individual sessions because the music therapist is a familiar face. At the start of the school year, only group sessions commence. This period serves to identify children exhibiting trauma-related problems, who are then referred for individual therapy. Sometimes, what a child learns in individual sessions can be practised in group settings. Take, for example, Nadia, a ten-year-old who was quite reserved. She understood Dutch but became anxious when asked to speak it. In her individual sessions, she began to create a song in Dutch. This was also the moment she chose to record a part of the song in Dutch that the group was composing during their group sessions. Goals practised in individual sessions can therefore be effectively tried out in group sessions.

Learning Dutch

Children attend school primarily to learn Dutch. Learning a new language under challenging circumstances is not easy for the children. Safe & Sound initially focuses on the well-being of the children, while also recognizing the importance of learning Dutch. The songs are composed in Dutch using words most children are familiar with to improve language skills. For example, during one session, a song about making friends with Dutch children was composed, where they sang phrases they could use when meeting Dutch peers:

- What's your name?

- How are you doing?

- How old are you?

- Will you play with us?

Language barrier solutions

In group sessions, there are children with many different languages. Within Safe & Sound we don't seek assistance from an interpreter, and only use one when there are meetings with parents who don't speak Dutch. Next to music, we make use of other art forms like drawing, dancing, and theatre. Translation applications are also used. Miscommunication has to be accepted as part of the process. Not everything the therapist says, or children say to each other, or all the lyrics in the song will be understood by everybody. Communication can be stimulated by using gestures. In group sessions, children support each other with translating.

Culture-sensitive approach

Next to a lot of different languages, the children come from different countries, with different cultural backgrounds and religions. It's important for the music therapist to be curious and interested in the children's cultural background. Within Safe & Sound, a safe space is established where children can share music from their own countries and languages in group sessions as well as in individual sessions. In song composition, there is room for cultural differences and similarities – for instance, songs about weather or food in their home countries and in the Netherlands. Sometimes, translations of Dutch words are included in their languages in creating the songs. For example, in a song about friendship in Dutch, there's a part where everyone sings the word 'friend' in their own language as well as in Dutch.

Trauma-sensitive approach

The length of this chapter limits a detailed exploration of the term 'trauma'. However, a brief introduction is essential to understand how music therapy works within the intervention Safe & Sound, which focuses on a trauma-sensitive approach. The term 'trauma' is derived from the word 'wound', signifying the consequences of intense events such as abuse, violence, war, and displacement (Lindauer & Boer, 2013). Trauma relates to the repercussions of an individual resulting from the 'traumatic' event (Lindauer & Boer, 2013). It's important to note that not every intense event will lead to trauma-related problems (Coppens *et al.*, 2016). Hence, these events are called potentially traumatic events (PTEs). Although it is impossible to change the occurrence of the events, the capacity to alleviate the traumatic aftermath exists, offering hope.

To grasp the foundation of trauma, it is crucial to understand the neurological and physiological responses occurring in our brains and bodies during PTEs. Van den Ouwelant (2023) has developed a psychoeducational method to understand trauma, incorporating the use of symbols for the neurologic responses. The primary brain region involved in PTEs is the amygdala, which can be symbolized as the brain's 'alarm bell'. If everything is safe, calm, and okay, the bell remains silent. If it is not okay, or even unsafe, threatening, or dangerous, then the bell will ring. By ringing, it sends a warning signal to the brain and the body (van den Ouwelant, 2023). During PTEs, the stress reaction flight, fight, and freeze is activated, while specific parts of the brain are 'switched off', such as the prefrontal cortex and memory (van den Ouwelant, 2023), which can finally result in trauma-related problems.

Children and young individuals from refugee backgrounds have usually endured PTEs over an extended duration. This includes experiencing war, leaving their homeland, parting with family and friends, facing hazards during the escape, encountering stress throughout the asylum process, and managing stress during the integration in a new country. This can cause chronic trauma. During chronic trauma, the alarm bell rings continuously due to frequent situations of danger. This means the brain and the body are always in survival mode (van den Ouwelant, 2023). Crucial for these children and young people is to experience moments the alarm bell can calm down. Re-establishing connections, introducing structure and pre-dictability, incorporating movement, and providing a sense of control are four key elements that can contribute to calming the alarm bell. These four elements are integrated into the group sessions as well as the individual sessions of Safe & Sound.

VIGNETTE
Song: I can't wait to be friends with you
(refugee children from 10 to 12 years old)

The children were asked, 'How was your first day here at school?' They all related to the topic and began to share their stories.

I can't wait to be friends with you
Hi I'm new, I hope you like me, I'm entering a new world like you did
Can we be friends, we can work it out, we went through the same
Maybe our feelings reach each other, never
got this feeling when I'm near you
I can't wait to be friends with you, I can't wait to be friends

I can't wait to be friends with you
I can't wait to be friends with you
I can't wait
I can't wait to be friends

When I first met you we were strangers,
strangers that never knew each other
But now I want to be friends with you, friends forever and ever
When I first entered this class, everybody stared at me
I was scared, I was silent

Didn't know what's going to happen

I can't wait to be friends with you
I can't wait to be friends with you
I can't wait
I can't wait to be friends

I'm happy that you helped me
Show me around, show me the school
One more step, and we will be friends
Yeah, we will be friends

THE THREE PHASES OF SAFE & SOUND

Both group and individual sessions of Safe & Sound include three phases:

1. Establishing safety

2. Composing

3. Integration

Group sessions

During group sessions, the music therapist focuses on creating a positive group climate aiming to optimize conditions for the learning process, such as a sense of safety, relaxation, and openness to learn new experiences (Beld *et al.*, 2019). Collaboratively, the therapist and children work on interpersonal goals that are generic to the programme, including active listening, mutual assistance, and building trust. Each session revolves around a specific theme, such as forging new friendships, sharing personal stories, addressing challenging situations and emotions, and exploring individual talents and strengths. These themes come from the children's own preferences or in reflection of the group dynamics. In collaboration with the children, songs are co-created based on their stories, ensuring their active involvement in the composing process and fostering a sense of ownership. The recorded songs are complemented with a video clip. The session content is tailored to the language and experience level of the children. The learning process occurs incrementally, fostering successful experiences and enjoyment.

In these schools, children come and go on a regular basis. Once their Dutch proficiency reaches a certain level, they transition to a regular school. Occasionally, children are referred to another asylum-seeker centre, or they move to a different location within the Netherlands. Additionally, new children will arrive who have just recently settled in the asylum-seeker centre or moved to a house in the neighbourhood of the school. This means that during the school year, the safety in the class can change and earlier phases may need to be revisited.

Phase 1: Establishing safety

The first phase involves establishing a safe space/secure environment for the children. This is done using music and movement, connection, giving back control, and being predictable – the four elements that can help to calm down the alarm bell. Being predictable is an essential step towards a positive alliance – show what's coming, tell what's coming, tell what you do, and do what you say (Horeweg, 2017). All sessions follow a clear structure with three steps: the beginning, the core, and the closure of the session. The beginning consists of two parts: a check-in, followed by a warm-up. The check-in is needed to observe the group's overall mood and to identify the individual needs. This is the moment you observe if there are any alarm bells ringing. You may notice that some children are physically or behaviourally overly active, stressed, or withdrawn, and their levels of motivation may also vary.

There are different ways to do a check-in; for example, by introducing a 'hello song' where every participant sings their name. Children can express their feelings through words, gestures, body movements, or music. All responses of the children are accepted without judgement, recognizing that there are no right and wrong answers. Even if a child doesn't want to participate, that's perfectly acceptable. The warm-up levels children's energy and is a way to help calm down the alarm bell so that they are prepared for the core of the session. The warm-up consists of easily accessible music activities with movement, adapted to the energy level of the group. Through musical interaction with the music therapist, the children establish a safe connection.

The setup of Safe & Sound involves working in a circle, allowing everybody to see and connect with each other. The core of the session consists of a learning part, a creative part, and a moment to reflect. The music therapist introduces the theme of the session and the music exercises. For example, one theme is based on working with rhythm and body percussion. Initially, the music therapist instructs the children on various rhythms and demonstrates body percussion techniques they can imitate. In the creative part, the music therapist guides the children in creating their own rhythms while using their bodies. Creating is a way to give control to the children.

Near the end of the group, there is a chance to reflect on their experiences and to present what they made. Finally, at the end of the session, there will be a 'check-out'. That can also be an ending song, a game they like to play, or a moment to share the plan for the next session. The first phase might need several weeks or even months. Many of the refugee children haven't been able to attend school during their flight or during the war in their home country. They might need time to adjust to working in a group, and it is important that they get this time. Additionally, during the first phase, it is important to make agreements about the boundaries of the group with the children. This also provides predictability and a sense of control. For example, when one person talks or plays music, the rest of the group listens. This can even be done using a song or a rap. This might follow a structure, such as 'When one person talks, the rest is... (the music stops, and every child is quiet). We listen to each other.'

The themes of the songs during the first phase aim to build on the children's inner resources, such as children's own talents, giving compliments, the weather, learning Dutch, getting to know each other, and exploring happiness, pride, and calmness. By utilizing relatable topics, individuals can easily connect and comprehend, enabling them to share insights about these topics. For example, at school they are learning words and sentences about the weather in Dutch, so during the session a song about the weather in the Netherlands can be produced. The second part of the song is about how the weather is different in their land of origin. In this song, every child can sing about where they come from and talk about the weather in their country of origin. These songs are called 'Fill in Songs'. They all originate from conversations with the children about the subject. They are short, one chorus, or sometimes extended by one verse. Then there is space for children to fill in their subjective part about the subject.

Song: 'We All Have Talents'

> *We all have talents! Talents! Talents!*
> *We all have talents! Together a lot of talent!*
> *Everybody in the world*
> *It doesn't matter where you are from*
> *With talents you are born*
> *You'll discover them all*

Fill in part (suggestions): I'm good at football, I can help other children, I'm good at keeping a secret, I am good at dancing, I care for animals.

Phase 2: Composing

During this phase, the creative process of composing a song is initiated. The themes of these songs focus on resilience. In Safe & Sound, Ungar's (2005) definition of resilience is used. Resilience is the process and outcome of successfully adapting to difficult or challenging life experiences, especially through mental, emotional, and behavioural flexibility, and adjustment to external and internal demands. More specifically, it is a resource that everybody has, and which is influenced by the people and the context in which we surround ourselves (Ungar, 2005). Focusing on resilience in the context of potentially traumatic experiences, there can be a distinction between individual resilience sources (e.g. self-confidence, future self, dealing with emotions, dealing with others, dealing with difficult experiences, dealing with behaviour) and environmental resilience sources (supportive environment, role model, participation, culture and religion) (Vandamme, 2019). These individual and environmental resilience sources are the subjects that are explored through songwriting, with the active involvement of the children. Together, the music therapist and the children decide the theme of the song through conversations in which the children share their experiences. The music therapist documents these discussions, serving as a foundation for the lyrics. Drawing is also integrated into the process of composing. The songs explore individual resilience factors, as well as addressing the difficulties they've encountered, how they cope with anger, and their hopes for the future. Additionally, environmental factors are considered, by exploring questions like: Who provides support? What holds significance in your life? Where do you find a sense of security? How do your culture and faith contribute to your strength?

During the composing process, it's crucial to monitor children's stress level, considering that certain topics may be challenging or might trigger emotional reactions (Schottelkorb *et al.*, 2012). For example, children may take part in composing a song about the pets they had to leave behind in their home country. Children love to share stories about their beloved animals, but at the same time, it's obvious that they miss their pets. To prevent overwhelming them, delving too deeply into their emotions is avoided. When they express missing their pets, it's essential to first acknowledge that such feelings are entirely normal. One effective approach is the game 'Rumble if...' Rumbling refers to tapping your legs with your hands. You ask a question, and if that resonates with you, you can rumble. 'Who had a dog?' And then the children who had a dog rumble with their hands on their legs. 'Who misses their pets?' This often leads to a collective rumbling among the children, creating a sense of shared experience and recognizing that they are not alone in their emotions. Following this, a musical activity unrelated to the topic is performed, aiming to either stimulate or bring calmness. This allows the children to channel their emotions and can reduce stress through collaborative music-making.

It is important to give the children the feeling that they have a strong sense of ownership over the song. To achieve this, they are presented with various choices for the musical segments and can actively contribute to shape the song according to their preferences. This can, for example, be realized by using the colours of boomwhackers, which are colourful tubes that produce different tones. The children can choose a colour pattern which becomes the chord progression. The music therapist plays the chords in different musical styles and parameters like slow or fast, loud or soft, major or minor, and in different rhythms, while following the choices of the children. Finally, the music therapist composes the song, integrating all the chosen lyrics, words, drawings, and musical choices of the children. When they hear their song for the first time, they are often very excited.

Song: 'My Pet and I' (refugee children aged from eight to ten years)

> *I have a beautiful pet*
> *But unfortunately,*
> *It's not here with me*
> *It's far away in my home country*
> *And when I think of him,*
> *I miss him oh so much*
> *Because we shared so much joy,*
> *My pet and I*

Phase 3: Integration

In the third phase, the song is finalized and the rehearsal and recording process can begin. The children are often proud of their song and eagerly participate in rehearsals. Ensuring a safe environment during recording is crucial. The music therapist explains and demonstrates how recording equipment works. During the recording, there are essential agreements and gestures that the children need to learn, including signals for silence, starting to sing, and to stop. Some practice is needed to ensure a smooth recording process. The music therapist also helps children who may feel hesitant to sing, providing support in small steps or encouraging them to imitate the therapist. It's completely acceptable not to sing, and alternative activities such as playing an instrument or clapping are offered. And even that is optional, as they might say no.

Once the recording is completed, a video clip is produced. The children actively participate in deciding what to film, often featuring drawings, glimpses of them playing games, or capturing their movements. For privacy reasons, no footage of the children's faces is captured. When the song and the video clip are finished, it is evaluated on aspects such as whom they intend to share the song with, their experience in creating the song, the elements that make them proud, their perception of teamwork, and insights gained about the theme of the song. As a result of this process, there is a noticeable decrease in their stress levels and an increasing sense of belonging to the group (Heynen *et al.*, 2022). Discussing the theme becomes more comfortable and safer. The song has become a way to express their feelings and their stories with resilience.

Song: 'Our Story' (Ukrainian refugee children
aged from eight to ten years)

> *Oh no! There is war in Ukraine*
> *What happens to my school and my friends?*

We packed up quickly and had to go
The Netherlands welcomed us into their home
A new school, a new language
Music lessons, peace and confidence
But the end of the war will come
Back to my friends and pets
We help each other
Being together again, drawing together
Working together, building together
For peace, for humanity
For goodness, for our motherland Ukraine

Individual sessions

The children who are indicated for individual music therapy sessions often show trauma-related problems like aggressive behaviour, rebellious tendencies, difficulties in controlling their emotions, resistance to corrections, withdrawal, challenges in receiving compliments, limited social skills, desire for control, making demands on teachers or peers, perfectionism, concentration and planning issues, impulsiveness, and a lack of insight into cause and effect (Coppens *et al.*, 2016). These problems are automatic responses of the nervous system which can be explained as 'normal' reactions to abnormal situations. These problems may stem from the potential traumatic experiences they have undergone. The individual sessions are tailored to the specific needs and capabilities of the child. The main objective of the individual sessions is to calm down the alarm bell and promote feelings of safety and stability. Before the start of individual work, it is important to establish any underlying information to determine the therapeutic goals during the session. These may include:

- The purpose for indicating individual music therapy, the request for help.

- The child's objectives of the therapy.

- The personal characteristics and interests of the child.

- Information about the system around the child.

- What is already helpful in dealing with the trauma-related problem of the child, from individual and environmental perspectives.

- The level of Dutch language.

This information is gathered through the observations of the music therapist during group sessions, as well as through discussions with teachers, other caregivers, and family members. The teacher plays a crucial role in inviting children for individual therapy. They engage in conversations with the children about their behaviour and the challenges they encounter at school. By informing the children that the music therapist can also assist them in addressing these issues, the teacher encourages them to attend individual sessions.

Sessions for children who have a stable environment (permanent residency, living together in a house with a supportive family, good contact with the school) can go more in depth. Many children in asylum-seeker centres often arrive in the host country alone or with only part of their family. This means that they often rely on survival mechanisms which help them to cope with difficult situations. It is then important to seek opportunities to calm down the alarm bell and explore ways that others can provide support. During individual sessions, we provide moments to calm down the alarm bell by making music together. Besides this, the emphasis can be placed on one potential traumatic event the child feels safe enough to share, especially in the individual therapy sessions.

Phase 1: Establishing safety

In the first phase, the primary goal is to re-establish a safe connection, which is needed to create a safe learning environment for the child in a one-to-one setting (Beld *et al.*, 2019; Horeweg, 2017). It is important to calm down the alarm bell by being predictable, giving back control, using movement, and establishing a safe connection. The music therapist ensures predictability by explaining the purpose of the sessions together with the teacher, prior to the therapy. When the child wants to attend, they walk together to the therapy room. The first time in the room the music therapist shows the instruments and the musical activities that are optional. The initial focus is on what the child wants to play, rather than getting them to talk. The music activities are easily accessible and some of them the child already knows from the group sessions. For instance, the therapist plays the child's name in a rhythm on a drum, and the child repeats it. Then, the child plays their own name, and the therapist repeats it. This can lead to an improvisation in which the music therapist helps the child to create his or her own melodies and rhythms. The music therapist structures the music to match the child's pace, dynamics, and energy level. Whether the child plays calmly or energetically, the therapist adapts the music accordingly. This provides the child with a sense of being acknowledged and heard by the therapist. The child also experiences success in how to make music with the support of the music therapist. This contributes to the growth of the connection between the therapist and the child. The child is given choice to get the feeling of control during the therapy. The child also has the option to decide that the therapist can make a choice. Creating melodies and rhythms gives a sense of regaining control. Music inherently involves movement, even if it's subtle. From moving fingers to dancing, everything is possible.

In addition to or instead of making music, the child can also choose to listen to music they prefer. This could be music that makes them feel happy or calm or that brings back memories. It can be any type of music, in any language or from any cultural background. The music therapist and the child will listen to it together, and the therapist may ask questions about the song, the band, the singers, or the lyrics. They might ask: What do you like about this song? Why does it make you happy? How often do you listen to it? What do you do while listening to this music? But instead of talking, the music therapist can also learn a part of the song and play and sing this with the child.

Besides making and listening to music, there are also verbal interventions. First, we start with easy questions that the child might know the answer to, such as what is the name of this instrument or the colour of the instrument. Then the music therapist can ask closed questions about easy facts such as age, the child's preferences, country of origin, companions, current living situation. If the child chooses not to talk, or is not able to talk, that is perfectly acceptable. When stress reactions occur, even slightly, we stop talking and start making the child's preferred music to calm down the alarm bell. If the child feels safe enough to tell more, then you can go into feelings and help the child in how to deal with this. This is what happens in the composing phase.

Phase 2: Composing

The second stage is commonly known as the composing phase, and resembles the second phase in group sessions. Music is used to target the objectives of the therapy, essentially composing the path to achieve them. The act of composing music serves as a tool to ease this process. The focus is on recognizing the child's individual and external resources. Achieving this through the creation of music is one way to work. For example, a child who is very shy might play softly in the beginning. In the second phase, children learn step by step to play louder. Another example is a child who plays unstructured music to begin with, and learns to play with more structure, how to follow the music of the music therapist, and to play or sing a song. When needed, the therapist explains the concept of the alarm bell to the child, helping them to understand brain and body reactions with a tangible symbol. This helps the child in realizing that automatic reactions when the alarm rings are not their fault. With music therapy, the child becomes able to calm the alarm bell down. The therapist also educates teachers and caregivers about the alarm bell, working together to develop strategies for managing in the classroom or at home. Psychoeducation to teachers, parents, and children about the physical and emotional reactions of experiencing a shocking event can help them understand the reactions and respond appropriately (GGZ standaarden, 2024).

Composing a song about the child's story is another way to reach therapy goals. We focus on a PTE the child is able to share within the safety of the therapy. We use solution-focused questions to help the child find personal and environmental resources. Questions are adapted to the child's age and verbal capacity and language barrier solutions as described before are used:

1. What makes you so brave and strong that you're still here, even after facing difficult times?

2. Who/what helped you through this difficult time?

3. Who did you help during tough times?

4. What have you learned about yourself through everything you've experienced?

5. What do you hope for in the future?

During the process of composing song lyrics, it might be possible that the alarm bell starts to ring. To prevent the child getting overwhelmed by stress reactions and emotions, the music therapist uses the preferred music that can help to calm the alarm bell down. Once calm, they can proceed with composing the song.

Phase 3: Integration
In this phase, the positive impact of music therapy sessions in the child's classroom and living environment is assessed. This involves effective communication with teachers, parents, and other caregivers. During therapy, the child's needs are identified, and the music therapist helps the environment of the child to better meet those needs.

FICTIONAL CASE EXAMPLE: AMIR, 10 YEARS OLD, FROM SYRIA
Amir fled Syria with his family during the war. Separated from his father for three years, he, his mother, and his younger brother walked long distances

and took a boat to reach Europe. The boat's motor broke, leaving them stranded at sea for several days. Amir endured bombings at his school and in his neighbourhood, losing family members and friends. Amir and his family members lived in an asylum-seekers centre in the Netherlands for nearly a year. After receiving their residence permit, they moved to a house near the school.

When he began the Safe & Sound sessions, Amir's Dutch was good, but he got stressed when talking. He was quiet, let other children go first, and struggled to share his emotions and thoughts. He had one close friend and was very helpful to others. His parents mentioned that he suffered from nightmares and didn't play outside with others.

Amir enjoyed the group sessions. Using simple instruments like shakers and boomwhackers, he could play easily together with other children. Initially quiet, he gradually expressed himself more through music. He liked listening to music and was interested in other instruments like the piano and percussion. He was more expressive in Safe & Sound group sessions than in class. Due to his nightmares and difficulty making friends and sharing feelings, he was referred to individual Safe & Sound sessions.

When asked about participating in individual sessions, he immediately said yes. He already was familiar with the music therapist, and he had seen other children having individual sessions, and that they enjoyed it.

During the establishing safety phase, he tried different instruments and preferred the piano. Initially, he played softly and slowly. With the music therapist's support, together they created short improvisations in his way of playing. During these sessions, he began playing louder and more expressively, exploring new ways to play. He also opened up verbally, sharing themes like friends, what he liked to do, and his favourite meal.

In the composing phase, Amir agreed with the music therapist to make songs about his life. Knowing how to use music to calm down the alarm bell, he felt safe to open up and share more about himself. Initially, they composed a song about his grandparents in Syria, whom he dearly missed. The song was in Dutch and Arabic. Gradually, he shared his life story, before, during, and after the war, telling of how he fled his country to find safety in the Netherlands. The song also embraced his hope for the future.

During the integration phase, the song was completed and presented to his teacher, remedial teacher, and parents. He asked the music therapist to sing, while he played percussion. They also recorded the song so he could listen to it whenever he wanted and share it with others. The song, dedicated to his grandparents, was sent to them, and everyone was incredibly proud of Amir.

After the individual sessions, he became more engaged in the class.

Teachers noticed he was speaking more and making new friends. His parents reported that he no longer had nightmares, slept better, and was happier, also making friends in the neighbourhood.

CONCLUSION

Safe & Sound has proved to be a promising intervention for children and youth who experience negative and traumatic events. It has successfully been implemented in Dutch primary language schools to support the well-being of children and adolescents growing up in challenging circumstances, like refugee children. The use of music in Safe & Sound can serve to bridge the gap between languages and cultures and strengthen the sense of belonging. Safe & Sound aims to focus on resilience factors, such as dealing with others, future self, self-confidence, and dealing with difficult situations, especially in the group sessions. In individual sessions, children with trauma-related problems can focus on more safety and stability by being helped to calm down the alarm bell. Music therapists can advise and support teachers, parents, and family members to support the child in this process.

In the future, it is important to train more music therapists to be able to facilitate Safe & Sound and to implement the intervention in more language schools in the Netherlands. Furthermore, we should build on research that sheds more light on the effectiveness of Safe & Sound to build a solid base for a more general implementation of the intervention, not only in language schools, but also in regular schools and schools in problem areas with high potential of trauma in children and their families.

REFERENCES

Beld, M. H. M., Van den Heuvel, E. G., Van der Helm, G. H. P., Kuiper, C. H. Z., *et al.* (2019). The impact of classroom climate on students' perception of social exclusion in secondary special education. *Children and Youth Services Review*, 103, 127–134.

Blackmore, R., Boyle, J. A., Fazel, M., Ranasinha, S., *et al.* (2020). The prevalence of mental illness in refugees and asylum seekers: A systematic review and meta-analysis. *PLoS Medicine*, 17, e1003337.

Bogic, M., Njoku, A., & Priebe, S. (2015). Long-term mental health of war-refugees: A systematic literature review. *BMC International Health and Human Rights*, 15(1), 1–41.

Center for Substance Abuse Treatment. (2014). Understanding the Impact of Trauma. In *Trauma-Informed Care in Behavioral Health Services*. Rockville, MD: Substance Abuse and Mental Health Services Administration.

Coppens, L., Schneijderberg, M., & van Kregten, C. (2016). Lesgeven aan getraumatiseerde kinderen. *Een praktisch handboek voor het basisonderwijs*. Amsterdam: Uitgeverij SWP.

Crepet, A., Rita, F., Reid, A., Van den Boogaard, W., *et al.* (2017). Mental health and trauma in asylum seekers landing in Sicily in 2015: A descriptive study of neglected invisible wounds. *Conflict and Health*, 11(1), 1–11.

GGZ Standaarden. (2020, 1 December). *Psychotrauma – en Stressorgerelateerde Stoornissen.* www.ggzstandaarden.nl/uploads/pdf/project/project_ab077dad-ae18-4c96-a07e-3fdf5b406ceb_psychotrauma-en-stressorgerelateerde-stoornissen__authorized-at_01-12-2020.pdf.

Heynen, E., Bruls, V., van Goor, S., Pat-El, R., Schoot, T., & van Hooren, S. (2022). A music therapy intervention for refugee children and adolescents in schools: A process evaluation using a mixed method design. *Children*, 9(10), 1434.

Horeweg, A. (2017). *De Trauma Sensitieve School.* Amsterdam: Lannoo Campus.

Idemudia, E. S., Williams, J. K., & Wyatt, G. E. (2013). Migration challenges among Zimbabwean refugees before, during and post arrival in South Africa. *Journal of Injury and Violence Research*, 5(1), 1–17.

Lindauer, R. & Boer, F. (2013). *Trauma bij kinderen.* Tielt, Belgium: Lannoo Meulenhoff-Belgium.

Marley, C. & Mauki, B. (2019). Resilience and protective factors among refugee children post-migration to high-income countries: A systematic review. *European Journal of Public Health*, 29(4), 706–713.

Schottelkorb, A. A., Doumas, D. M., & Garcia, R. (2012). Treatment for childhood refugee trauma: A randomized, controlled trial. *International Journal of Play Therapy*, 21(2), 57–73.

Solberg, Ø., Nissen, A., Vaez, M., Cauley, P., Eriksson, A. K., & Saboonchi, F. (2020). Children at risk: A nationwide, cross-sectional study examining post-traumatic stress symptoms in refugee minors from Syria, Iraq and Afghanistan resettled in Sweden between 2014 and 2018. *Conflict and Health*, 14(1), 1–12.

Thomason, M. E. & Marusak, H. A. (2017). Toward understanding the impact of trauma on the early developing human brain. *Neuroscience*, 342, 55–67.

Tiems, J. (2016, 3 maart). Muziek als traumaverwerking: Muziektherapie voor asielzoekerskinderen. *Dagblad de Limburger*, p 2.

Ungar, M. (ed.) (2005). *Handbook for Working with Children and Youth: Pathways to Resilience Across Cultures and Contexts.* Thousand Oaks, CA: Sage Publications.

Vandamme, N. (2019). Veerkracht bij kindertrauma. In M. Serra (2020), Gezien en gelezen. *Kind & Adolescent Praktijk*, 19(2), 47–49.

van den Ouwelant, A. (2023). When the (Alarm) Bell Rings. https://trauma-company.store/product/when-the-alarm-bell-rings/?lang=en.

van Oudheusden, H. (2023). *Teaching Refugee Children.* New York, NY: Apollo Books.

Wiess, C. & Bensimon, M. (2020). Group music therapy with uprooted teenagers: The importance of structure. *Nordic Journal of Music Therapy*, 29(2), 174–189.

Yayan, E. H., Düken, M. E., Özdemir, A. A., & Çelebioğlu, A. (2020). Mental health problems of Syrian refugee children: Post-traumatic stress, depression and anxiety. *Journal of Pediatric Nursing*, 51, e27–e32.

SUPPORTING SOCIAL TRANSFORMATIONS

Music Therapy Perspectives on Music-Based Interventions with Displaced Youth

The Heidelberg 'Bridges' Project

SAMUEL GRACIDA, DIANE J. PITZER,
CORDULA REINER-WORMIT, AND ALEXANDER F. WORMIT

INTRODUCTION

This chapter delves into the practices employed by the Bridges project, an initiative located in Heidelberg, Germany. The project is committed to offering refugee children and young people various musical opportunities and relationship-building experiences – to build bridges that help them transition from their old world to their new one. This includes community music therapy groups, individualized musical instrument instruction, immersive band workshops, and community music concerts. A central focus of this chapter is to explain the concepts that have informed the Bridges project. These include 'safe(r) spaces', adverse childhood experiences (ACEs), the Heidelberg model of heuristic working factors in music therapy (Hillecke & Wilker, 2007), resilience, and regulation. The chapter aims to bridge theoretical knowledge with empirical evidence to offer a multidimensional view that integrates neuroscience, therapeutic best practices, and real-world applications to enrich and nuance the ongoing conversations surrounding the Bridges project and its broader implications.

Germany hosts a substantial refugee population exceeding 2.2 million individuals in a total population of approximately 84 million, ranking among the highest globally (UNHCR, 2023). Approximately 450 refugees are currently assigned to Heidelberg by the state of Baden-Württemberg. Refugees in Heidelberg are provided with housing either within one of the main complexes for refugees or in private housing (Heidelberg, n.d.). The Bridges project was conceived in 2022 and funded with grants to operate in these main complexes for refugees. It traces its origins to the foundational concept of the so-called 'Spielraum Musik – ein Stück Heimat' (roughly translated as 'Music Playroom – A Piece of Home'), a special music group programme initiated by Cordula Reiner-Wormit (music therapist) and Jutta Glaser (jazz and world musician) in 2015. With additional support garnered in 2022, the project experienced significant expansion, extending its reach to the three main complexes for refugees in Heidelberg. What began as a weekly special music group programme with a music-therapeutic approach has blossomed into a multifaceted endeavour, encompassing ongoing Spielraum-Musik sessions, music lessons, band workshops, and community concerts.

Bridges provides sustained support to individuals aged 2 to 29 with refugee backgrounds through its music-centred programmes. The hallmark of Bridges lies in its commitment to long-term engagement with participants, some of whom may benefit from its services for months or even years. This prolonged involvement allows for the cultivation of meaningful relationships, the development of tailored interventions, and the implementation of comprehensive, future-oriented plans to support individuals on their journey to integration and empowerment.

The team at Bridges comprises professionally qualified, seasoned experts in their respective fields, including culturally and trauma-sensitive musicians, music educators, and music therapists. They undergo specialized training and receive ongoing supervision to uphold rigorous standards of practice. This chapter endeavours to outline the core offerings of Bridges while shedding light on key concepts underpinning how these interventions bolster the resilience and regulatory skills of displaced youth.

Positioning – introducing ourselves

The Bridges team currently consists of nine members, encompassing a diverse range of expertise. This includes music therapists as well as music pedagogues and accomplished local musicians. The interdisciplinary composition of the team is intended to leverage the unique perspectives of different professionals. Four of the nine members have actively contributed to the crafting of this chapter. We aim to briefly contextualize our involvement, underscoring how our backgrounds, professional histories, and experiences with Bridges inform our approach to the topics delineated herein.

Samuel Gracida

I am a music therapist trained in an international programme in Germany but originally from Mexico. I first moved out of Mexico when I was 16 years old. I lived in China for two years, in the USA for four years, and have been in Germany for seven years as of 2025. My extensive global experiences have deeply influenced my work, particularly in my interactions with displaced youth. I joined Bridges in 2019 as a volunteer during my academic studies at SRH University. In 2022, I officially became a member of the Bridges team, and since then, I have been heavily involved in all the activities offered by Bridges. My roles often include leading the Spielraum-Musik groups, providing weekly lessons, and conducting band workshops with aspiring instrumentalists in our programme. The work in Bridges inspired me to write my Master's thesis on the topic of displaced persons and led to my involvement as co-editor of this book.

Diane Jeeranut Pitzer

I was born in Thailand and raised in Germany. I am a trainer and practitioner for trauma-informed bodywork, a singer-songwriter, anti-racism trainer, and activist. I joined the Bridges team in 2019 as a trauma-sensitive musician, especially in leading the Spielraum-Musik groups.

Cordula Reiner-Wormit

I was born in Germany as a granddaughter of grandparents who were expelled from their home in what was then East Germany at the end of the Second World War. I studied music therapy in Heidelberg and I have been offering music therapy in the context of crisis intervention, prevention, health promotion, inclusion, and participation at a music school for 25 years. I am a lecturer for musical relationship work and early childhood education at the University of Education in Heidelberg. I also work as a musician and composer.

Professsor Dr Alexander F. Wormit

I was born in Germany to a father who was forced to flee his home in what was then East Germany with his family at the end of the Second World War (Wormit is a family name originating from East Prussia). I studied music therapy with a diploma in Heidelberg and have been a Professor of Clinical Music Therapy since 2008. I am currently Vice Dean for Research at the Faculty of Therapy Sciences. My research and publications focus on music therapy in geriatric care and evidence-based music therapy, especially in the areas of chronic pain and palliative care. I joined the Bridges team in 2023 as part of project funding via the Ferry Porsche Challenge, in which project funds were administered and coordinated via the SRH University of Applied Sciences Heidelberg.

Introducing Noor and Alina

We would also like to introduce Noor and Alina, two fictional children we have created who will accompany the reader throughout this chapter.

Noor

Noor was born in Herat, Afghanistan in 2009 to a family with three other children. He was not particularly troublesome and even as a four-year-old he enjoyed playing soccer with his siblings. Herat was never particularly safe, but the situation became more extreme when the NATO forces withdrew and the Taliban and Islamic State expanded. After a nasty encounter with someone from the Taliban, Noor's father decided that it was time to leave Afghanistan and seek asylum in Europe. It was a long and arduous journey, but eventually Noor and his family arrived in Heidelberg, Germany in 2015. They now live in one of the residence complexes for refugees. Noor struggled initially with language barriers and cultural differences, but within a few months, he was able to speak good German and communicate without issues. He now goes to school, enjoys listening to German rap, and occasionally indulges in Afghani music.

Alina

Alina was born in Mariupol, Ukraine in 2012, into a family facing economic hardship. She always enjoyed playing outside and started learning guitar when she was six years old. Her parents worked tirelessly to make ends meet and were barely able to get by. Yet, they were always loving to Alina and rarely showed her that anything was wrong or that they were struggling. Their lives took a drastic turn when conflict erupted in eastern Ukraine. Alina heard the sirens and bombs go off and felt the urgency in her parents' voices as they came to her and told her to quickly pack her things. While going to the train station, even though her parents were trying to keep her from seeing things around her, she caught a glimpse of a destroyed house and a body on the ground. The biggest shock came when she realized at the train station that her dad would not be coming along. Alina, accompanied only by her mother, embarked on a westbound journey by train, while her father remained to participate in the war effort. In 2023, Alina arrived in Heidelberg, Germany, and moved into the same residence complex as Noor. Alina encountered a warm reception from the local community and her new school. She has been picking up some German but still struggles to make herself understood in this new language.

CHILDHOOD ADVERSITY

Having endured the horrors of war, being forced to flee their homes, and potentially confronted with stigma, isolation, rejection, and racism in their new homes, displaced children often have trauma-related symptoms on resettlement (Bashir, 2000; Brough *et al.*, 2003; Dokter, 1998; Sirin & Rodgers-Sirin, 2015). These symptoms are often displayed through issues with self-regulation, increasing the likelihood of these children engaging in high-risk behaviours (Layne *et al.*, 2014).

The events and circumstances that displaced children face fall under the umbrella of childhood adversity. A subset of childhood adversity is the so-called adverse childhood experiences (ACEs). ACEs are well-documented risk factors for poorer health and adjustment in adulthood. A study by Bager *et al.* (2022) in Denmark found that children with refugee parents have a higher ACEs Hazard Ratio (HR). Olivia Yinger (2022) has emphasized the importance of understanding ACEs and their relationship to resilience within a trauma-informed music therapy framework.

The experiences of Noor and Alina illustrate how childhood adversity can vary greatly. Noor left Afghanistan at the age of six. Despite his long and arduous journey, he has now been in Germany for over six years and speaks German fluently, indicating significant adjustment and integration into German society. Noor's fluency in German after six years highlights the importance of language proficiency for successful integration (Stanat & Edele, 2016). Without effective communication skills, refugees may struggle to access education, employment, and social services, leading to social isolation and exclusion.

In contrast, Alina left Ukraine at the age of 11. While her journey to Germany was relatively easier, she still experienced the hardship of displacement and separation from her father. Alina has only been in Germany for a few months and is just beginning to learn the language, facing additional challenges as she adjusts to her new environment and culture. Additionally, her family is planning to return to Ukraine as soon as the war is over. She potentially faces greater hardship in learning the language than Noor, but while she might face challenges with integration into German culture, her skin colour also means she might experience less stigma and racism.

Racism in Germany

Germany has a significant history of racism. The National Discrimination and Racism Monitor of the German Centre for Integration and Migration Research (Deutsches Zentrum für Integrations und Migrationsforschung (DeZIM), 2023) published a survey revealing that 90% of respondents believe racism exists in Germany. Additionally, 65% of respondents identified racial discrimination within authorities, while 61% noted racism in everyday life. Moreover, 47% have contradicted a racist statement in the last five years, and 22% reported experiencing racism, especially young people considered 'racialized persons'.

According to Mediendienst Integration (2024), Islamic and Muslim people, along with Black people, are often associated with aggression and criminality in the news, perpetuating insecurity and fear against these groups. Refugees arriving in 2015 from Syria and Afghanistan, such as Noor, faced a different 'welcome culture' compared to Ukrainian refugees like Alina. The German government, in support of Ukraine against Russia, voluntarily accepted and continues to accept Ukrainian refugees as a sign of loyalty to Ukraine, providing them with work-related infrastructure and basic income support. In contrast, refugees from third countries face complex bureaucracy and often encounter injustice. For instance, a 26-year-old man from Congo, despite being accepted for nursing training, was arrested and faced deportation (Woitsch, 2024).

REGULATION

A central theme in the work at Bridges is exploring emotional regulation and dysregulation, especially in the context of childhood adversity and trauma. Understanding self-regulation and co-regulation is crucial when designing and implementing group and individual interventions for displaced children and youth. The objective is to facilitate self-regulation and help transition the autonomic state toward a social engagement system (Porges, 2010, 2021; Porges et al., 1994; Porges & Rossetti, 2018; Wentling & Behrens, 2018). The reader is encouraged to read Chapter 2 by Gene-Ann Behrens for an in-depth explanation of the concepts described in this section.

Porges and Rossetti (2018) proposed that music can help down-regulate the sympathetic nervous system, which is associated with mobilization behaviours such as fight or flight responses. It can also up-regulate the ventral vagal complex, which promotes social engagement behaviours and optimizes homeostatic processes. They emphasized the role of prosody or cadence in music, similar to infant-directed speech, in regulating emotional states. They concluded that 'music may functionally "retune" our nervous system's capacity to regulate visceral organs, shift mood states, and optimise social behaviour, trust, and connectedness' (ibid., p.117).

Uhlig et al. (2017) in the Netherlands suggest that 'Rap and Sing Music Therapy' support self-regulation among adolescents in school settings.

To grasp regulation and music's effects, one has to consider the intricate connection between the body and cognition. Embodiment theory underscores how bodily experiences influence psychological processes and vice versa, shaping attitudes, behaviours, and emotional experiences. Adverse experiences often result in hyperactive brain responses and cognitive dysregulation. Awareness of children's behaviours and their underlying causes can enable tailored interventions (Brown *et al.*, 2022; Moore, 2013; Moore & Hanson-Abromeit, 2015; Williams, 2018; Yinger, 2022).

During the critical and delicate transition period for children on arrival in a new country, they are often grappling with a myriad of unfamiliar experiences and emotions. This adjustment phase can be particularly challenging, with children potentially entering a state of absent-mindedness or dorsal vagal freeze. To support these children during this vulnerable period, it is crucial to provide orientation and regulation through attention modulation techniques (Hillecke, 2020). We explain further what these techniques are in the next sections of this chapter. In short, we have observed that non-verbal communication and activities, accompanied by a warm and genuine smile, can serve as powerful tools for engaging children and gradually bringing them out of this state. Simple gestures, such as offering paper and markers or musical instruments, can serve as initial prompts to spark their interest. Once a child displays an initial impulse, such as tapping a drum, responding to this action in a supportive manner can lay the groundwork for co-regulation.

Fischer (2010) has advocated for therapists to be 'neurobiological regulators', emphasizing the interplay between caregivers' and therapists' responses and children's regulation. She drew on neuroscience and attachment research, as well as sensorimotor psychotherapy, an approach developed by Ogden *et al.* (2015) to argue that the nervous and somatic system responses and reactions of parents/caregivers and therapists play a crucial role in the regulation (or dysregulation) of the other. This understanding informs Bridges' approach to working with dysregulated children. This may entail acknowledging that complex interventions, such as musical question-and-answer or cognitively demanding tasks, might not be feasible for all children. It is also important to note that we always have two team members for all groups. Typically, one person is responsible for maintaining the music's cohesion, while the other focuses more on the needs of specific children. Usually, this second group leader can offer more individual support to children and potentially create an opportunity for one-on-one co-regulation, while the first group leader contains the whole group with its dynamic.

Following Noor

The first time we met Noor and invited him to the Spielraum-Musik group, he looked at us absent-mindedly, probably not understanding what we meant. He did not come at that first invitation, but the week after he saw the instruments set up and curiously approached the circle. At intervals, we looked at him and offered something, whether an instrument, a smile, or a simple question, such as: 'What is your name?' No response came the first time he came to the group. One more week passed by and Noor appeared again, this time at the beginning of the session. He sat on a chair and we casually put a djembe in front of him and showed him he could hit the top to make a sound. He again looked at us blankly. We started the group, and as we sang 'Salam alaikum', a greeting that works for most individuals from a Muslim background, he looked curiously at us and for the first time seemed to have a hint of an expression on his face. During the session, Noor lightly tapped a rhythm on the djembe. A group leader imitated the exact rhythm and looked at Noor. At this, Noor looked up with surprise on his face and he cautiously tapped another rhythm. The group leader tapped it right back at him. The first communication had been established! Noor was engaging socially and co-regulating with this group leader.

Safe(r) spaces

While the notion of 'safe spaces' (Kok, 2020; Scrine & Koike, 2022; Yinger, 2022) has garnered attention in the field of music therapy, existing literature seldom addresses its applicability to displaced and refugee populations. This significant gap in scholarly discourse underscores the importance of exploring this subject matter. Safety is not merely an auxiliary benefit but serves as a foundational element, allowing children to confront an array of challenges and foster resilience (Yinger, 2022).

Herman (2015) has written about the need for safety as a first step in treating trauma. At Bridges, this is often discussed in terms of 'safe(r) spaces' as we recognize the limitations that we have. While in our project we are not offering 'treatments' for trauma, creating safe spaces is a first step in fostering regulation and building resilience. We try to create safe(r) spaces through consistency, continuity, reliability, and the therapeutic relationships that arise from repeated encounters with the children. We provide orientation in that we are always in the same room, we provide a similar structure to our offers, and the same team members go to the same residence complexes. We provide continuity and reliability by bringing our activities every week, come rain or come shine. We encounter those who come to the group and give them an opportunity to feel seen and felt by others, build trust, and provide emotional discharge (Kok, 2020; Lutz Hochreutener, 2018).

HEURISTIC EFFECT FACTORS IN MUSIC THERAPY

The Heidelberg Model of heuristic effect factors in music therapy by Hillecke and Wilker (2007) offers a framework for understanding how music facilitates regulation and its application in therapeutic contexts, such as the Bridges programme. The model summarizes the specific effects of music through five overarching factors, which can be differentially utilized based on various indications and integrated into individualized intervention plans. These factors include:

- Attention modulation (A)

- Behaviour modulation (B)

- Emotional modulation (E)

- Cognition modulation (C)

- Interpersonal communication (I).

These factors are described in Hillecke (2020) and Hillecke and Wilker (2007) and set out below.

(A) Attention modulation

Throughout the natural world and certainly in humans and children, auditory signals naturally attract attention, functioning as a 'warning system' to detect dangers or relevant information in the environment. The perception of music is rooted in this evolutionary function of the auditory system. Music activates brain structures such as the thalamus and the anterior cingulate gyrus, which are crucial for vigilance and maintaining an awake state. Auditory experiences can override other sensory perceptions, even during sleep and anaesthesia, highlighting the primacy of auditory attention.

Application in Bridges: At the beginning of the Spielraum-Musik groups, attention is modulated with the welcome song, performed with a guitar and two harmonizing voices. The song incorporates greetings in the mother tongues of those present. The group often becomes quite focused during the performance, attempting to imitate unfamiliar languages. You may remember the story from Noor earlier and how his attention was engaged when hearing us singing hello in his mother language. Another example of attention modulation is the 'Conductor' game. The game's structure fosters a heightened sense of awareness and responsiveness, requiring participants to remain alert and engaged, thus effectively modulating their attention through controlled auditory and behavioural cues.

(B) Behaviour/motor modulation

Music functions as a potent signal capable of inducing movement, often prompting involuntary rhythmic responses in listeners. The perception of music as positive or negative can significantly impact the motivation for behaviour and movement. The staged way music is processed in the brain means that one aspect closely correlates or aligns with early stages of action planning. It exerts influence on timing processes within areas of motor control and action execution.

Application in Bridges: Music-supported movement activities such as drumming circles are utilized to activate the sympathetic nervous system, facilitating stress regulation while assisting individuals in managing feelings of restlessness (Bensimon *et al.*, 2008). Another beloved activity among the children in our programme is the 'Stop Dance' game. This activity combines enjoyment with competitiveness, fostering self-control over body movements, attentive listening to the music's cues, and self-awareness to avoid distraction or reacting to mistakes made by others. Through these engaging exercises, participants develop essential regulatory skills while enjoying the benefits of music-supported movement.

(E) Emotional modulation

Music is renowned for its profound capacity to evoke and intensify emotions. It possesses the remarkable ability to elicit pleasant sentiments, enrich visual imagery, and, under specific circumstances, provoke hostility. In music therapy, both positive and negative emotions can be activated, possibly mediated by brain regions implicated in emotion processing. Individuals may exhibit diverse responses to music, influenced by factors such as their musical background and personal experiences.

Application in Bridges: We acknowledge the unpredictability of participants' emotional states on arrival. Therefore, we afford participants the autonomy to select songs they wish to sing or listen to, empowering them to modulate their own emotions. As a team, we remain attuned to the group's emotional dynamics, offering avenues for emotional release through interventions like group drumming or solo performances within songs. Interestingly, we've observed that younger children (under six years old) often gravitate towards upbeat and cheerful songs, such as chart-toppers or children's tunes, while older children and teenagers explore a diverse range of selections, spanning love songs to traditional melodies.

(C) Cognition modulation

Music serves as a powerful medium for stimulating imagination and often plays a supportive role in facilitating creative thought processes. Artists frequently harness music to enhance their creative endeavours, leveraging its emotive qualities and expressive potential. Furthermore, music plays a significant role in activating episodic memories, forging a strong connection between music and the recall of personal experiences. It serves as a vehicle for conveying meanings across generations, functioning as a subcultural language that transcends linguistic barriers and fosters cultural continuity. Moreover, music has the capacity to evoke dreaming and daydreaming, inviting listeners into imaginative realms of introspection and reverie. In many indigenous cultures, music is utilized to induce altered states of consciousness, leading to trance-like states of heightened awareness and spiritual exploration. Additionally, musical ability, often regarded as talent, reflects cognitive competence, with the acquisition of musical skills posing complex cognitive demands. Contemporary scientific insights suggest that the processing of music in the brain parallels that of language, with musical pieces acquiring meaning comprehensible to the listener.

Application in Bridges: Music lessons and band workshops offer a significant cognitive challenge to children in the Bridges project. It is common for children to feel frustrated when they struggle with difficult passages. However, with encouragement, they eventually master these challenges, showcasing their progress. Band workshops present an added difficulty, as students must not only know their parts well but also synchronize with others. Singing songs in German further supports language acquisition, which is crucial for some children who continue to face language and speech barriers years after arriving in Germany. Alongside speech therapy, they are encouraged to practise singing their favourite German songs. Additionally, songwriting serves as a cognitive exercise, requiring children to organize their thoughts and emotions into musical expression.

(l) Interpersonal communication

Music often serves as a potent form of interpersonal non-verbal communication, transcending linguistic boundaries and facilitating interaction through emotive expression. Concerts and youth groups, in particular, perceive music as a unifying force, providing a sense of identity and belonging, especially among teenagers navigating the complexities of adolescence. In therapeutic settings, music improvisation serves as a valuable tool for non-verbal communication, complementing verbal therapy by allowing patients to express symptoms, thoughts, behaviours, and emotions through musical expression. This non-verbal mode of communication enhances interpersonal understanding and promotes therapeutic rapport.

Application in Bridges: In the Bridges project, the profound interpersonal communication facilitated by music plays a pivotal role in our interventions. This non-verbal mode of communication allows individuals to convey thoughts and feelings that may be difficult to articulate through words alone. Moreover, music has the ability to promote trust and rapport between participants and project leaders. By harnessing music as a medium for interpersonal expression, the Bridges project cultivates a supportive and inclusive space where participants can explore and address their psychological needs.

RESILIENCE

Alongside considerations of regulation, we prioritize the cultivation of resilience among our participants. According to Fröhlich-Gildhoff and Rönnau-Böse (2022), resilience refers to the ability of individuals to develop psychologically healthy lives despite adverse life circumstances and successfully cope with the negative consequences of stress. Key components of resilience include a positive self-concept, emotional self-regulation, and self-control. Additionally, experiences of self-efficacy, social skills, active coping mechanisms, and problem-solving abilities are integral to resilience. Moreover, the presence of at least one stable attachment figure and having positive relationship experiences are repeatedly highlighted as crucial factors for resilience. Music and music therapy, serving as a medium for expression and communication, hold immense potential for fostering resilience. For a further exploration of the neurobiological basis of resilience, the reader is encouraged once more to read Chapter 2 by Gene-Ann Behrens.

In the discourse surrounding resilience within developmental contexts, Ginsburg and Jablow (2020) have introduced the 7 Cs of Resilience Model, encapsulating crucial factors influencing resilience in children and adolescents. These factors encompass character, competence, confidence, coping, control, connection, and contribution. Character embodies an ethical compass, guiding individuals towards discerning right from wrong, fostering a commitment to ethical conduct rooted in respect and accountability. Competence, integral to confidence-building, signifies individuals' adeptness in confronting challenges, empowering them to navigate life's complexities autonomously. Control and coping, both under the umbrella of regulation, highlight the importance of understanding and addressing emotional dysregulation in children. Connection underscores the significance of interpersonal bonds in fostering reliance on others and nurturing a sense of belonging and support. Contribution emphasizes instilling in children an awareness of their capacity to effect positive change, fostering a sense of purpose and agency. In practical application, this model resonates in initiatives like Bridges, where children cultivate resilience through experiential learning.

We can now go back to Alina and consider how these 7 Cs are addressed through her participation in Bridges:

- Coping: Coping skills are woven throughout all of Bridges' offerings. In Spielraum Musik, Alina is able to share songs that evidence how she is feeling. In lessons, she is taught how to cope with frustration in not being able to play a certain passage immediately. Through the therapeutic relationships she creates with the Bridges teams, she is able to co-regulate, an important coping skill and a precursor to self-regulation.

- Control: Being forced to flee her home, not knowing how permanent her current living situation would be, and so many other factors create a sense in Alina of not having control over her life. In the Bridges project, Alina can choose the songs she wants to bring to the group, the instrument she wants to play, and what she wants to learn. She also experiences control when she 'directs' the group in the 'Conductor' game.

- Confidence: Even before learning to play an instrument or speak German, Alina demonstrates some of the things she already knows on the guitar from when she was in Ukraine. The other children regard her with surprise and she receives praise for it, strengthening her self-confidence.

- Competence: Through music lessons, Alina continues to build her competence on the guitar, and occasionally also on the piano. This again feeds into her self-confidence.

- Character: Alina often plays the drums quite loudly with a stick rather than with her hands. This behaviour is understood from a neuro-biological point of view. Through an informed stance and several conversations, Alina starts to understand why some behaviours are less desirable. It is explained, for example, that if she hits the drum as she does and it breaks, then nobody will be able to play the drum anymore and that would be sad.

- Connection: There seems to be little contact between children from Ukraine and children from other countries. That being said, they do all come together to the Spielraum-Musik groups. In one particular instance, Alina surprises all by singing a song in German from memory. This is a current hit, and all children join in. Through this and other moments, Alina is seen to get along better with the other children.

- Contribution: In band workshops, Alina is one of the most advanced children and demonstrates this in the parts she plays. She feels as if she has important contributions to the group.

Regulation and resilience: Two sides of the same coin

Artuch-Garde *et al.* (2017) explored the connection between self-regulation and resilience in a study in Spain and found a significant and positive relationship between these two constructs. In the context of the Bridges project, these findings hold profound implications for our approach to supporting children and adolescents in their journeys. Understanding the critical link between self-regulation and resilience, we prioritize the development of self-regulatory skills as a fundamental aspect of our therapeutic interventions. By equipping participants with tools to effectively manage their emotions and behaviours, we empower them to navigate the challenges of their new environment with greater resilience and adaptability. Through activities that promote self-awareness, emotional regulation, and coping strategies, we foster the resilience necessary for children and adolescents to thrive despite the complexities they may encounter. By integrating these insights into our programmatic offerings, we aim to cultivate a nurturing environment where participants can build the internal resources needed to overcome adversity and flourish in their new surroundings.

WHAT BRIDGES OFFERS
Spielraum Musik

Spielraum-Musik groups (Reiner-Wormit, 2017) follow a community music therapy approach that is low-threshold, open, or semi-open, with a music-therapeutic attitude designed to be inclusive and accessible. There is no official referral process and any individuals in the community are welcome to attend the group and leave at any point. Its format is adaptable, taking place outdoors or indoors depending on weather conditions and the desired atmosphere and objectives. The sessions are conducted weekly for one hour by two team members. It is ideally staffed by a music therapist and a musician who dedicate time to preparation and follow-up, including detailed documentation. Framed in a resource-oriented manner (Rolvsjord, 2006), Spielraum Musik serves as a targeted initiative for promoting health and well-being.

The Spielraum-Musik groups follow a minimally structured format designed to engage participants and achieve specific objectives. As mentioned earlier in the chapter, the session begins with a greeting song performed in various languages. Following the introduction, the activities commence, offering a range of engaging experiences for the participants. Our approach considers child and youth group dynamics, which frames and contains very different content rather than prescribing a structured programme. Our supervisor, who is a music therapist, child and adolescent psychotherapist, and group analyst, also supports us professionally with this approach.

One popular activity is the 'Stop Dance' or 'Statues' game, a playful exercise where participants dance or move to music and freeze when the music stops. Those who move during the pause are eliminated from the game. This game encourages active participation, enhances listening skills, and promotes coordination. Another key activity is the 'Conductor' game, where participants take turns leading the group in creating music through gestures and movements and controlling the loudness of the sounds produced by other participants, instructing them when to stop. This activity fosters control, leadership skills, and collaboration. Throughout the session, improvisation plays a significant role, allowing participants to explore their musical creativity freely. Additionally, participants engage in listening activities, where they listen to and discuss songs from different cultures, promoting cross-cultural understanding and appreciation.

Embedded within the structure of the session are the overarching objectives of the group. These include fostering a cross-cultural and cross-generational community experience, promoting intercultural understanding, and conveying appreciation for all cultural identities with cultural sensitivity. Moreover, the sessions aim to integrate aspects of participants' countries of origin with their new home country. The creation of safe and welcoming spaces within the complexes where the youth live is essential, as these complexes are intended to provide safety but often fall short due to neglect by city administrations. While voluntary organizations strive to offer support through activities like German courses and childcare, these efforts often lack continuity and reliability due to their voluntary and non-professional nature.

Noor and Alina start coming to Spielraum Musik

Noor and Alina arrived at different times in Heidelberg. Noor arrived in 2020, followed by Alina in 2023. In the initial weeks after their arrival, both Noor and Alina found themselves grappling with feelings of confusion, exhaustion, and low spirits as they adjusted to their new surroundings. Amid their uncertainty, they received an unexpected visit bearing news of a 'music' activity. As you read earlier, Noor initially felt hesitant to trust his new environment and it took some time before he felt comfortable enough to join the music sessions. In contrast, Alina, aided by a translator app, found it somewhat easier to communicate and she came at the first invitation. By the time Alina began attending the music groups, Noor had already been a regular participant for three years. Despite his initial shyness, Noor's true personality became quickly evident, revealing his innate energy and inability to stay still during the sessions. As Alina acclimated to the group, it became apparent that while she joined the group right away, she seemed to be weighed down by a sense of melancholy.

In a particular session in which both Noor and Alina were present, we were able to see how specific songs and music activities addressed their feelings. Noor's restlessness translated into him taking a drum and starting to play on it as loudly as he could. One of the group leaders took this energy, stood in the middle, and played along with him as loudly as he could and invited the rest of the group to do the same. He then gestured by crouching and playing softly that they should follow as well. They did, and he continued gesturing different loudness levels a few times before inviting Noor to be in the middle and conduct the group. He happily did this, and after the activity, he seemed to be more regulated. As the group continued, the group leader noticed that Alina seemed to be down in mood and she had barely played along with the conductor activity. She was invited to share a song with the group and she shared 'Stefania', a Ukrainian song that speaks to the maternal bond but also expresses melancholy and sadness towards the situation in Ukraine.

Music lessons

The possibility to receive music lessons through Bridges started in 2022. Unlike the Spielraum-Musik groups, these lessons typically involve one-on-one sessions, allowing teachers to provide personalized attention and cater to individual needs. While the primary focus is on learning an instrument, the lessons often become a platform for addressing emotional, cognitive, and developmental aspects. Learning an instrument involves various elements that extend beyond musical proficiency. First, discipline plays a pivotal role, as consistent practice at home is crucial for skill development. Additionally, children inevitably encounter challenges and frustrations during their musical journey, presenting opportunities to cope with negative feelings. As they navigate these obstacles, they enhance their musical competence and bolster their confidence, with many children deriving a sense of identity and pride from their newfound musical abilities. Furthermore, learning an instrument instils a sense of control, an essential component of emotional regulation. By mastering an external skill, a sense of autonomy and self-efficacy is fostered.

Noor and Alina start having music lessons

Introducing instrument lessons within the Bridges project sparked immediate interest from Noor, who eagerly seized the opportunity to explore music. Among the first to enrol, he sampled different instruments until he found his muse: the bass guitar. Noor's commitment to his lessons was among the most consistent of all the students at Bridges. Over time, he was able to accompany several of the songs he liked and started to play more complex melodies. Alina's path to instrument lessons was more nuanced and complex. While she had already learned guitar back in Ukraine, her interest in continuing instrument lessons seemed to ebb and flow. At times, she displayed genuine enthusiasm, and she did seem to be proud when she played something for the group and received praise for it. Yet, amid the challenges and uncertainties of resettlement, Alina often cancelled lessons or did not show up. There were moments when she seemed to lose motivation but then she would have periods where she would be more consistent. Navigating these obstacles proved to be a test of resilience for Alina. Despite the setbacks and uncertainties, she persisted. Alina gradually found her footing, and while she continued learning the guitar, she also occasionally had piano lessons.

Band workshops

Transitioning from individual instrument lessons to group band workshops marks a significant milestone in the musical journey of the children participating in the Bridges project. Unlike the low-threshold accessible and minimally structured Spielraum-Musik groups, which foster a sense of inclusivity and exploration, band workshops are more structured and goal-directed, requiring children to collaborate and synchronize their efforts to create cohesive musical performances.

Forming groups based on the instruments played by each child, the workshops aim to cultivate teamwork and ensemble skills, with each participant assuming a specific role within the band. However, assembling successful bands has posed its challenges, as children must learn to focus beyond their individual impulses and desires. They are tasked with paying attention to the music director and their peers, while also considering the song being played and its arrangement. This demands a level of self-regulation that can be difficult for some children to attain.

Despite these challenges, the ultimate goal of the band workshops is to instil a sense of collective achievement and connection among the children. By participating in group performances, they experience the gratification of contributing to something greater than themselves and forge meaningful connections with their peers. The culmination of these efforts is often showcased in end-of-workshop 'concerts', where the children proudly display their musical prowess to the wider community.

Noor and Alina join band workshops

For Noor, the transition from individual bass guitar lessons to the collaborative environment of band workshops proved to be a thrilling yet challenging endeavour. Accustomed to the autonomy of solo practice, he initially struggled to synchronize his playing with that of his bandmates and to maintain focus amid the collective energy of the group. As the band rehearsals progressed, Noor's confidence and competence increased over time, and he found himself eagerly anticipating the end-of-workshop concerts, where he could showcase his newfound skills to the community with pride.

For Alina, the journey from tentative lessons to the structured setting of band workshops was a step she was initially not ready to take. Despite her initial reservations and occasional lapses in focus, Alina persevered. Being able to play melodies and chords on the guitar, she was able to showcase her competence and gain confidence from the praises of her bandmates. As the band rehearsals culminated in the experience of performing in front of an audience, Alina felt a sense of belonging and validation.

Concerts

The final pillar of the Bridges project centres around concerts. This pillar is still in the developmental stages as of writing this chapter. Initially, the project relied on the band of a Bridges team member to perform at various refugee residence complexes. These concerts served as powerful community-building events, drawing together residents from diverse backgrounds, with neighbours and citizens of Heidelberg, fostering a sense of unity and belonging. However, due to the logistical complexities involved, such events have been infrequent, occurring only on rare occasions. One memorable concert on 3 February 2024 at the Karlstorbahnhof Heidelberg featured a unique blend of performances, with some of the children showcasing their vocal talents while members of the Bridges team provided musical accompaniment.

The students from the Bridges team were featured as instrumentalists in their debut concert, also at the Karlstorbahnhof. This was an exciting milestone in the project's evolution, as it provided the children with an opportunity to take centre stage and share their musical talents with the wider community. Through these concerts, the Bridges project continues to foster a sense of empowerment, pride, and accomplishment among its participants, while also promoting inclusivity and cultural exchange within the refugee community.

Noor and Alina play at a concert

Noor and Alina were excited when we announced the possibility for them to perform at a concert. In the weeks leading up to the concert, Noor would ask about it every time he saw the Bridges team, which showed his excitement. Alina, despite her initial hesitations and sporadic engagement, found herself fully committed to the performance. The concert allowed her to overcome her shyness and channel her emotions through the piano. For this first concert, the students needed to find common ground, so they learned a universally popular song: 'Wellerman'. The band workshops proved to be challenging as most students were still learning the basics of their instruments and their concentration would often not last long. The day of the concert Noor, Alina, and the rest of the band were picked up by the Bridges team and taken to the venue. They all received a warm welcome and could not believe that they were able to get drinks and ice cream for free as they were performers. The time came, the band came on stage, and with a smile on their face, Noor and Alina played their hearts out. Weeks after the concert, Alina and Noor were still talking about what a great experience it was.

CONCLUSION

Ten years ago, Jutta Glaser and Cordula Reiner-Wormit planted a seed that has since blossomed into the project you have just read about in this chapter. This initiative continues to make a profound impact on children like Noor and Alina, who have faced – and continue to face – significant challenges. We are privileged to witness our participants' growth, both externally and internally, as they navigate their unique paths. Each child's journey is distinct, and while some trajectories take them beyond our reach – due to deportation or other circumstances – others bring them closer, deepening their engagement with our programmes. Although many questions persist, and the journey is not always easy, we remain committed to learning and evolving to better serve the youth in our project.

In 2025, the Bridges project stands at a pivotal moment. We have received a critical European grant that enables us to sustain and expand our services for the next three years. This funding is essential to preserving the momentum and stability of our initiatives. We are looking forward to seeing how this funding will allow us to expand the work of Bridges.

While this chapter cannot cover every topic we regularly address at Bridges, it's important to acknowledge the significant challenges we face – issues of identity, the imperative for professional supervision, and numerous other aspects that shape our daily work. However, we hope that the concepts discussed here – such as the creation of safe spaces, fostering resilience, promoting self-regulation, and building community – offer a meaningful insight into our efforts. Our ultimate aim is to inspire others working with displaced populations worldwide, demonstrating the transformative power of music therapy and music.

REFERENCES

Artuch-Garde, R., González-Torres, M. D. C., de la Fuente, J., Vera, M. M., *et al.* (2017). Relationship between resilience and self-regulation: A study of Spanish youth at risk of social exclusion. *Frontiers in Psychology*, 8, 612. https://doi.org/10.3389/fpsyg.2017.00612.

Bager, L., Laursen, T. M., Palic, S., Nordin, L., & Høgh Thøgersen, M. (2022). Adverse childhood experiences among children of parents who are refugees affected by trauma in Denmark: A register-based Cohort Study. *The Lancet Public Health*, 7(10). https://doi.org/10.1016/s2468-2667(22)00194-3.

Bashir, M. (2000). *Immigrant and refugee young people: Challenges in mental health*. Paper presented at Deeper Dimensions: Culture, Youth and Mental Health, Transcultural Mental Health Centre.

Bensimon, M., Amir, D., & Wolf, Y. (2008). Drumming through trauma: Music therapy with post-traumatic soldiers. *The Arts in Psychotherapy*, 35(1), 34–48. https://doi.org/10.1016/j.aip.2007.09.002.

Brough, M., Gorman, D., Ramirez, E., & Westoby, P. (2003). Young refugees talk about well-being: A qualitative analysis of refugee youth mental health from three states. *Australian Journal of Social Issues*, 38(2), 193–209.

Brown, E. D., Blumenthal, M. A., & Allen, A. A. (2022). The sound of self-regulation: Music program relates to an advantage for children at risk. *Early Childhood Research Quarterly*, 60(3), 126–136. https://doi.org/10.1016/j.ecresq.2022.01.002.

Deutsches Zentrum für Integrationsund Migrationsforschung (DeZIM). (2023, 1 January). Rassismus und seine symptome. www.rassismusmonitor.de/fileadmin/user_upload/NaDiRa/Rassismus_Symptome/Rassismus_und_seine_Symptome.pdf.

Dokter, D. (1998). Being a Migrant, Working with Migrants: Issues of Identity and Embodiment. In D. Dokter (ed.), *Arts Therapists, Refugees and Migrants. Reaching Across Borders* (pp.217–235). London: Jessica Kingsley Publishers.

Fischer, J. (2010). Brain to brain: The therapist as neurobiological regulator. *Psychotherapy Networker*.

Fröhlich-Gildhoff, K. & Rönnau-Böse, M. (2022). *Resilienz*. Munich, Germany: Reinhardt Verlag.

Ginsburg, K. R. & Jablow, M. M. (2020). *Building Resilience in Children and Teens: Giving Kids Roots and Wings*. Itasca, IL: American Academy of Pediatrics.

Heidelberg. (n.d.). *FAQ. Frequently asked questions*. www.heidelberg.de/english/Home/Life/frequently+asked+questions.html.

Herman, J. L. (2015). *Trauma and Recovery: The Aftermath of Violence; From Domestic Abuse to Political Terror*. New York, NY: Basic Books.

Hillecke, T. K. (2020). Effect Factors in Music Therapy. In A. F. Wormit, T. K. Hillecke, D. von Moreau, & C. Diener (eds) *Music Therapy in Geriatric Care: A Practical Guide* (E-book) (pp.38–48). Munich, Germany: Reinhardt Verlag.

Hillecke, T. K. & Wilker, F.-W. (2007). Ein heuristisches Wirkfaktorenmodell der Musiktherapie. *Verhaltenstherapie & Verhaltensmedizin*, 28, 62–85.

Kok, M. (2020). Der sichere Ort. Ein traumasensibles Musiktherapie-Projekt in einer Schulkooperation. In *Verband deutscher Musikschulen (Hg.): Spektrum Musiktherapie. Grundlagen und Arbeitshil-fen.* VdM, S. 123–126.

Layne, C. M., Greeson, J. K. P., Ostrowski, S. A., Kim, S., *et al.* (2014). Cumulative trauma exposure and high risk behavior in adolescence: Findings from the National Child Traumatic Stress Network Core Data Set. *Psychological Trauma: Theory, Research, Practice, and Policy,* 6(Suppl 1), S40–S49. https://doi.org/10.1037/a0037799.

Lutz Hochreutener, S. (2018). Musiktherapie im Schulischen Kontext. Fakten – Heraus-forderungen – Chancen. In A.-K. Jordan, E. Pfeifer, T. Stegemann, & S. Lutz Hochreu-tener (eds) *Musiktherapie in Pädagogischen Settings. Impulse aus Praxis, Theorie und Forschung* (pp.15–30). Munich, Germany: Waxmann.

Mediendienst Integration (2024). Mediendienst Integration – Informations-Plattform für Medienschaffende. https://mediendienst-integration.de.

Moore, K. S. (2013). A systematic review on the neural effects of music on emotion reg-ulation: Implications for music therapy practice. *Journal of Music Therapy,* 50(3), 198–242. https://doi.org/10.1093/jmt/50.3.198.

Moore, K. S. & Hanson-Abromeit, D. (2015). Theory-guided therapeutic function of music to facilitate emotion regulation development in preschool-aged children. *Frontiers in Human Neuroscience,* 9. https://doi.org/10.3389/fnhum.2015.00572.

Ogden, P., Fisher, J., Del Hierro, D., & Del Hierro, A. (2015). *Sensorimotor Psychotherapy: Interventions for Trauma and Attachment.* New York, NY: W.W. Norton & Company.

Porges, S. W. (2010). Music Therapy and Trauma: Insights from the Polyvagal Theory. In K. Stewart (ed.) *Symposium on Music Therapy & Trauma: Bridging Theory and Clinical Practice* (pp.3–15). New York, NY: Satchnote Press.

Porges, S. W. (2021). *Polyvagal Safety: Attachment, Communication, Self-Regulation.* New York, NY: W.W. Norton & Company.

Porges, S. W., Doussard-Roosevelt, J. A., & Maiti, A. K. (1994). Vagal tone and the physio-logical regulation of emotion. *Monographs of the Society for Research in Child Devel-opment,* 59(2/3), 167–186. https://doi.org/10.2307/1166144.

Porges, S. W. & Rossetti, A. (2018). Music, music therapy and trauma. *Music and Medicine,* 10(3), 117. https://doi.org/10.47513/mmd.v10i3.635.

Reiner-Wormit, C. (2017). Spielraum Musik: ein Stück Heimat. *Musiktherapeutische Umschau,* 38, 187–188.

Rolvsjord, R. (2006). Therapy as empowerment: Clinical and political implications of empowerment philosophy in mental health practices of music therapy. *Voices: A World Forum for Music Therapy,* 6(3). https://doi.org/10.15845/voices.v6i3.283.

Scrine, E. & Koike, A. (2022). Questioning the Promise of Safety in Trauma-Informed Music Therapy Practice. In L. E. Beer & J. C. Birnbaum (eds) *Trauma-Informed Music Therapy and Practice* (pp.37–44). New York, NY: Routledge.

Sirin, S. & Rogers-Sirin, L. (2015). *The Educational and Mental Health Needs of Syrian Refugee Children.* Washington, DC: Migration Policy Institute.

Stanat, P. & Edele, A. (2016). Language proficiency and the integration of immigrant stu-dents in the education system. *Emerging Trends in the Social and Behavioral Sciences,* 1–15. https://doi.org/10.1002/9781118900772.etrds0407.

Uhlig, S., Jansen, E., & Scherder, E. (2017). 'Being a bully isn't very cool...': Rap & Sing Music therapy for enhanced emotional self-regulation in an adolescent school set-ting – a randomized controlled trial. *Psychology of Music,* 46(4), 568–587. https://doi.org/10.1177/0305735617719154.

UNHCR. (2023). *Global trends report 2023.* www.unhcr.org/global-trends-report-2023.

Wentling, B. & Behrens, G. A. (2018). Case study of early childhood trauma using a neu-robiological approach to music therapy. *Music Therapy Perspectives,* 36(1), 131–131. https://doi.org/10.1093/mtp/miy003.

Williams, K. E. (2018). Moving to the beat: Using music, rhythm, and movement to enhance self-regulation in early childhood classrooms. *International Journal of Early Childhood*, 50(1), 85–100. https://doi.org/10.1007/s13158-018-0215-y.

Woitsch, K. (2024, 29 February). Abschiebung von Münchner Pflegehelfer im letzten Moment verhindert. www.merkur.de/lokales/muenchen/abschiebung-von-muenchner-pflegehelfer-im-letzten-moment-verhindert-92855760.html.

Yinger, O. S. (2022). I Am Safe and I Am Strong: Understanding Adverse Childhood Experiences and Building Resilience through Trauma-Informed Music Therapy. In L. E. Beer & J. C. Birnbaum (eds) *Trauma-Informed Music Therapy Theory and Practice* (pp.47–55). London: Routledge. https://doi.org/10.4324/9781003200833-8.

CHAPTER 7

Researching Safe Spaces, Addressing Ethical Challenges

Music with Children on the Move in Transit Camps

MITSI AKOYUNOGLOU

Welcome to Greece, a country on the European periphery after a decade of crisis.

CARASTATHIS *ET AL.*, 2018, P.33

A refugee could be anybody. It could be you or me. The so-called refugee crisis is a human crisis.

AI WEIWEI, 2018, P.2

THE SOCIO-POLITICAL CONTEXT: 'WE ARE ALL REFUGEES'

In Europe, we witnessed a massive flow of refugees and migrants during the second half of 2015. More than 850,000 people arrived by inflatable boats that year to Greece alone, crossing the Aegean Sea from the Turkish shorelines (UNHCR, 2015a), and over 120,000 people arrived in Chios Island (UNHCR, 2015b), my place of residence. As documented by the United Nations High Commissioner for Refugees (UNHCR), people were mainly from Syria, Afghanistan, Iraq, and Iran. Children, either accompanied by their families, or unaccompanied minors, made up about 37% of the total arrivals to Chios. Behind these numbers and facts are actual people struggling for their survival, security, and future.

Many terms have been used in the literature to describe people on the move, such as refugees, asylum seekers, displaced persons, informal migrants, border crossers, persons of concern, and illegal or undocumented immigrants (Callister *et al.*, 2022; Douglas *et al.*, 2019; Papataxiarchis, 2016a). Even though the term 'refugee' has been specifically defined since the 1951 Convention Relating to the Status of Refugees,[1] all these different terms have been used interchangeably in the Greek media discourse to describe people on the move. Acknowledging that each term has a distinct meaning and significance, the term 'refugee' will be used throughout this chapter for the sake of simplicity and conciseness, without taking legal or other factors into account, and without considering refugees or refugee children to be a homogenous group. In addition, the term 'refugee children' is used, as stated in paragraph 8 of the Note on Refugee Children (UNHCR, 1987), to describe refugees, asylum seekers, and displaced persons of concern up to the age of 18.

In this chapter, I describe my experience as a community music therapist, based on my voluntary involvement in the 'refugee crisis' as a grassroots activist in Chios, standing in solidarity with refugee children. Although I led open-to-all children's music groups from 2015 to 2019, I limit my narrations to groups that took place from June 2015 to March 2016, the 'open borders' period. Specifically, during 'the first phase of mass migration and solidarity' and the 'second phase of a dual management of the "refugee crisis" with humanitarian and securitization terms' (Souzas *et al.*, 2021, p.25), the European borders were open, and refugees were able to move from Greece to other countries. With the need to reduce the pressure on Europe's borders, the EU and Turkey deal was signed on 18 March 2016, as a joint agreement to address the refugee crisis. This agreement changed the landscape of the migratory flow and enforced the 'hotspot' approach. By 2016, Greece was referred to as the 'hotspot of Europe', having shifted from providing a transit area to a place of detention for refugees (Carastathis *et al.*, 2018, p.29).

I chose a self-reflexive approach to write and describe my personal experience, with the intention of making meaning of working as a music therapist in the field, following the interpretative paradigm (Pino Gavidia & Adu, 2022). My narrations are based on an extensive journal that I kept during these years, enriched with data from journals kept by five other

---

[1] Any person who, 'owing to well-founded fear of being persecuted for reasons of race, religion, nationality, membership of a particular social group or political opinion, is outside the country of his nationality and is unable or, owing to such fear, is unwilling to avail himself of the protection of that country; or who, not having a nationality and being outside the country of his former habitual residence as a result of such events, is unable or, owing to such fear, is unwilling to return to it' (article 1, para. A2).

volunteers who supported the groups. As Pino Gavidia and Adu (2022, p.2) posit, 'a description of sociality, temporality, and place acknowledges the lived experience of participants as the knowledge source'. In other words, the aim of my descriptions is to gain a deeper understanding of the particular social conditions of the music therapy groups, during the particular time period and in the particular environments. In addition, I would like to recognize that my narratives simply convey my understanding and interpretations after engaging as a music therapist with refugee children in the transit camps. To fully understand the refugee experience, one would have to be a person on the move. Since I am describing from the position of a participatory observer, I acknowledge my limitations, as well as the challenge of representing solely with words the various facets of the interventions.

As a music therapist living and working in Greece, I have witnessed various crises during the last couple of decades, from the 'financial crisis' in 2008 to the 'refugee crisis' in 2015 and the 'health crisis' in 2020. Yet, it has been argued in the literature that each crisis has found Greece in a tougher position that resulted in a rise in solidarity every time (Katsanidou & Lefkofridi, 2020). The slogan that has been used in marches and protests in Greece since 2015, *Eimaste oloi prósfyges* (We are all refugees), reflects a collective understanding of the refugee experience as a universal one. Volunteerism, activism, and a collective grassroots perspective have been the driving forces of the music therapy project that I will narrate in the following paragraphs.

THE ACT OF STANDING IN SOLIDARITY

Allylengýi, the Greek word for solidarity, identifies the 'horizontal, egalitarian attitude' of support offered to someone (Papataxiarchis, 2022, p.163), and the neologism *allyléngioi* describes the solidarians, the people who stand in solidarity. The refugee crisis in Greece in 2015 stirred up a movement of locals who provided *allylengýi stous prósfyges* ('solidarity with refugees'). As an after-effect of the so-called 'European refugee crisis', the act of solidarity with refugees promoted a new sense of community, forged at a grassroots level (Gkionakis, 2016), in this case from the local people of Chios Island. During the summer of 2015 in Chios, an interesting transition from xenophobia to the new patriotism of 'solidarity' was observed (Papataxiarchis, 2016c; Souzas *et al.*, 2021). Refugees, regardless of age, gender, social position, race, or colour, were seen as vulnerable human beings in need (Papataxiarchis, 2022).

Solidarity with refugees was a phenomenon driven from the bottom up, through spontaneous self-organized social mobilizations of support

(Papataxiarchis, 2016a) based on altruistic and humanistic motives (Papa-taxiarchis, 2016b). As part of a wider solidarity movement that had evolved in Greece in the previous years of austerity, groups of locals formed collec-tivities based on solidarity. In Chios, the summer of 2015 was characterized as 'the summer of solidarity' (Souzas *et al.*, 2021), during which time many locals actively expressed their support. Considering its size, Chios, an island with a population of about 50,000 people, welcomed 120,000 refugees in 2015 alone. There was no provision from the state at that time, nor was there any space properly prepared to welcome and host refugee people, especially given the large numbers that were arriving.

It was interesting to observe how the local people took action and very soon several working groups were formed. Spaces like the Municipal Square, Souda, and the harbour became hosting areas. The locals took it on them-selves to pitch tents, provide food, create a kitchen, provide clothing and other supplies, offer transport to and from the hospital, and attend to the needs of the refugees. These were grassroots projects run by solidarians who got together because they wanted to help. The question is whether it was an ephemeral solidarity, as Papataxiarchis (2022) describes it.

In October 2015, the Greek state, along with the UNHCR, started taking initiatives to minister to the needs of refugees, and formal refugee camps were established. Most locals who were involved as volunteers were either absorbed into humanitarian non-governmental organizations (NGOs) or opted to step aside. The landscape changed after the European Union-Turkey agreement in March 2016, and even more after the change in the migration policy in the summer of 2019 when the new conservative gov-ernment came to power. Thus, we saw that '"refugee solidarity" was both born and concluded at low levels of politics' (Papataxiarchis, 2022, p.179).

THE PRECARIOUSNESS OF THE REFUGEE EXPERIENCE
As described by UNHCR (2024):

> Refugees are people forced to flee their own country and seek safety in another country. They are unable to return to their own country because of feared persecution as a result of who they are, what they believe in or say, or because of armed conflict, violence or serious public disorder. (para. 1)

From the three phases commonly identified in this involuntary dislocation journey – pre-flight, flight, and post-flight – the time living in a transit camp is what has been described as the 'survival' stage (Papadopoulos, 2021, p.255) and the 'asylum phase of hope and fear' (Jalonen & La Corte, 2018, p.23). Life in a transit host country holds for refugees many uncertainties and risks while they wait for their asylum claim to be concluded, and they focus on surviving, and striving for a long-term future (Hieronymi, 2008).

Forced migration has been documented as being a particularly vulnerable situation for refugee children (Dangmann *et al.*, 2022), since all acts of violence jeopardize children's well-being and compromise their healthy development. Children face many challenges on the refugee journey. They must quickly, and often without prior notice, understanding, or planning, abandon their home life, leaving behind their room and toys, neighbourhood, friends, school, and activities. Papadopoulos (2021), in discussing the significance of the concept of home and all that it encompasses in their lives, highlights the complex reality that refugee children experience: homelessness, involuntary dislocation, the hostility and unfamiliarity of the environment of the various transit refugee camps during their journey, and the anxiety, challenges, and acculturation stressors faced when adjusting to a new life in another country.

The flight phase is a multifaceted and difficult period for the children. Life in a transit camp might be accompanied by deprivation of food, water, and shelter. Children may sustain injuries, assaults, or diseases, be separated from their caregivers, lose their community (friends, relatives, neighbours), live with uncertainty about the future, and might even face harassment from authorities and be placed in detention centres. During this time, refugee children might experience traumatic stress related to these adversities, but also from the effort to adjust and integrate to a new culture while holding on to their culture of origin. These could include cultural misunderstandings, language difficulties, problems trying to fit in at school, isolation stress as minorities in the host country, lack of a social support network, discrimination and harassment from the local communities, and feeling unwelcome (Papastathopoulos, 2020; Patel *et al.*, 2023).

Although children are very resilient and can often cope with difficult experiences in healthy and productive ways (Mohammed & Thomas, 2017; Zolkoski & Bullock, 2012), exposure to traumatic events can elicit a variety of symptoms. These could include stomach aches, headaches, or other pains in the body that don't seem to have a physical cause, crying a lot, exhibiting anxiety, sadness, or uneasiness, trouble falling asleep or sleeping too much, trouble paying attention, lack of desire to play or engage in activities, and persistent thoughts or emotions about the traumatic events (Dangmann *et al.*, 2022; Jensen *et al.*, 2019; Richter *et al.*, 2020).

The temporality of life in a transit camp
Closed controlled access centres and formal and informal transit refugee camps have been described as converging spaces of global displacement

(Huq & Miraftab, 2020). These are temporary spaces that host temporary lives. Using Van Gennep's (1960) contextualization, the refugee journey can be viewed as a passage, a transition from one stage of life to another, or from one condition to another. He theorized that the rites of passage can be divided into three phases: separation, transition, and incorporation, resembling the three phases of the refugee journey: before, during, and after resettlement. During the flight phase and living in a transit camp, refugees are held in the margins of society, or in a state of liminality. While they are in transition, the in-between, or this liminal period, Turner (1979) characterizes refugees as being 'invisible', at least 'structurally, if not physically' (p.235), since 'they are at once no longer classified and not yet classified' (p.236), being not here nor there. Papastathopoulos (2020) has used an interesting metaphor of refugees being transformed into ghosts within transit host countries, 'excluded from participation in social life and assimilated, [...] far away from the town' in the closed controlled-access refugee camps (p.10). And as Präger (2024, p.113) describes, 'migrants awaiting outcomes of their asylum-seeking processes frequently circle in the loop of permanent liminality' within these closed detention centres, and are isolated on an island.

Being in this liminal space of no longer having a home and not knowing where one is going makes the period of being in a transit camp a time of fear, stress, uncertainty, and an unknown tomorrow. Refugee camps are never intended to provide permanent living (Ramadan, 2013; Tsoni, 2016). Temporality, insecurity, and marginality characterize life in these camps, where people are suspended between what their lives used to be and what their lives will be in the future. For refugee children, life in a transit camp is quite taxing on many levels, in terms of restrictions, limitation of mobility, deprivation of control, loss of individual identity, and absence of life purpose (Arvanitis *et al.*, 2019). Although children's natural resilience plays an important protective role, trauma, extreme stress, and anxiety can interfere with their development, mental health, and overall well-being (Dangmann *et al.*, 2022; Jensen *et al.*, 2019). This lack of stability, security, infrastructure, and psychosocial support makes music therapy, as a strengths-based approach, a valuable and much-needed intervention within these camps.

THE OPEN-TO-ALL MUSIC THERAPY GROUPS FOR CHILDREN

Taking into account the difficulties that children had encountered during the refugee journey and had to face once they landed at Chios Island, in June 2015, jointly with a group of educators, I decided to provide groups open to all children. We aimed to offer psychosocial support through non-verbal means of communication since we did not share a common language. I facilitated the first group in June 2015 at the overcrowded detention camp in Mersinidi. The informal arrivals of refugees continued in unprecedented numbers for the following months, and we decided to continue our visits to formal and informal camps, once, twice, or even three times a week. We named our team the SamSam group.

During these months, refugees stayed for a maximum of two to three days before they continued their journey to Athens and then to the borders. The groups ran twice or even three times a week. However, the children participating in each group were never the same due to the short duration of their stay. This necessitated the development of a trauma-sensitive music therapy intervention based on the Psychological First Aid (PFA) principles (Else & Gonzales, 2023) and informed by cultural humility (Edwards, 2022). Since transit camps cannot be seen as environments that can foster children's healthy development, regardless of the length of stay, it was important to offer groups that mitigated distress, promoted a sense of safety, instilled hope, and allowed for children to build connections.

To meet the needs of the children, I designed and implemented music therapy groups in various camps on the island (Mersinidi, Municipal Garden, Souda, Chios Port), which hosted refugees from June 2015 to March 2016. Since the groups were open to all children, any child at the camp was welcome to join if they so desired, and depending on the arrivals of each day, the groups would have anywhere from a few children to more than 90.

Music therapy groups: The approach

Trauma-informed care (Else & Gonzales, 2023; Miller *et al.*, 2019) with a culturally humble stance (Edwards, 2022) was adopted to offer psychosocial support to children, integrated into the PFA principles (a sense of safety, calmness, a sense of self and community efficacy, connectedness, and hope) and actions (looking, listening, and connecting) (Akoyunoglou & Paida, 2019; Ramirez *et al.*, 2013). Trauma-informed care is recommended as a best practice in the care of refugee youth (Miller *et al.*, 2019), and guides care providers with six principles: safety, trustworthiness and transparency, peer support, collaboration and mutuality, empowerment (voice and choice), and cultural, historical, and gender sensitivity (Else & Gonzales, 2023). In addition, it is accompanied by a perspective of cultural humility that fosters inclusivity and gives room to examine one's personal biases and be considerate of the children's experiences (Edwards, 2022).

Examining the integration of the three PFA actions with the trauma-informed care principles, one can see interrelatedness and progressiveness. Looking refers to checking for safety issues or potential threats in the environment, locating a safe space to form the group and be with the children, and attending to obvious needs first before moving to the next step. Listening includes sensitively approaching children and asking about their needs, being attentive and listening carefully to them, providing a sense of calmness through presence and attitude, and responding with empathy to what the children say. Connecting or linking refers to providing an environment that can enhance connectivity and collaboration among children, strengthen resilience, and promote feelings of hope.

Music therapy groups: The design

As members of the SamSam team, we attended a training offered by UNHCR in collaboration with the War Trauma Foundation in October 2015 (Gkionakis, 2016). This training equipped us with the important tools to provide groups targeted at the specific needs of the children. Even though no particular PFA model has been created for refugee children, the flexibility that characterizes the application of the PFA actions can prove helpful in fostering emotional safety, allowing for expression and communication, and enhancing feelings of trust (de Freitas Girardi *et al.*, 2020). While the PFA principles and actions cannot be seen as evidence based (Hermosilla *et al.*, 2023), their use within music therapy in humanitarian settings has been documented as beneficial (Else & Gonzales, 2023).

In particular, music therapy in transit refugee camps can be seen as a strengths-based approach to care. Acknowledging children's strengths, resilience, and agency, the goals set for the open-to-all children's music therapy groups aimed to promote children's resilience, foster healthy development, and empower individual and collective identities of children living in the hostile, temporary, liminal, and strange environment of the camp.

Taking into account the emotional, developmental, and psychosocial needs of the children, I followed a process of planning, assessing, designing, implementing, evaluating, reassessing, and redesigning for each group. Considering the setting and the context, the interventions were chosen in order to address the children's needs. The autoharp, a non-threatening and unfamiliar instrument, was used to provide an opportunity for initial non-verbal communication via a relational object. Hand-made small shakers allowed for the development of a common group sound; singing permitted the musical inner child to emerge; and movement enabled the awakening of the body.

Music therapy groups: The implementation

Every time the number of children differed. Not knowing in advance the number of children, I arrived at the camp with two or three volunteer educators and members of the SamSam team. The duration of each group was from one and a half to two hours, depending on the number of children, the energy of the group, and the weather conditions. All groups took place outdoors, in an open area that we evaluated as appropriate. The criterion for the space we chose was to provide ample room for children to gather. Then, we placed one, two, or three tarpaulins depending on the number of children who were at the camp that day. Children who gathered were mostly from two to fourteen years of age. Sometimes their parents or other teenagers or adults would gather around and observe the group. The tarpaulins defined the boundaries of the group, set the space for the intervention, and made the area friendlier for all. On the tarpaulins, three- to four-metre-long pieces of paper were taped, and colourful markers were spread on the sheets. The tarpaulins, the paper, and the markers acted as gathering agents, and on their initiative, children would come, sit, and start drawing. Starting the group this way encouraged children who did not know other children to sit and work individually, draw whatever they wanted, and use as many markers as they wanted. Drawing within a group setting around a long piece of paper shared with others fostered concentration, involvement over time, and a sense of quietness and stability, and it provided an avenue for individual expression.

Once the drawings were completed, the music would begin by singing an improvised hello song accompanied by the autoharp. Children were already seated in a circle and the autoharp provided a non-threatening, one-on-one interaction. Children who wanted to play the autoharp were welcome to do so. The hello song was the first of a number of easy call-and-response songs that followed. The songs we used were mostly African songs with easy syllabic structure and repetitive lyrics and melodies to ensure success in the participatory experience. There were about four to five songs, in which simple rhythmic patterns were improvised in various forms such as body action, body percussion, or using hand-made instruments. The musical instruments were created by the children with the help of our team members. Once the group was rhythmically synchronized and coordinated, we began adding body and dance movements, and the children would either follow movements that the music therapist showed or improvise their own. A simple goodbye song, leading to synchronized loud voices, marked the ending of the group and all children helped in folding the drawing papers and putting the tarpaulins in the bag.

Music therapy groups: The supports

To ensure individual and collective reflective practice, all members of our team kept journals after every group, and weekly or bi-weekly meetings were organized with the whole team. Since it was an emotionally and psychologically demanding setting that we did not have prior experience with, we relied on supporting each other throughout those months. 'Feelings of guilt', of 'witnessing stressful situations', and 'seeing unprotected children separated from family members' were some of the issues documented in the journals. Thoughts, beliefs, biases, actions, and reactions were documented in our journals. By extension, our meetings took the form of peer group supervision, where all issues and fears were discussed and analysed. This allowed us to collectively face our uncertainties, recognize our limitations, deepen our understanding, and evolve as a team.

Emotional burnout was a threat for all of us, so we decided to run groups only when at least two members and myself were available, and team members alternated. The team acted as a support system, reducing the levels of stress and feelings of helplessness in these environments. Supervision and self-care were my personal support systems. From the beginning, I realized how important supervision was in order to offer community music therapy to refugee children in a transit camp. It was important for me to acknowledge that there would be times when I would not be able to help in the way I wanted or provide what was needed, and I realized that there was much that we could not address due to the overall circumstances. The more knowledgeable I became on how to facilitate the groups, the more confident I felt in managing unexpected or challenging situations.

Music therapy groups: The outcomes

The structure of the intervention followed the three stages proposed by PFA: look, listen, and connect. In the beginning, we concentrated on looking and observing. As children would gather on their own to sit and draw, we would just observe how they sat, if they were alone, with a sibling, or with a parent, if they drew in a small or bigger area of the paper, the number of markers used, and what themes they drew. Drawing gave them an avenue for non-verbal expression. Then we would sit down at available spaces in the circle, introduce ourselves, and begin to discuss with them what they had drawn and get an idea of their emotional state. Since children were of various ethnicities (from Syria, Afghanistan, Iran, Iraq, and others), our communication was either with the help of a parent in English or through joint drawing as a non-verbal way to communicate. The music followed and enabled the children to become a group. We aimed to use songs that were age and culture-appropriate. Due to the diversity of ethnicities and the different languages and cultures, easy African songs proved to be a good choice. Since musical instruments permit further engagement with the music, we used hand-made instruments, so that children could take them with them after the group was over, if they chose to. The focus of the music therapy intervention was to bring children together to meet other children living in the camp, enhance their social skills, build a sense of community, and help children sustain hope. One team member documented in her journal, 'music offers moments of fun, a space for venting negative feelings, releasing anxiety, while creating islands of joy' for refugee children. At the end of one of the many groups we did then, one girl, around 13 years old, came to me and said: 'Thank you for making us smile,' reminding me of their need to feel, act, and be children.

REFLECTIONS ON SAFE SPACES AND ETHICAL CHALLENGES

How do we position ourselves within a transit camp? Are we there for self-serving purposes? How do we understand belongingness and differentiation? And how do we give meaning to the musical event as an experience of encountering the 'other'? These questions were reflected on every time I facilitated groups for refugee children. This self-reflective approach during the initial ten months allowed for a deeper understanding of cultural diversity, multiculturalism, vulnerability, and disorientation.

Every group, every visit, and every discussion formed my personal story. As a solidarian during those months, I observed multiple context-situated and fluid identities emerging in the field: a volunteer, an activist, a grass-roots responder, a musician, and a community music therapist. Positionality, or how one views the self and the other, is informed by moral and personal qualities (Van Langenhove & Harré, 1999) and is influenced by the interaction of context, space, and identities (Bayeck, 2022). Considering both reflexivity and positionality as dynamic elements of development (Davies & Harré, 1990; Osbeck & Nersessian, 2017), my understanding of personhood and identity was shaped by these social interactions.

Working in the field, I realized that the term 'refugee' is often used to label and marginalize the 'other' (i.e. the victim, the vulnerable, in need of humanitarian assistance), which might lead to removing the human subjectivity, and in the process, dehumanizing them (Baak, 2021). I agree with Pieloch et al. (2016, p.337) who state that 'to help promote resilience we must first see children as children and as refugees second'. Challenging as it may be, redefining the socially constructed term 'refugee' would allow us to rehumanize our understanding of the refugee, avoid the act of 'othering', and view them as individuals (Baak, 2021).

A question that often surfaced in my mind regarding the groups I facilitated was whether music had the capacity to ensure a sense of safety and consequently promote a safe space for children in transit camps. In defining a safe space, one can view it as a 'place intended to be free of bias, conflict, criticism, or potentially threatening actions, ideas, or conversations' (Merriam-Webster, n.d.). Applied to an educational setting, a safe space can be viewed as one that allows participants to feel secure enough to take risks, honestly express their views, and share and explore knowledge, attitudes, and behaviours (Holley & Steiner, 2005). By extension, it contains the aspect of protecting all members of a group from psychological or emotional harm, and in an even broader sense, it is 'concerned with the injuries that individuals suffer at the hands of society' (Rom, 1998).

A definition that echoes the notion of a safe space, as I contextualized it in the open-to-all children music therapy groups, is articulated by Bustamante Duarte *et al.* (2021), who describe it as an environment that promotes 'open communication, knowledge exchange, and beneficial engagement among all participants' (p.192). In other words, it can be comprehended as creating spaces for musical dialogues, musical engagement, and musical belongingness, aspects that were reinforced in all the music therapy groups I offered. For children residing temporarily at transit camps in dire conditions, safe environments and resiliency-focused approaches allow for healthy development, empowerment, and an enhanced sense of well-being (Pieloch *et al.*, 2016). The structure of the groups aimed to foster non-judgemental environments, enhance feelings of safety, and promote acceptance and a culture of equity, all features of a space that can be characterized as safe for all participants.

Furthermore, it is documented that music has the capacity to promote social inclusion and social integration essential to those who are cut off from their countries, communities, and families (Crooke *et al.*, 2024; Grebosz-Haring & Gaul, 2024). But can music guarantee a feeling of safety since musicking involves meeting the other? Music-making has been described as a process accompanied by 'ethical responsibilities [that] arise from these encounters' (Warren, 2014, p.1). Thus, ethical concerns and moral dilemmas accompany the use of community music therapy in transit refugee camps. The way that I live and see, make sense of, and interact with the world as a music therapist informs my ethical perspective (Papadopoulos, 2002). For music therapists to engage in ethical thinking, Dileo (2021) has accurately expressed that they need to balance several inputs: feelings and perceptions, self-awareness, virtues, and moral values, knowledge and judgement, cultural location, the clients' values and input, the fundamental ethical principles, the ethical codes, the situational context, as well as the law. These multiple areas of concern form the ethics mosaic that has guided my personal and professional growth.

As a professional music therapist working in Greece, I practise according to the ethical code of the Hellenic Association of Professional Music Therapists. Yet, these codes do not directly address issues that accompany music therapy services in this specific context. To ensure ethical issues were addressed, various steps were taken. Once in the field, it was important to scan for immediate needs of children and their families before offering our groups. Since interventions that follow an ethical orientation should address the needs of individuals in crisis (Sommers-Flanagan, 2007), essentials such as food, clothing, and shelter were of top priority. Once these were taken care of, groups had a space and a need to be offered to children regardless of their age. The interventions provided were sensitive to the developmental and cultural needs and were constantly adapted to meet the requirements of each particular group. The open character of the groups allowed children to decide at their own will whether they wanted to participate or not. The place given to each child permitted them to decide where to sit and how close to other children. The open space gave children the freedom to form subgroups with other children of the same nationality. Children were able to come and go at their own free will during the groups. The voluntary and open-to-all features of the community music therapy groups fostered inclusion and acceptance of all, adapting every time the musicking to match the needs of each group.

Empathy was a guiding principle, and empathic understanding was essential for an ethics of care. Cobussen and Nielsen (2012, p.155) mention: 'Music can teach us to listen more carefully; it can make us receptive and responsive to the voices of others and to the voice of otherness, to other voices and to the otherness of the voice.' Furthermore, music fosters a sense of community and solidarity among active and receptive participants (Trondalen, 2023). The combination of these elements allows for community music therapy in formal and informal camps, as an ethical practice of care, to become a political, environmental, and social act.

CODA

Sites of confinement, such as refugee camps and places of detention, are characterized by flows and enclosures of people – dislocated, confined, encamped, imprisoned, detained, trapped, stuck, or forcibly removed – who are doing their utmost to cope, survive, or escape. These people 'are caught between the temporary and the permanent; between exclusion and inclusion; and between boundaries and their transgression' (Jefferson et al., 2019, p.2). During the phase of survival, life in transit camps hides many developmental threats for children, who seem to have the worst experiences

(Papadopoulos, 2002). It is essential to provide 'more child-friendly accommodations and services, especially for children waiting for claims to be processed' (Vaghri *et al.*, 2019, p.12).

Art and music can be an effective means of non-verbal communication for refugee children during this challenging and pervasive experience (Akoyunoglou, 2019; Akoyunoglou & Tsiris, 2024). Music's expressive and non-verbal qualities can help people communicate their emotions, break through feelings of loneliness, improve their emotional state, and boost hope (Davis, 2010; Garrido *et al.*, 2015; Wiess & Bensimon, 2020). They can also help children learn new cultures and maintain their cultural identity while enhancing their social skills, self-esteem, and self-trust, nurturing their collaborative skills, and reducing their anxiety (Akoyunoglou, 2019; Akoyunoglou & Tsiris, 2024; Altschuler *et al.*, 2002; Enge & Stige, 2022; Heynen *et al.*, 2022).

There is growing empirical research that shows that by engaging in music-making while living in a makeshift refugee camp, children are aided in building relationships, developing a positive sense of self, and strengthening their cultural identity and their sense of agency (Akoyunoglou & Tsiris, 2024; Enge, 2015; Lenette & Sunderland, 2014; Millar & Warwick, 2018). Although multidimensional challenges accompany community music therapy interventions in transit refugee camps, as a strengths-based approach, community music therapy can prove to be effective as psychosocial support, a means to cultivate a culture of belonging and transform the hostile and strange environment into a friendlier, safer, and maybe even pleasurable place for the children.

REFERENCES

Akoyunoglou, M. (2019). The 'Circle of Music' with Refugee Children in Chios: Description and Account of Three Years of Actions [in Greek]. In Th. Raptis & D. Koniari (eds) *Music Education and Society: New Challenges, New Orientations. Proceedings of the 8th Conference of the E.E.M.E.* (pp.94–101). E.E.M.E.

Akoyunoglou, M. & Paida, S. (2019). Approaching refugee children in educational settings informed by the principles of Psychological First Aid [in Greek]. *Proceedings, Panhellenic Interdisciplinary Conference, 'The multicultural school in the 21st century'*, 4–6 October 2019, Corfu (pp.208–219).

Akoyunoglou, M. & Tsiris, G. (2024). Community Music Therapy with Refugee Children in Transit Camps on the Greek Island of Chios. In U. Herrmann, M. Hills de Zarate, H. M. Hunter, & S. Pitruzzella (eds) *Arts Therapies and the Mental Health of Children and Young People: Contemporary Research, Theory, and Practice* (volume 2, first edition, pp.30–50). London: Routledge.

Altschuler, J., Agnoli, M., Halitaj, M., & Jasiqi, I. (2002). In the Aftermath of Violence. In R. Papadopoulos (ed.) *Therapeutic Care for Refugees and Asylum Seekers: No Place Like Home* (pp.271–291). London: Karnac Books.

Arvanitis, E., Yelland, N. J., & Kiprianos, P. (2019). Liminal spaces of temporary dwellings: Transitioning to new lives in times of crisis. *Journal of Research in Childhood Education*, 33(1), 134–144. https://doi.org/10.1080/02568543.2018.1531451.

Baak, M. (2021). Once a Refugee, Always a Refugee? The Haunting of the Refugee Label in Resettlement. In J. Silverstein & R. Stevens (eds) *Refugee Journeys: Histories of Resettlement, Representation and Resistance* (pp.50–71). Canberra, Australia: ANU Press.

Bayeck, R. Y. (2022). Positionality: The interplay of space, context and identity. *International Journal of Qualitative Methods*, 21. https://doi.org/10.1177/16094069221114745.

Bustamante Duarte, A. M., Ataei, M., Degbelo, A., Brendel, N., & Kray, C. (2021). Safe spaces in participatory design with young forced migrants. *CoDesign*, 17(2), 188–210. https://doi.org/10.1080/15710882.2019.1654523.

Callister, A. H., Galbraith, Q., & Carlile, A. (2022). Politics and prejudice: Using the term 'undocumented immigrant' over 'illegal immigrant'. *International Migration & Integration*, 23, 753–773. https://doi.org/10.1007/s12134-021-00852-y.

Carastathis, A., Spathopoulou A., & Tsilimpounidi, M. (2018). Crisis, what crisis? Immigrants, refugees and invisible struggles. *Refuge: Canada's Journal on Refugees*, 34(1), 29–38.

Cobussen, M. & Nielsen, N. (2012). *Music and Ethics*. Farnham, Surrey: Ashgate Publishing.

Crooke, A. H. D., Thompson, W. F., Fraser, T., & Davidson, J. (2024). Music, social cohesion, and intercultural understanding: A conceptual framework for intercultural music engagement. *Musicae Scientiae*, 28(1), 18–38. https://doi.org/10.1177/10298649231157099.

Dangmann, C., Dybdahl, R., & Solberg, Ø. (2022). Mental health in refugee children. *Current Opinion in Psychology*, 48, 101460. https://doi.org/10.1016/j.copsyc.2022.101460.

Davies, B. & Harré, R. (1990). Positioning: The discursive production of selves. *Journal for the Theory of Social Behaviour*, 20(1), 43–63. https://doi.org/10.1111/j.1468-5914.1990.tb00174.x.

Davis, K. M. (2010). Music and the expressive arts with children experiencing trauma. *Journal of Creative Mental Health*, 5, 125–133.

de Freitas Girardi, J., Miconi, D., Lyke, C., & Rousseau, C. (2020). Creative expression workshops as Psychological First Aid (PFA) for asylum-seeking children: An exploratory study in temporary shelters in Montreal. *Clinical Child Psychology and Psychiatry*, 25(2), 483–493. 10.1177/1359104519891760.

Dileo, C. (2021). *Ethical Thinking in Music Therapy* (second edition). Cherry Hill, NJ: Jeffrey Books.

Douglas, P., Cetron, M., & Spiegel, P. (2019). Definitions matter: Migrants, immigrants, asylum seekers and refugees. *Journal of Travel Medicine*, 26(2), taz005. https://doi.org/10.1093/jtm/taz005.

Edwards, J. (2022). Cultural Humility in Music Therapy Practice. In L. B. Beer & J. C. Birnbaum (eds) *Trauma-Informed Music Therapy: Theory and Practice* (pp.28–36). London: Routledge.

Else, B. A. & Gonzales, M. (2023). Global Trends in Music Therapy for Disaster Preparedness, Response and Recovery. In L. B. Beer & J. C. Birnbaum (eds) *Trauma-Informed Music Therapy: Theory and Practice* (pp.19–27). London: Routledge.

Enge, K. E. A. (2015). Community music therapy with asylum-seeking and refugee children in Norway. *Journal of Applied Arts & Health*, 6(2), 205–215. doi:10.1386/jaah.6.2.205_1.

Enge, K. E. A. & Stige, B. (2022). Musical pathways to the peer community: A collective case study of refugee children's use of music therapy. *Nordic Journal of Music Therapy*, 31(1), 7–24. https://doi.org/10.1080/08098131.2021.1891130.

Garrido, S., Baker, F. A., Davidson, J. W., Moore, G., & Wasserman, S. (2015). Music and trauma: The relationship between music, personality, and coping style. *Frontiers in Psychology*, 6, 977. https://doi.org/10.3389/fpsyg.2015.00977.

Gkionakis, N. (2016). The refugee crisis in Greece. *Intervention*, 14(1), 73–79. https://doi.org/10.1097/wtf.0000000000000104.

Grebosz-Haring, K. & Gaul, M. (2024). Musical Activities in the Acculturation Processes of Children and Adolescents with Migration Experiences. In W. Gratzer, N. Grosch, U. Präger, & S. Scheiblhofer (eds) *The Routledge Handbook of Music and Migration: Theories and Methodologies* (pp.420–458). London: Routledge.

Hermosilla, S., Forthal, S., Sadowska, K., Magill, E. B., Watson, P., & Pike, K. M. (2023). We need to build the evidence: A systematic review of psychological first aid on mental health and well-being. *Journal of Traumatic Stress*, 36, 5–16. https://doi.org/10.1002/jts.22888.

Heynen, E., Bruls, V., van Goor, S., Pat-El, R., Schoot, T., & van Hooren, S. (2022). A music therapy intervention for refugee children and adolescents in schools: A process evaluation using a mixed method design. *Children*, 9(10), 1434. https://doi.org/10.3390/children9101434.

Hieronymi, O. (2008). Refugee children and their future. *Refugee Survey Quarterly*, 27(4), 6–25. https://doi.org/10.1093/rsq/hdn058.

Holley, L. C. & Steiner, S. (2005). Safe space: Student perspectives on classroom environment. *Journal of Social Work Education*, 41(1), 49–64. https://doi.org/10.1093/rsq/hdn058.

Huq, E. & Miraftab, F. (2020). 'We are all refugees': Camps and informal settlements as converging spaces of global displacements. *Planning Theory & Practice*, 21(3), 351–370. https://doi.org.

Jalonen, A. & La Corte, P. C. (2018). *A Practical Guide to Therapeutic Work with Asylum Seekers and Refugees*. London: Jessica Kingsley Publishers.

Jefferson, A., Turner, S., & Jensen, S. (2019). Introduction: On stuckness and sites of confinement. *Ethnos*, 84(1). https://doi.org/10.1080/00141844.2018.1544917.

Jensen, T. K., Skar, A. M. S., Andersson, E. S., & Birkeland, M. S. (2019). Long-term mental health in unaccompanied refugee minors: Pre- and post-flight predictors. *European Child & Adolescent Psychiatry*, 28, 1671–1682. https://doi.org/10.1007/s00787-019-01340-6.

Katsanidou, Al. & Lefkofridi, Z. (2020). A decade of crisis in the European Union: Lessons from Greece. *JCMS: Journal of Common Market Studies*, 58, 160–172. https://doi.org/10.1111/jcms.13070.

Lenette, C. & Sunderland, N. (2014). 'Will there be music for us?' Mapping the health and well-being potential of participatory music practice with asylum seekers and refugees across contexts of conflict and refuge. *Arts & Health*, 8(1), 32–49. https://doi.org/10.1080/17533015.2014.961943.

Merriam-Webster. (n.d.). Safe space. In *Merriam-Webster.com dictionary*. www.merriam-webster.com/dictionary/safe-space.

Millar, O. & Warwick, I. (2018). Music and refugees' wellbeing in contexts of protracted displacement. *Health Education Journal*, 78(1). https://doi.org/10.1177/0017896918785991.

Miller, K. K., Brown, C. R., Shramko, M., & Svetaz, M. V. (2019). Applying trauma-informed practices to the care of refugee and immigrant youth: 10 clinical pearls. *Children (Basel, Switzerland)*, 6(8), 94. https://doi.org/10.3390/children6080094.

Mohammed, S. & Thomas, M. (2017). The mental health and psychological well-being of refugee children and young people: An exploration of risk, resilience and protective factors. *Educational Psychology in Practice*, 33(3), 249–263. https://doi.org/10.1080/02667363.2017.1300769.

Osbeck, L. M. & Nersessian, N. J. (2017). Epistemic identities in interdisciplinary science. *Perspectives on Science*, 25(2), 226–260. doi:10.1162/POSC_a_00242.

Papadopoulos, R. (2021). *Involuntary Dislocation: Home, Trauma, Resilience, and Adversity-Activated Development*. London: Routledge.

Papadopoulos, R. K. (2002). Refugees, Home and Trauma. In R. K. Papadopoulos (ed.) *Therapeutic Care for Refugees. No Place Like Home.* London: Karnac Books.

Papastathopoulos, S. (2020). The phantomized presence of refugees in spaces of passage. *Misfit: Strange Ideas*, 1, 6–15.

Papataxiarchis, E. (2016a). Being 'there': At the front line of the 'European refugee crisis' – part 1. *Anthropology Today*, 32(2), 5–9. doi:10.1111/1467-8322.12237.

Papataxiarchis, E. (2016b). Being 'there': At the front line of the 'European refugee crisis' – part 2. *Anthropology Today*, 32(3), 3–7. doi:10.1111/1467-8322.12252.

Papataxiarchis, E. (2016c). A major upheaval: The European refugee crisis and the new patriotism of solidarity. *Syhrona Themata*, 132–133, 7–28.

Papataxiarchis, E. (2022). An Ephemeral Patriotism: The Rise and Fall of 'Solidarity to Refugees'. In M. Kousis, A. Chatzidaki, & K. Kafetsios (eds) *Challenging Mobilities in and to the EU During Times of Crises: The Case of Greece* (pp.163–184). IMISCOE research series. Cham, Switzerland: Springer.

Patel, S. G., Bouche, V., Thomas, I., & Martinez, W. (2023). Mental health and adaptation among newcomer immigrant youth in United States educational settings. *Current Opinion in Psychology*, 49, 101459.

Pieloch, K. A., McCullough, M. B., & Marks, A. K. (2016). Resilience of children with refugee statuses: A research review. *Canadian Psychology*, 57(4), 330–339. https://doi.org/10.1037/cap0000073.

Pino Gavidia, L. A. & Adu, J. (2022). Critical narrative inquiry: An examination of a methodological approach. *International Journal of Qualitative Methods*, 21. https://doi.org/10.1177/16094069221081594.

Präger, U. (2024). Liminality. In W. Gratzer, N. Grosch, U. Präger, & S. Scheiblhofer (eds) *The Routledge Handbook of Music and Migration: Theories and Methodologies* (pp.110–114). London: Routledge.

Ramadan, A. (2013). Spatialising the refugee camp. *Transactions of the Institute of British Geographers*, 38(1), 65–77.

Ramirez, M., Harland, K., Frederick, M., Shepherd, R., Wong, M., & Cavanaugh, J. E. (2013). Listen protect connect for traumatized schoolchildren: A pilot study of psychological first aid. *BMC Psychology*, 1, 1–9.

Richter, K., Baumgärtner, L., Niklewski, G., Peter, L., *et al.* (2020). Sleep disorders in migrants and refugees: A systematic review with implications for personalized medical approach. *EPMA Journal*, 11, 251–260. https://doi.org/10.1007/s13167-020-00205-2.

Rom, R. B. (1998). 'Safe spaces': Reflections on an educational metaphor. *Journal of Curriculum Studies*, 30(4), 397–408.

Sommers-Flanagan, R. (2007). Ethical considerations in crisis and humanitarian interventions. *Ethics & Behavior*, 17(2), 187–202.

Souzas, N., Mermigka, I., & Diakoumakou, T. (2021). *'Because my loneliness is considered a safe country': Asylum seekers' struggles and local reactions to the border status of Chios (2015–2016)* [in Greek]. Thessaloniki: Psifides.

Trondalen, G. (2023). *Ethical Musicality*. London: Routledge.

Tsoni, I. (2016). 'They won't let us come, they won't let us stay, they won't let us leave.' Liminality in the Aegean borderscape: The case of irregular migrants, volunteers and locals on Lesvos. *Human Geography*, 9(2), 35–46. https://doi.org/10.1177/194277861600900204.

Turner, V. (1979). Betwixt and Between: The Liminal Period in Rites de Passage. In W. A. Lessa & E. Z. Vogt (eds) *Reader in Comparative Religion: An Anthropological Approach* (fourth edition, pp.234–243). New York, NY: Harper & Row Publishers.

UNHCR. (1987). *Note on Refugee Children EC/SCP/46.* www.unhcr.org/publications/note-refugee-children.

UNHCR. (2015a). *Greece – Sea arrivals 2015.* https://data.unhcr.org/en/documents/details/46733.

UNHCR. (2015b). *Greece: Chios island snapshot (31 Dec 2015)*. https://reliefweb.int/report/greece/greece-chios-island-snapshot-31-dec-2015.

UNHCR. (2024). *Who we protect: Refugees*. www.unhcr.org/about-unhcr/who-we-protect/refugees.

Vaghri, Z., Tessier, Z., & Whalen, C. (2019). Refugee and asylum-seeking children: Interrupted child development and unfulfilled child rights. *Children (Basel, Switzerland)*, 6(11), 120. www.unhcr.org/about-unhcr/who-we-protect/refugees.

Van Gennep, A. (1960). *The Rites of Passage*. Chicago, IL: The University of Chicago Press.

Van Langenhove, L. & Harré, R. (1999). Introducing Positioning Theory. In R. Harré & L. van Langenhove (eds) *Positioning Theory* (pp.102–115). Malden, MA: Blackwell.

Warren, J. R. (2014). *Music and Ethical Responsibility*. Cambridge: Cambridge University Press.

WeiWei, A. (2018). *Humanity*. Princeton, NJ: Princeton University Press.

Wiess, C. & Bensimon, M. (2020). Group music therapy with uprooted teenagers: The importance of structure. *Nordic Journal of Music Therapy*, 29(2), 174–189. https://doi.org/10.1080/08098131.2019.1695281.

Zolkoski, S. M. & Bullock, L. M. (2012). Resilience in children and youth: A review. *Children and Youth Services Review*, 34(12), 2295–2303. https://doi.org/10.1016/j.childyouth.2012.08.009.

CHAPTER 8

Interactive Therapeutic Music-Making in Palestine

Insights and Considerations Amid Conflict and Displacement

ELIZABETH COOMBES AND SAPHIA ABOU AMER

INTRODUCTION

Contemporary music therapy practice offers a range of ways to share under-pinning thinking, theories, and practical music-based skills with communities where access to music therapy as a regulated profession is limited (Coombes, 2020; Coombes *et al.*, 2023). These can include music therapists trained to the required level of this profession in their own country offering briefer, tailored training opportunities through in-person or online courses. It may also include visits by music therapists to settings where music therapy might be indicated to offer advice and support. Many of these practices could be considered to sit at an interface between music therapy and arts in health work, or as part of a continuum of music therapy practice (Moss, 2008). Other authors have also written on this topic, exploring these practices and projects in a range of different countries (Coombes, 2011; Coombes & Tombs-Katz, 2015; Hesser & Bartleet, 2020; Quin & Rowland, 2016; Shrubsole, 2017; Strange *et al.*, 2016).

One such area of practice is the development of music therapy skill-shar-ing training projects in international contexts. The goal of these projects is to enable local people to deliver music-based work underpinned by music therapy techniques and principles in their communities. In Coombes and Tombs-Katz's article from 2015, the term 'interactive therapeutic music-making' (ITM-M) was coined as an umbrella term for this work. This chapter will describe a series of projects in the Occupied Palestinian Territories (OPT). OPT refers to Gaza, East Jerusalem, and the West Bank, territo-ries occupied by Israel after the 1967 war. It acknowledges the ongoing occupation of Palestinian lands and the hoped-for two-state solution where a Palestinian state will be formed.

WHAT DO WE MEAN BY ITM-M?

In ITM-M practice, interactive music-making is offered to those who may benefit from the therapeutic aspects of such work where access to clinical music therapy is not possible. This often requires training to be delivered by individuals or organizations. The initial stages of this work consist of delivering sessions where music therapists share knowledge and skills with others working in education or caring roles. Underpinning theories and techniques linked to music therapy are explored and taught in a variety of ways with a range of aims and outcomes depending on context. There is no one model or any consensus on what should be included in such training, or how groups should be run. As can be seen from earlier references, many such programmes or projects arise organically after long periods of discussion with local organizations. Each has its specific structure and goals tailored to the needs of the setting. These could be as broad as offering new ways for care to be provided to those who are in need. Those participating in such training come from a range of professional backgrounds and experiences. They may be musicians, healthcare workers, teachers, classroom assistants, parents, or volunteers. From the evidence available, it seems that the overarching aim for these programmes is to enable access to music therapy-influenced practices and enjoy the benefits of music-making or 'musicking' (Small, 1998). Some focus more on aspects of social justice and equitable distribution of knowledge. What all have in common is the use of interactive music-making with elements of therapeutic practice at their core.

ITM-M may support the future development of music therapy training in parts of the world where this is limited. Sustainability can, therefore, be a part of these projects. This, however, is not the goal of the work *per se*. Rather, it could be described as the development of a music-based psychosocial intervention to support healthy development within social environments (Coombes *et al.*, 2023).

ITM-M PROJECTS IN THE OPT

The training projects in the OPT described here involved teaching participants how to run music groups for small numbers of children. The groups typically aimed to support between four and six children under the age of ten who may have been disabled or who had emotional challenges due to their living conditions. They were developed and run under the auspices of Music as Therapy International (MasT).[1] These MasT training projects enabled Palestinians from a range of backgrounds, including teachers, school counsellors, classroom assistants, and musicians, to lead the groups and offer them to children who might benefit from such provision.

MasT has been working in international development for 30 years, providing training and support activities rooted in music therapy practice. All the charity's activities are developed in response to direct requests from people who may fulfil a range of roles worldwide (including care practitioners, teachers/educators, psychological support workers, social workers, school counsellors, activity leaders, family members, etc.) and who wish to embed music into the support they offer to children and adults living in vulnerable situations.

The overarching goal of projects in the OPT was to explore ways in which music might be used by practitioners to broaden their offer to those in their care. A hoped-for outcome of this work was for it to be embedded in a range of settings. The authors view this work as being linked to social justice in that the practice of music therapy programmes such as these facilitates a fairer distribution of knowledge in this field through shorter and more accessible training.

The projects in this chapter include the following:

1. A six-week-long project delivered in 2009 in one school and one children's home in the Bethlehem area (Coombes, 2011). The project was led by Elizabeth Coombes.

2. Another six-week-long project delivered in three schools in Beit Sahour, Beit Jala, and Ramallah (Coombes & Tombs-Katz, 2015). This project was led by British music therapists Hazel Child and Teleri Dyer.

3. A distance learning programme (DLP) which ran from 2015 to 2019 in Bethlehem.

Elizabeth led an in-person music-making weekend during each iteration, with Saphia as a training partner on one occasion. Saphia carried out a two-stage evaluation of the experiences of those who participated in the training. This evaluation received ethical approval from the University of South Wales (Coombes *et al.*, 2023).

This chapter draws on the data collected within the aforementioned two-stage evaluation and reflection and discussion of the projects in the

---

1   www.musicastherapy.org

OPT. In relation to these provisions, the chapter will reflect on historic issues of the displacement of the population in Palestine and the resultant trauma arising from this.

OUR POSITIONING
Saphia Abou Amer

I am a British music therapist of mixed English and Palestinian heritage. I grew up in London, but as a child, we visited my father's family in the Gaza Strip and visited the OPT every summer until the beginning of the Intifada in 2000. I experienced the unpleasant questioning in the airport on arrival and departure, I saw the illegal Israeli settlements and checkpoints, and I visited numerous refugee camps, seeing the conditions people lived in. These experiences impacted me from an early age. I became acutely aware of discrimination, racism, social inequality, and poverty in the OPT, and then the privilege I was returning to in London while my Palestinian family continued to live in vastly different conditions with much less freedom and fewer human rights than I enjoyed. This shaped the way I viewed the world and made me alive to issues of social justice early on in life.

Initially, I found it challenging to integrate social and political dimensions into my music therapy work, thinking they were separate from therapeutic practice. However, with increasing awareness that therapists can and do incorporate social justice into their therapeutic approaches and practice, I have developed a more inclusive and integrated approach. I subscribe to the position that when addressing social justice, it is essential to take into consideration gender, social class, sexuality, economic status, age, disability, ethnicity, and neurodiversity so that justice can be realized through fairness, equal opportunity, and equitable outcomes (Moodley, 2009; Winter & Charura, 2023).

Elizabeth Coombes

From an early age, I was hooked on music-making, beginning with the recorder and piano and then moving on to the oboe. A Bachelor's degree in music solidified my music skills, enabling me to develop my singing and guitar playing as well as engaging in a host of musical genres that were new to me. Although post-degree I didn't immediately move into music-related work, I subsequently trained as a community musician in Wales, my homeland, moving on to develop and deliver projects with a whole host of participants. I also became a project manager and fundraiser, developing valuable new skills. It was after a period of this work that I found out about music therapy and trained in this profession, becoming a music therapist in 2000. Since then, I have had the opportunity to work primarily with children and young people and their families in a range of contexts. I began teaching at university level in 2008, becoming Programme Director of the MA Music Therapy training in Wales in 2012. When I saw an opportunity advertised by MasT in 2009 to develop work in the OPT I realized I wanted to be part of this type of work. My application for the project said: 'I do not pretend that my career to date in the UK has fully prepared me for work in a war-torn country; however, I believe that my skills and experience, and my maturity, together with the support of MasT and the host organization mean that I can fulfil the project aims.' I could not have foreseen at the time that working in the OPT would form such a large part of my life, with over ten visits taking place in subsequent years up to the Covid-19 pandemic in 2020 to support and develop projects linked to MasT and other local organizations. My work in the OPT has been a core part of my professional life, enabling me to be a part of the equitable distribution of knowledge and skills in the area of music therapy.

PALESTINE: AN ONGOING HISTORY OF DISPLACEMENT

Palestine has a long-standing and ongoing history of displacement due to the settler colonialism which it has experienced for over one hundred years (Khalidi, 2020). The initial displacement of Palestinians took place as a result of the first war of the Israeli-Palestine conflict in 1948. This led to approximately 750,000 Palestinian refugees being forcibly removed to neighbouring countries as well as the West Bank and Gaza Strip (United Nations Relief and Works Agency for Palestine Refugees, n.d.). The subsequent 1967 conflict with Israel led to the displacement of even more Palestinians and saw the beginning of Israel's occupation of the West Bank, East Jerusalem, and the Gaza Strip, often referred to as the OPT (United Nations Conference on Trade and Development, n.d.). The refugee population here is a large and increasing one; a 2021 United Nations Relief and Works Agency for Palestine Refugees report stated that there were 2,400,208 Palestinian refugees living in the OPT, 1,516,258 in the Gaza Strip and 883,950 in the West Bank, a number which has increased by 2.2% since 2020 (United Nations Relief and Works Agency for Palestine Refugees, 2021). Displacement is thus an intrinsic part of Palestinian society, with themes of returning to their family homes and villages being ever present for Palestinians.

The Israeli military occupation of the territories means that Palestinians residing in the West Bank and Gaza Strip do not have freedom of movement and frequently experience violence and oppression from the Israeli military, sometimes on a daily basis (Agbaria *et al.*, 2021). Such circumstances do not allow for political stability and thus render the area a conflict zone (Khalidi, 2020; Punamaki *et al.*, 2014). Aside from the ongoing daily violence, there have been periods marked by a notable intensification of violence, such as the two Palestinian uprisings (Intifadas in Arabic), which occurred across the occupied territories in response to the occupation, between 1987 and 1993 and between 2000 and 2005, and there have been numerous wars on the Gaza Strip, in 2008, 2012, 2014, and 2021. The current situation in Gaza since 7 October 2023 has meant an intensified period of displacement, with a ripple effect of increased conflict in the West Bank, as well as a spilling over of this conflict into neighbouring Arab countries (Agbaria *et al.*, 2021).

The impact of intergenerational displacement and exposure to war trauma, linked to the dream of returning to their former homes and once again connecting with the land now lost to them, makes for a complex melange of experiences for Palestinian families. Psychological support is recommended for children in these situations, and music therapy skill-sharing training as part of this support is one aspect of treatment that can be offered.

Specifics related to the work in Palestine described here are issues related to displacement and intergenerational trauma. Palestinian children living under the occupation are highly likely to experience trauma-derived developmental disorders. Symptoms include anxiety and depression, nightmares and bedwetting, and peer relationship and concentration difficulties (Abdeen *et al.*, 2008; Al-Krenawi *et al.*, 2009). Participating in arts-based initiatives has been shown to offer ways of mitigating the degree of such trauma (Coombes, 2011; Soulsby *et al.*, 2019; Storsve *et al.*, 2010; Sutton, 2002; Van Eck, 2013). Although there is currently no research on the impact on children receiving this kind of psychosocial intervention, there is sufficient other evidence related to music therapy (Porter *et al.*, 2012; Porter *et al.*, 2017) and music-based interventions (Sena Moore & Hanson-Abromeit, 2015) to suggest that this approach has positive outcomes.

MUSIC AS THERAPY – INTERNATIONAL PROJECTS IN THE OPT

In these projects in the OPT, participants were supported through training to use a range of musical activities and improvisation with percussion instruments and voice to enhance the well-being of those referred to the groups by the institution. These projects had a theoretical underpinning based on the tenets of music therapy, such as developmental theories of communicative musicality (Malloch & Trevarthen, 2009), vitality affects

(Stern, 2010), and a humanistic perspective of unconditional positive regard (Rogers, 1959). They drew from music therapy principles such as mirroring and matching, and dialoguing and holding (Wigram, 2004). These MasT training projects enabled Palestinians from a range of backgrounds, including teachers, school counsellors, classroom assistants, and musicians, to lead the groups and offer them to children who might benefit from such provision.

They provided training in building music groups with therapeutic aims using child-centred techniques. Examples of activities used in these groups include greeting and ending songs, newly composed songs or existing ones, conducting and following activities, development and use of the musical elements, sharing and turn-taking, and improvisation-based work. The aim of these activities was to provide a secure environment that nurtured the children's play and creativity, enabling them to express and process emotions through a musical relationship. Furthermore, the activities were designed to enhance social skills, foster positive relationships among peers and adults, and develop attention and awareness of others. Practitioners received guidance on how to best select group members and activities and shape sessions for the specific goals they identified for their participants.

ITM-M: CONSIDERATIONS IN PRACTICE

Given Palestine's history of experiencing colonialism, it is important to consider the impact of this on such projects, and to consider the umbrella term ITM-M more broadly in the sphere of international development (Comte, 2016). First, a critical approach is needed concerning how we think about and refer to countries outside the Global North, which is where much ITM-M takes place. These may be referred to as 'developing countries'. The United Nations (UN) classifies countries as developed or developing by using global economic benchmarks and the Human Development Index. These measures problematically ignore vital aspects of context and the diversity of skills and resources that are already available in a country (Bolger & Murphy, 2023). Music therapists practising or facilitating music therapy projects in countries categorized as 'developing' might benefit from reflecting on their views of 'developing countries' to assess any pre-existing biases or notions, ensuring that they do not approach the work with a saviour mindset.

Colonial history continues to influence and have an impact on many aspects of the world in which we live, including music therapy. While the profession has begun to acknowledge and reflect on this (CAMTI Collective, 2022), de Cruz (2023) highlights the lack of contribution to this discourse from British music therapists. Similar criticisms have been made of the psychological professions by Winter and Charura (2023) who highlight 'a lack of adequate responses to content on social justice, wider global injustices, diversity, culture, and ethnicity' (p.5).

Criticism has also been levelled at international music therapy initiatives, questioning whether they are undertaken from a white saviour perspective, viewing the beneficiaries as passive victims (CAMTI Collective, 2022). Eurocentric music therapy practices and theories, and their relevance and applicability in other contexts, have also been brought under scrutiny. For instance, Sabbah, a Palestinian music therapist, argues that 'healing' is a Western concept and therefore not a worthy goal in the context of relentless violence (CAMTI Collective, 2022).

Consequently, music therapists must engage in ongoing self-reflection and reflective practice, as well as intercultural musical engagement, to avoid perpetuating colonial dynamics when conducting international music therapy projects (Bolger & Murphy, 2023). Tsolka (2022), who participated in a music therapy project in the OPT, emphasized the importance of recognizing intersecting identities. Through Crenshaw's intersectionality lens (1989), she called for an awareness of and reflection on one's privilege while undertaking work in an intercultural context. This is indeed important as intersectionality seeks to recognize the complex and multiple facets of social identity that impact people's experiences of the world. The primary focus of this concept lies in its use for achieving social equity and justice (Winter & Charura, 2023).

The concept of social justice extends into healthcare and education, where there is a focus on advocating for equitable access to quality healthcare and education (Wang, 2015; Wilkinson, 1996). In the OPT, the lack of access to music therapy training programmes serves as an example of such inequalities and is therefore a social justice issue. The broader socio-political challenges in the OPT, such as resource allocation, access to education, and the ongoing occupation, impede the development of the music therapy profession. This not only stunts the professional growth of Palestinian practitioners wishing to train as music therapists but also impedes direct access to music therapy services by a population affected by an ongoing conflict. This highlights the need for systemic changes to enhance access to specialized therapy training in the OPT.

Nonetheless, despite the increase in ITM-M skill-sharing projects being conducted internationally, much of the literature informs us of the music therapist's experience instead of that of local stakeholders and participants (Bolger & Murphy, 2023; Coombes, 2011; Coombes & Tombs-Katz, 2015). Coombes and Tombs-Katz (2015) have argued that examining participants' motivations and expectations supports the sustainability of skill-sharing projects, exploring whether the training resources are in fact fit for purpose. Despite potential barriers and challenges, such as language and the fear of burdening practitioners, it is crucial to hear and understand the experience of local practitioners and stakeholders to avoid the marginalization of their voices and to try and foster an intercultural engagement that is collaborative (Bolger & Murphy, 2023; Mansvelt, 2022).

IMPACT OF MAST PROJECTS IN THE OPT
Anecdotal reflections
As stated above, the first OPT project under the auspices of MasT took place in the Bethlehem area in 2009. It was a six-week project, where a music therapist and musician stayed in the area. Elizabeth Coombes and a colleague delivered a project that was a mixture of seminars and demonstration sessions, with the trainee practitioners gradually taking over the sessions until by the end of the project they had sufficient competency to run groups themselves. The training took place during the usual working days of the trainees. By the very nature of the six-week project design, there was an intensity to it for training participants and trainers, but this enabled practitioners to build skills in a short space of time, with the opportunity for reflections and questions about the sessions taking place when the trainees' workload allowed. A return visit of a week's duration in 2010 saw an evolution of the work in some settings; a social worker was using some of the activities in bigger groups, while a music teacher remained close to the smaller group work that had been used.

Implementation of the work in another setting was low level. Some practitioners simply had no time in their workload to run groups, and while they found the training interesting, it didn't seem to fit at that time with their job requirements. They had not been given a choice about undertaking the training in the first place. This gave Elizabeth food for thought when thinking about further work in the OPT.

Changes to the programme
Elizabeth undertook research in a further iteration of the same model in 2012 to explore how trainee practitioners were selected by the host organizations, how they felt about doing the training, and their subsequent practice (Coombes & Tombs-Katz, 2015). Through this research, it transpired that few of those selected by management had the space in their workloads to deliver groups, although all highly rated the training and said they had taken away thinking around working in a more child-centred way from it. In each of the three settings, the school counsellors subsequently became

the driving force behind sustaining these groups, and have continued to run them until the present day. This represents 12 years of continued use of music groups. Kindergarten teachers in one school also use the activities they learned with whole class groups for the prosocial skill development of their students. Further recruits to this way of working have been those who teach children with additional learning needs. These have been trained by the school counsellors, evidencing how sustainable this work can be with staff and management support.

It is worthy of note that the relationships between the British music therapists who initially delivered the training and the practitioners have continued, and informal exchanges of thinking about the work, offers of support, and sharing the work with British music therapy students have been additional outcomes of this project. Perhaps these unanticipated relationships have in a way supported the continuation and development of the work. MasT also continues to offer support, encouraging reflection on practice and designing support activities, sometimes also using social media posts on a variety of platforms.

In 2015, staff from Musicians Without Borders asked if it would be possible for them to undertake the distance learning programme (DLP) that MasT had been running in Romania since 2010. This had been developed by two music therapists, the Director of MasT, Alexia Quin, and Emma Lovell, together with other members of the charity's Advisory Panel. The DLP had seven monthly online tutorials and a practical weekend of music-making, followed by a practicum of group work. The curriculum focused on child development, developing observation skills, group dynamics, therapeutic goal setting, and session design, with an emphasis on enhancing music appreciation and skills among group leaders. A pilot project was run with four participants. The DLP ran in the OPT until 2019 when it halted due to the Covid-19 pandemic. Trainees received support with written assignments from the Musicians Without Borders staff member, Fabienne Van Eck, who had undertaken the pilot OPT-based DLP. The group work was supported by British music therapists using written responses translated into Arabic on receipt of reports from the trainees.

EVALUATING THE DLP: PRACTITIONERS' VOICES
An evaluation of the impact of this particular project in 2018 and 2019 on those who participated in the training was undertaken with three cohorts of practitioners. Saphia conducted face-to-face interviews and focus groups with practitioners at their workplaces, at times convenient for them. When practitioners could not speak English, a translator facilitated the process. Interviews

and focus groups were transcribed, and a thematic analysis was performed on the data, which yielded codes, master themes, and superordinate themes, reflecting patterns and meanings that emerged from the data, and capturing common and divergent experiences (Braun & Clarke, 2022). This process was supervised by Elizabeth, who reviewed the coding and themes.

Findings

Practitioners (2015–2019) said that the training substantially enhanced their professional practices, nurturing professional development and personal growth. Three themes emerged from the evaluation of these projects:

- Practitioners gained new skills and knowledge.

- A therapeutic stance was developed by the practitioners.

- The projects influenced aspects of the personal and professional lives of practitioners.

New skills and knowledge

The training cohorts explained how the acquisition of new skills in working with children appealed to them; it seems this was a primary motivator for participating in the projects:

'I thought it would help me out a lot in my field of work; I work in refugee camps with kids.'

'It's a new thing to know about, it's a way how to deal with the special needs because music is an essential part of how to work with them.'

'I thought I could use it with children who are hard cases.'

'I thought it would help me with students in our classes: how to listen, how to be with each other, and how to respect each other.'

Musicians with an interest in music therapy viewed the training as a valuable opportunity to further explore the discipline and its practical applications. In the OPT, the absence of music therapy training programmes presents a significant barrier for Palestinians aspiring to become qualified music therapists. The DLP gave them the chance to gain some additional knowledge in this field of study:

'I chose to do the training because I was already interested to know what's music therapy.'

'I was so interested in it and I thought okay, this my chance because I cannot do the complete study, but this could be a way to figure out if I like it or not.'

After the DLP, training practitioners said that they had increased their knowledge and skills:

> 'It taught us how to set aims that help us with all of the programmes we run across the school. We can help students in class to improve their self-confidence and self-esteem.'

They acknowledged gaining new knowledge and skills, particularly valuing experiential aspects of the training, such as the sessions that demonstrated and engaged them in music-making.

Practitioners running groups after the training continued to develop skills and knowledge, demonstrating initiative, creativity, and the embedding of therapeutic thinking in their everyday practice.

> 'I have increased my skills... The activity I did with the hoops, could it be a music-as therapy activity? Because this activity has the same goals – concentration, listening, appreciating one another.'

> 'I developed them over time. I searched for more ideas and I saw many different things, I learned things.'

> 'I think it also helped the children develop social skills and how to express their feelings. I felt I could solve a lot of problems by using these groups.'

> 'We can help students in class through this groupwork: how to listen, how to be with others, and how to respect each other. It also builds their self-confidence and self-esteem.'

Conversely, those who ceased practice maintained, rather than advanced, their skills and knowledge over time.

> 'It's still in my mind, maybe I need to read it more, refresh my mind to do it again, but yeah I remember the main things.'

A therapeutic stance

Many of the practitioners talked about developing a different stance to their work. Rather than positioning themselves as teachers or experts in behaviour, they began to understand the children's behaviour was communicating emotion and to respond to this rather than labelling it as 'naughty'. They unanimously identified unconditional positive regard (Rogers, 1959) as a pivotal concept which enhanced their own potential to develop therapeutic qualities, resulting in a more therapeutic and child-centred approach towards children.

> 'To accept children and whatever kind of thing they do which might upset

us, that we should just take a step back and try to understand them as children, what are they trying to tell us? I mean, before (the training) we would scold them, we would tell them not to do this, we would give them a hard time, but without really understanding what message they're trying to give us.'

'How to respect the desires of children. Like some of them don't want to participate, so I don't have to force them to participate, maybe to use different activities to let them participate but it's their choice.'

'For me, it's the positive regard because it's hard when you deal with the children. Like if you see the education here in Palestine, the relation between the teacher and the student, and when you speak about the positive regard, you will not find a lot.'

This was a paradigm shift in approach for practitioners, many of whom were working in a didactic and performative framework. It led to notable changes in how practitioners engaged with and responded to children. The embedding of unconditional positive regard into their practice led to a marked increase in their way of relating with the children in their care at work. Traits such as tolerance, patience, acceptance, and empathy were awakened and developed, and it brought about an understanding of children's behaviour as a form of communication, thereby enriching their professional practice.

Personal and professional influence of the DLP

The practitioners noticed a change in how they interacted with colleagues as they began to demonstrate more empathy and utilize the listening skills they had learned in the training. They were also imparting this to the children in the groups. One practitioner who was in a managerial position noticed that her management style became more holistic; she could see how the well-being of her staff needed to be considered and supported by the organization. Additionally, a participant in an administrative position for an organization working with children reported interacting more with children at work following the training; despite not having a child-facing role, they felt more confident in spending time with the children.

Furthermore, practitioners began to apply what they described as the concept of unconditional positive regard in their personal relationships with adults and children, both in their family and friendship groups. Perhaps this was also related to the musical components of training on the practical weekend they had received as part of the DLP, where listening and responding were core components of the work.

'It's helped me a lot to think about my own children and how I can play with them and support them with their feelings. This is a difficult life here; they need support.'

'Also, in dealing with colleagues, we're trying to give them space... It helps to calm things down because you give someone the opportunity to share without attacking ... it's the whole culture around the training...'

'I use unconditional positive regard with my family; it helps you to change in a better way, you'll start thinking in a different way, not why the people do this and just focus on what he did ... not just reacting and judging ... My sister's daughter, if she doesn't want to play, you will find all the family continue to ask her "just come". After this theory, you will find like okay, there are one thousand ways to deal with a child who doesn't want to play, or just give them space.'

Music and dance teachers noticed that there was a change in how they approached teaching their art form, as therapeutic thinking became embedded into their practice. This led to a greater understanding of the needs and abilities of their students and feeling better prepared to adapt their teaching and teaching material accordingly. Irrespective of whether they were running music groups or not, all practitioners integrated principles from the projects into their work, particularly in teaching. This integration involved employing music more and using it therapeutically, crafting activities with therapeutic underpinnings, and engaging with music more inventively and confidently with children.

'I took ideas, activities from the training but I changed them a little bit to make them fit more with the group I am working with.'

'In the past, I would ask them to be in the line, just come here in the line, look please, listen, and you speak a lot ... now maybe I'll start using my hands or using rhythm, using voice. So, you start to use new ways, new strategies.'

'Before, I was looking at the music, I have to do dance, dabkeh [traditional Palestinian dance] just for performance. Now I am looking at the children, thinking about how they will participate in the activities with music. So, for me it was like changing focus on the children.'

Challenges for DLP practitioners
It is to be expected that practitioners encountered challenges in engaging with the programme. Some arose in the practical aspects of the training, particularly while running the sessions and knowing how to manage and respond to behaviours in sessions, such as hyperactivity, withdrawal, and

non-participation. Practitioners largely appreciated the written assignment support provided in their own language by someone who had undertaken the training themselves, and the written responses from British music therapists were also helpful. They used it to explore these challenges. Strategies for overcoming or sitting with these challenges included employing musical techniques, leveraging children's strengths, and fostering mutual support among group members.

> 'The first time it was really difficult, I wasn't sure if I was doing it right and I felt scared, but then the second, third, fourth times, I started to realize, like it became much, much easier... I relaxed, and I felt I could do it.'

> 'You need to use unconditional positive regard, but sometimes, to tell you the truth, nothing works. I still acknowledge it, I use the three who are staying to sing for that person to come, to encourage him to come. Sometimes it works...but sometimes they will not come.'

Significant challenges were faced with the theoretical aspects of the training, with practitioners citing feelings of overwhelm due to the volume of information and feeling pressured by tight deadlines. Also, many were trying to undertake the tutorials using their phones as they did not have access to a laptop. Several female practitioners spoke of the stress of balancing these assignments with responsibilities at work and in the home.

> 'The challenge was that many times I was really stressed with time because they gave us the assignment while I needed to work here and then I needed to go back home and help my parents, or I needed to help in the house.'

DISCUSSION
The thoughts and feelings of the DLP practitioners offer a range of insights into a project designed to enable therapeutic music groups to be run in Palestine. Covid-19 impacted the continuation of the DLP in the OPT, but the practitioners trained, along with the 2012 cohort, continue to either run groups or have developed their own practices in after-school clubs and work with children and young people.

It is interesting to reflect on the importance of the concept of motivation to learn (Noe, 1986), the expectations of training (Colquitt *et al.*, 2000), and the reasons for undertaking the training. From the interviews, focus groups, and personal communications with practitioners, it emerged that a willingness to increase skill levels and a deep interest in the work showed a strong correlation with the successful completion of the training and utilization of the new skills.

There was a passion for the work that was demonstrated in those who completed and continued to use these new skills with significant management support, enabling these areas of practice to be developed. The 2012 project still maintains the closest way of working to that which was developed in training; these practitioners work with small groups that meet regularly, completing weekly notes and termly reports. It is unclear why this is the case, but it is likely a combination of support from the setting combined with peer group support and links with MasT and British music therapists who worked originally with the teams in carrying out the training and subsequently supporting it. Also, the structure of the school year lends itself to such work. Perhaps those who work in after-school clubs or settings with less structure are not able to find time or don't see the need for this aspect of the work to take place.

Although no data has been gathered relating to the music subsequently created in the groups, observations by the project teams, both those from the UK and those in the OPT, emphasize the importance of culturally specific resources. When visiting the OPT and seeing how the groups are run, it's clear that Palestinian music is a vital part of the work. This is an element of the work that has been developed by practitioners and children together. Palestinian songs, games, instruments, rhythms, and melodies offer a place where the groups and leaders can feel at ease. These create a sense of belonging which is important in this land where simply being Palestinian is a struggle. While practitioners keep the structure of the groups clear with repeated activities to build safe spaces, they also use free improvisation linked to movement or just being together to offer a chance for freedom and creativity to flourish and true enjoyment of creating a musicking community to arise.

When considering the music that is created in these projects, the connection to music that belongs to the Palestinians is of great importance. It became clear early on in this work that the instruments and musical elements present in the music created in the groups were strongly based on that of the practitioner's and children's heritage. Arabic drums continue to be a favourite instrument for practitioners and children, and there are often a series of negotiations to be made so that each group member can have a chance to play these. Traditional Palestinian rhythms and songs as well as hand clapping and ululating are also underpinning elements of the music created. Much of Palestinian music is linked to celebrations of joyful events, such as weddings, and this shines through in the music that is created or reproduced. In training when there is the encouragement to become confident and familiar with using instruments, improvisations using culturally evocative rhythms and vocalizations seem to arise naturally and provide a sense of community and togetherness. As one person said on such an occasion: 'Think how much the children will enjoy this when we see how much we are enjoying it!'

As of yet, evidence from the children who attend the groups is anecdotal, as is feedback from teachers and parents. However, practitioners report that children often ask for the groups to continue, and to be run more frequently. Parents make requests for their child to be offered a place in the programme as they have seen such positive changes reported by other parents in their children. These include discovering joy in playing music and thereafter starting to learn instruments. One parent whose child attends a school where ITM-M groups are run wrote:

> 'My son has been in the programme for two years and since this year we have seen changes in his character. We also discovered his new hobby of playing drums... The programme helps my son develop his abilities in many ways and gives him the opportunity to make good use of his energy. It makes him more self-confident and his relationship with his friends improves.'

CONCLUDING THOUGHTS

We suggest that these trainings conducted in the OPT illustrate the significant benefits of disseminating and cultivating therapeutic knowledge and child-centred practices among professionals working with children in conflict-affected areas. Building sustainability contributes to aspects of social justice in providing opportunities for such work to be offered.

The psychosocial support of these groups for young Palestinian children has the potential to provide a useful support intervention for children experiencing a range of challenges. Practitioners have told us that the learning they undertook about music and music therapy supports them in this work. Ensuring that the groups are grounded in theory, such as person-centred and child-centred mechanisms, is of importance. The musical content of the groups naturally uses and develops idioms and musical material that are deeply embedded in the consciousness of the practitioners and children. This supports the development of identity, community building, and a sense of belonging in the group and wider setting. We believe that the umbrella term ITM-M offers a way to provide a new category of music therapy practice to be explored and evaluated. As these groups continue to be sustained by practitioners in the OPT, it is hoped that more understanding of the effectiveness of such psychosocial support will emerge and the work will be further developed in the OPT and globally. What is certain is that this additional tool that is being used in a range of settings offers new and different ways of supporting young children in their development in a conflict zone. The safe and secure space provided by these groups is appreciated by practitioners, settings, and participants, and continues to offer another way of working in the OPT.

REFERENCES

Abdeen, Z., Qasrawi, R., Nabil, S., & Shaheen, M. (2008). Psychological reactions to Israeli occupation: Findings from the national study of school-based screening in Palestine. *International Journal of Behavioral Development*, 32(4), 290–297. https://doi.org/10.1177/0165025408092220.

Agbaria, N., Petzold, S., Deckert, A., Henschke, N., *et al.* (2021). Prevalence of post-traumatic stress disorder among Palestinian children and adolescents exposed to political violence: A systematic review and meta-analysis. *PLoS One*, 16(8), e0256426. https://doi.org/10.1371/journal.pone.0256426.

Al-Krenawi, A., Graham, J. R., & Kanat-Maymon, Y. (2009). Analysis of trauma exposure, symptomatology and functioning in Jewish Israeli and Palestinian adolescents. *The British Journal of Psychiatry*, 195(5), 427–432. https://doi.org/10.1192/bjp.bp.108.050393.

Bolger, L. & Murphy, M. (2023). Understanding the impact of international music therapy student placements on music therapy practice and professional identity. *Nordic Journal of Music Therapy*, 32(5). https://doi.org/10.1080/08098131.2023.2268692.

Braun, V. & Clarke, V. (2022). *Thematic Analysis: A Practical Guide*. Los Angeles, CA: Sage.

CAMTI Collective. (2022). *Colonialism and Music Therapy*. Dallas, TX: Barcelona Publishers.

Colquitt, J. A., LePine, J. A., & Noe, R. A. (2000). Toward an integrative theory of training motivation: A meta-analytic path analysis of 20 years of research. *Journal of Applied Psychology*, 85(5), 678–707. https://doi.org/10.1037/0021-9010.85.5.678.

Comte, R. (2016). Neo-colonialism in music therapy: A critical interpretive synthesis of the literature concerning music therapy practice with refugees. *Voices*, 16(3). https://doi.org/10.15845/voices.v16i3.865.

Coombes, E. (2011). Project Bethlehem – training educators and health workers in the therapeutic use of music in the West Bank. *Voices: A World Forum for Music Therapy*, 11(1). https://doi.org/10.15845/voices.v11i1.291.

Coombes, E. (2020). A Continuum of Music Therapy Practice and Pedagogy. [Unpublished PhD, University of South Wales].

Coombes, E., Abou-Amer, S., & Pickard, B. (2023). I started to think in a different way: Analysis of the lived experience of Palestinian educators and social workers who received a therapeutic music training programme. *International Journal of Music, Health and Wellbeing*, 1–13.

Coombes, E. & Tombs-Katz, M. (2015). Interactive therapeutic music skill-sharing in the West Bank: An evaluation report of Project Beit Sahour. *Approaches: An Interdisciplinary Journal of Music Therapy*, 9(1), 57–79.

Crenshaw, K. (1989). *Demarginalizing the Intersection of Race and Sex: A Black Feminist Critique of Antidiscrimination Doctrine, Feminist Theory and Antiracist Politics*. Chicago, IL: University of Chicago Legal Forum, 1 (Article 8).

de Cruz, M. (2023). Book review: The colonialism and music therapy interlocutors (CAMTI) collective, colonialism and music therapy. *British Journal of Music Therapy*, 37(2), 101–113. https://doi.org/10.1177/13594575231194605.

Hesser, B. & Bartleet, B. (eds) (2020). *Music as a Global Resource: Solutions for Social Economic Issues* (fifth edition). New York, NY: Music as a Global Resource.

Khalidi, R. (2020). *The Hundred Years' War on Palestine.* London: Palgrave Macmillan.

Malloch, S. & Trevarthen, C. (eds) (2009). *Communicative Musicality: Exploring the Basis of Human Companionship.* Oxford: Oxford University Press.

Mansvelt, N. (2022). International service learning: Insights from the voices of host organizations. *The Journal of Transdisciplinary Research in Southern Africa*, 18(1). https://doi.org/10.4102/td.v18i1.1208.

Moodley, R. (2009). Multi(ple) cultural voices speaking 'outside the sentence' of counselling and psychotherapy. *Counselling Psychology Quarterly*, 22(3), 297–307. https://doi.org/10.1080/09515070903302364.

Moss, H. (2008). Reflections of music therapy and arts in health. *British Journal of Music Therapy*, 22(2), 83–87. https://doi.org/10.1177/135945750802200207.

Noe, R. A. (1986). Trainees' attributes and attitudes: Neglected influences on training effectiveness. *Academy of Management Review*, 11(3), 736–749. https://doi.org/10.2307/258393.

Porter, S., Holmes, V., McLaughlin, K., Lynn, F., *et al.* (2012). Music in mind, a randomized controlled trial of music therapy for young people with behavioural and emotional problems: Study protocol. *Journal of Advanced Nursing*, 68(10), 2349–2358. https://doi.org/10.1111/j.1365-2648.2011.05936.x.

Porter, S., McConnell, T., McLaughlin, K., Lynn, F., *et al.* (2017). Music in mind study group. Music therapy for children and adolescents with behavioural and emotional problems: A randomised controlled trial. *Journal of Child Psychology and Psychiatry*, 58(5), 586–594. https://doi.org/10.1111/j.1365-2648.2011.05936.x.

Punamäki, R. L., Peltonen, K., Diab, M., & Qouta, S. R. (2014). Psychosocial interventions and emotion regulation among war-affected children: Randomized control trial effects. *Traumatology*, 20(4), 241–252. https://doi.org/10.1037/h0099856.

Quin, A. & Rowland, C. (2016). Intercultural Skills-Sharing in Music Therapy. In D. Doktor & M. Hills De Zarate (eds) *Intercultural Arts Therapies Research: Issues and Methodologies* (pp.212–224). London: Routledge.

Rogers, C. (1959). A Theory of Therapy, Personality and Interpersonal Relationships as Developed in the Client-centred Framework. In S. Koch (ed.) *Psychology: A Study of a Science, Vol 3. Formation of a Person and the Social Context.* New York, NY: McGraw Hill.

Sena Moore, K. & Hanson-Abromeit, D. (2015). Theory-guided therapeutic function of music to facilitate emotion regulation development in preschool-aged children. *Frontiers in Human Neuroscience*, 9, 572. https://doi.org/10.3389/fnhum.2015.00572.

Shrubsole, B. (2017). A community music project's journey. *Approaches: An Interdisciplinary Journal of Music Therapy*, 9(1), 58–66.

Small, C. (1998). *Musicking: The Meanings of Performing and Listening.* Middletown, CT: Wesleyan University Press.

Soulsby, L. K., Jelissejeva, K., & Forsythe, A. (2019). 'And I'm in another world'. A qualitative examination of the experience of participating in creative arts groups in Palestine. *Arts & Health: An International Journal for Research, Policy and Practice*, 13(1), 63–72. https://doi.org/10.1080/17533015.2019.1624585.

Stern, D. N. (2010). *Forms of Vitality: Exploring Dynamic Experience in Psychology, the Arts, Psychotherapy, and Development.* Oxford: Oxford University Press.

Storsve, V., Westbye, I. A., & Ruud, E. (2010). Hope and recognition: A music project among youth in a Palestinian refugee camp. *Voices*, 10(1). https://doi.org/10.15845/voices.v10i1.158.

Strange, J., Richards, E., & Odell-Miller, H. (2016). *Collaboration and Assistance in Music Therapy Practice: Roles, Relationships and Challenges.* London: Jessica Kingsley Publishers.

Sutton, J. (2002). Trauma in Context. In J. Sutton (ed.) *Music, Music Therapy and Trauma. International Perspectives.* London: Jessica Kingsley Publishers.

Tsolka, E. (2022). Intersecting Identities in a War Zone: A Music Therapist's Perspectives on Working with a Group of Mental Health Professionals in the West Bank, Palestine. In J. Collier & C. Eastwood (eds) *Intersectionality in the Arts Psychotherapies* (pp.149–162). London: Jessica Kingsley Publishers.

United Nations Conference on Trade and Development. (n.d.). *The question of Palestine.* https://unctad.org/topic/palestinian-people/The-question-of-Palestine.

United Nations Relief and Works Agency for Palestine Refugees. (2021). *Health conditions of, and assistance to, Palestine refugees in the occupied Palestinian territory, including East Jerusalem.* https://apps.who.int/gb/statements/WHA75/PDF/UNRWA.pdf.

United Nations Relief and Works Agency for Palestine Refugees. (n.d.). *Palestine refugees.* www.unrwa.org/palestine-refugees.

Van Eck, F. (2013). The role of the musician working with traumatized people in war-affected areas: Let the music happen. *Journal of Applied Arts & Health*, 4(3), 301–311. https://doi.org/10.1386/jaah.4.3.301_1.

Wang, F. (2015). Conceptualizing social justice: Interviews with principals. *Journal of Educational Administration*, 53(5), 667–681. https://doi.org/10.1108/JEA-07-2014-0080.

Wigram, T. (2004). *Improvisation: Methods and Techniques for Music Therapy Clinicians, Educators and Students.* London: Jessica Kingsley Publishers.

Wilkinson, R. G. (1996). *Unhealthy Societies: The Afflictions of Inequality.* London: Routledge.

Winter, A. L. & Charura, D. (eds) (2023). *The Handbook of Social Justice in Psychological Therapies: Power, Politics, Change.* London: Sage.

CHAPTER 9

Music Therapy, Displacement, and Internal Conflict in Colombia

ANDRÉS SALGADO VASCO

The armed conflict in Colombia began in the 1950s and continues to this day. According to the Government's Unified Victim Registry (RUV), 8,219,403 people have experienced forced displacement due to events occurring from 1985 to 31 December 2021. Working in this context poses a significant challenge for music therapists. Nevertheless, various studies have addressed music therapy work at different stages of life and with diverse populations, including elderly women, displaced adolescents, individuals in post-conflict reintegration, the Jitnu indigenous population, and rural communities affected by socio-environmental conflicts. The goals addressed typically include:

- resignifying self-confidence

- strengthening support networks

- improving quality of life

- fostering coping skills

- projecting hopeful futures

- rebuilding social cohesion

- cultural revitalization

- community empowerment

- effectively addressing economic and symbolic reparations.

INTERNAL DISPLACEMENT IN COLOMBIA

According to the Comisión Interamericana de Derechos Humanos (2004), a violent confrontation between political groups in Colombia occurred in the 1950s. The persecution of members of the Liberal Party in rural areas led to the creation of armed groups. In 1957, a reconciliation period known as the National Front began, where both political parties (Liberals and Conservatives) alternated in power. During the 1960s, 70s, and 80s, new revolutionary groups emerged: The Revolutionary Armed Forces of Colombia (FARC), The National Liberation Army (ELN), the People's Liberation Army (EPL), the April 19 Movement (M-19), the indigenous guerrilla group Quintín Lame Armed Movement, the Workers' Self-Defense (ADO), and dissidents from these groups, such as the Ricardo Franco group, among others. The rise of these groups and the failure to reach peace agreements resulted in a new period of violence called Banditry (Bandolerismo).

By 1968, paramilitary groups had emerged, growing stronger by the late 1970s and early 1980s. Supported by some sectors of the public force, they committed various massacres of civilians. In the late 1970s, drug trafficking by drug cartels had also added to the conflict. By 1997, these groups consolidated into an organization called the United Self-Defense Forces of Colombia (AUC). Meanwhile, successive governments strived to negotiate peace. In the early 1990s, M-19, EPL, and Quintín Lame undertook a demobilization process following a series of agreements. FARC and ELN, however, did not demobilize. Illegal armed groups such as guerrillas and paramilitaries created a confusing mix of alliances and simultaneous clashes with both drug traffickers and the public force. FARC, ELN, and paramilitaries also engaged in extortion and kidnapping. The ongoing conflict, in addition to the impact of organized crime in recent decades, shows how violence in Colombia is long-standing and complex (Comisión Interamericana de Derechos Humanos, 2004).

Several attempts have been made to find a solution to this issue by seeking peace agreements. The first of these, known as El Caguán, was in 1998 between the Colombian Government and FARC and extended until 2002. This process took place in a demilitarized zone covering several municipalities and was developed in a climate of military confrontation, except in the demilitarized zone. The Common Agenda for Change towards a New Colombia included topics such as employment, human rights, agrarian policy, natural resources, economic and social development, justice and state reform, and international relations. Despite the active participation of social representatives, community leaders, and political movements, the process was complex and progressed slowly due to incidents that eroded trust between the parties. The process definitively broke down on 20 February

2002, when FARC kidnapped Senator Jorge Gechem, leading President Andrés Pastrana to end the negotiations (Indepaz, 2013).

Another notable attempt at resolving internal conflicts was the demobilization of the United Self-Defense Forces of Colombia (AUC). In late 2002, the AUC declared a ceasefire and began their disarmament and reintegration process in 2003. According to García (2010), although it was not a formal peace agreement, this process aimed to dismantle an illegal counter-insurgency deeply connected to drug trafficking. However, dissident groups that did not demobilize or that broke away from the DDR (disarmament, demobilization, and reintegration) process continued illegal activities and fought for territorial control (García, 2010).

In 2012, a new peace process with FARC-EP began in Havana, Cuba. In October of the same year, negotiating tables were established with representatives from both sides and international guarantors, and on 12 November 2016, the Final Agreement for the Termination of the Conflict and the Construction of a Stable and Lasting Peace was signed. Since the signing of this agreement, a fundamental objective has been the reconstruction of social cohesion, which involves restoring and strengthening social relationships and structures damaged by armed conflict. This process includes the reintegration of former combatants and displaced persons, and comprehensive reparations for victims through a range of material and symbolic benefits such as:

- the promotion of social cohesion and reconciliation
- community development through infrastructure and education projects
- transitional justice to clarify and judge the crimes of the conflict
- strengthening institutions to ensure peace
- establishment of historical memory projects to educate and honour the victims. (Jurisdicción Especial para la Paz, 2016)

Since then, this process has been implemented, but the conflict persists. Currently, the control and dispute over territories by armed actors continue to intensify, with the struggle to dominate drug-trafficking routes and crop production continuing to grow. The lack of guarantees and the absence of civilian state institutions, along with militarization and the development of large-scale infrastructure projects, places populations in vulnerable situations, forcing them to be displaced. Simultaneously, human rights, community, and environmental defenders, as well as those involved in land restitution processes, become military targets (Comisión de la Verdad, 2022).

According to the Government's Unified Victim Registry (RUV), 9,720,863 people have been victims of the armed conflict in the country, of which 8,665,884 have been displaced (Registro Único de Víctimas, 2024). This figure can be corroborated by the 2022 Global Report on Internal Displacement, which accounts for 8,219,403 people displaced due to events occurring from 1985 to 31 December 2021 (Internal Displacement Monitoring Centre, 2022).

Forced displacement occurs when an individual or group is compelled to leave their residence or place of habitual work through the use of force or intimidation. In Colombia, this happens primarily due to actions perpetrated by armed groups, human rights violations, breaches of humanitarian law, or to avoid the direct effects of the conflict. Victims of forced displacement had to change their lives to preserve them. Violence had a differential impact on the rural population, particularly indigenous, Afro-Colombian, and peasant communities, with women, girls, boys, and adolescents being especially affected (Comisión de la Verdad, 2022).

Colombia has restructured its territories and built its history through the dynamics of internal conflict. Over the last 185 years, the country has experienced 25 national civil wars and approximately 60 regional conflicts, leading to significant internal displacement. Internal forced displacement has become one of the most significant political, economic, and demographic phenomena for the country, resulting in a redistribution of territory. In the last decade, internal migration due to forced displacement has affected 8.36% of the total population, equivalent to the population of a large city being forced to migrate to another territory, with the consequent social, economic, and demographic implications (Ruiz, 2011).

Official figures on forced displacement in Colombia do not encompass all victims; they represent only an approximation since the Government's Unified Victim Registry (RUV) began recording these cases in 1985. During the period known as La Violencia (1948–1958), academic sources estimate that two million people were displaced, while the press at the time reported three million. The social costs of displacement are enormous, as millions of people are forced to survive in conditions of poverty and violence. The causes of displacement persist due to the country's social conditions, replicating from generation to generation. Each recorded number represents a person, a family, or a community forced to flee armed conflict, leaving an indelible mark (Comisión de la Verdad, 2022). Currently, the scourge continues, as shown by the fact that, in 2023, nearly 121,000 people in Colombia were victims of mass forced displacement and confinement (Defensoría del Pueblo, 2023).

TRANSFORMATIVE MUSICAL PROJECTS IN COLOMBIA

Before addressing the contribution of music therapy to this issue, it is crucial to highlight that various cultural programmes and foundations have
emerged in Colombia in response to the profound social crises and armed
conflicts that have marked its recent history. These programmes not only
seek to mitigate the impacts of conflict but also promote reconciliation and
the reconstruction of social cohesion through art. Therefore, they serve
as significant antecedents, especially considering that music therapy is a
developing discipline. In this context, the following initiatives stand out:

- The Art and Sport for Life by Animarte programme in San Carlos,
  Antioquia-Colombia, initiated in 2009, uses art and sports for the
  psychosocial recovery of conflict victims. This programme promotes
  activities such as theatre, dance, music, hip-hop, and sports like football and basketball to promote co-existence, educate in values, and
  reintegrate ex-combatants into the community. Through a range
  of community groups, it aims to transform attitudes and values to
  consolidate peace and minimize future conflict risks, thereby contributing to the reconstruction of social cohesion in the region (Programa de las Naciones Unidas para el Desarrollo, 2010).

- The Fundación Nacional Batuta was created in 1991 by the National
  Government and the private sector. This foundation aims to promote the enjoyment, practice, and teaching of music in Colombia,
  especially among children. Through the National System of Youth
  and Children's Symphony Orchestras – Batuta, the foundation has
  expanded orchestral training projects nationwide, with the collaboration of departmental organizations such as Fundación Batuta
  Caldas, Corporación Batuta Risaralda, and others. Besides its educational work, the Foundation offers training workshops for teachers,
  directors, and luthiers, in partnership with public and private entities, contributing to the development and sustainability of orchestral
  activity in the country (Batuta, 2003). Since its creation, Batuta has
  been involved in post-conflict work, using music as a channel to heal
  the wounds of conflict and provide support to children with disabilities who are also victims (Bienestar Colsanitas, n.d.). Batuta has
  been crucial in preventing children from becoming involved in the
  war and mitigating the pain caused by the conflict. Additionally, it
  works closely with entities such as the Colombian Institute of Family
  Welfare and health organizations to provide comprehensive care.

- Medellín Music Schools Network is a programme established

through municipal agreements in 1996 and 1998 by the Medellín City Hall to promote co-existence and advancement of citizen culture through the musical training of children and young people. Specific objectives include fostering attitudes of agreement, inclusion, participation, and social integration; forming citizens through art and culture; guaranteeing rights in the dimensions of being, doing, and knowing; and strengthening a public, social, and musical programme in Medellín. The Medellín Music Schools Network was established in response to the social crisis in Medellín in the 1980s, marked by violence and social conflicts stemming from both drug trafficking and deep social injustices. This programme seeks to transform human relationships through musical learning, building new forms of co-existence among children, young people, and their families. The initiative not only offers educational opportunities but also generates social bonds and a positive identity in a community that has faced despair and division (Red, 1998).

- The Music for Reconciliation programme is an initiative of the Fundación Nacional Batuta, funded by the Colombian Ministry of Culture, aimed at promoting peace and rebuilding the social fabric through music education. This programme targets children, adolescents, and young people who have been victims of the armed conflict or are in highly vulnerable situations. Its primary objective is to ensure cultural rights and foster the comprehensive development of these young individuals, using music as a transformative tool (Fundación Nacional Batuta, 2024). Through 132 Music Centres distributed across various regions of the country, Music for Reconciliation has benefited over 19,000 Colombians, 91% of whom are children and young people. The programme also includes Afro-descendant and Indigenous communities, as well as individuals with disabilities, reinforcing music as a tool for peace that bridges differences and transforms contexts of violence (Fundación Nacional Batuta, 2015).

MUSIC THERAPY IN COLOMBIA

The development of music therapy in Colombia began in the 1970s, marked by three key events: the arrival of music therapists trained abroad, the attempt to establish an undergraduate programme in music therapy at the University of Cauca, and the organization of academic events such as the First Colombian Symposium on Music Therapy in 1991 and the First Colombian Music Therapy Workshops in 1998. In response to the growing interest in the relationship between music and health in various faculties of the National University of Colombia, dialogues began that culminated in the creation of permanent seminars coordinated by Carmen Barbosa Luna at the Conservatory of the Faculty of Arts. These seminars, recognized by the university in 2000, explored interdisciplinary topics such as brain disorders and music, music pedagogy and health, and music as therapy (Luna & Salgado Vasco, 2023).

In 2000, Edgar Blanco, a music therapist who graduated in Spain, proposed the Second Colombian Music Therapy Workshops in collaboration with the National University, consolidating interest in this discipline. This event, held in March 2001, attracted more than 400 people and included conferences and workshops led by prominent international and local music therapists. Taking advantage of the curricular reform of 2003, the Conservatory created the Music, Health, and Pedagogy specialization track, which preceded undergraduate courses related to the graduate programme in music therapy. In 2006, the National University formally approved the Master's programme in music therapy, marking a significant milestone in the academic development of music therapy in Colombia and establishing its position as a recognized discipline at one of the country's most prestigious universities (Luna & Salgado Vasco, 2023).

Since its origins, the Master's programme has placed special emphasis on students engaging in practice with various communities, including victims of the Colombian armed conflict, ex-combatants from different armed groups, as well as children and adolescents affected by violence and/ or forced displacement (Luna & Salgado Vasco, 2023). Currently, music therapists and Master's students continue to show great interest in this work, especially from the perspective of community music therapy. The objectives of this approach include, among others, strengthening or rebuilding social cohesion, and fostering *communitas*. Turner (1969) defined *communitas* as relationships that occur naturally, without hierarchies or specific roles. Ruud (1998) applied this idea to music therapy, highlighting that improvisation generates equality and unity by eliminating differences in social roles and fostering empowerment (Salgado Vasco & Güiza, 2018).

MUSIC THERAPY AND DISPLACEMENT IN COLOMBIA
Beyond the musical initiatives mentioned earlier, music has played a fundamental role in Colombia's history, especially during periods of conflict and displacement. Over the years, it has served as a form of resistance, resilience, and hope for numerous communities affected by violence and social instability.

In times of adversity, music has enabled these communities to maintain their cultural identity, express their pain, and find solace amid chaos.

In this context, music therapy, as an emerging discipline in the country, is proving particularly effective in addressing these complex and profound issues. This therapeutic approach provides a significant space for emotional, social, and cultural expression, allowing individuals and communities to process trauma, express feelings, and reclaim a sense of identity and belonging. Furthermore, by facilitating dialogue and empathy, it helps to heal the divisions caused by conflict. Through music therapy sessions, people can share their stories, listen to others, and find common ground to rebuild trust and social cohesion.

To illustrate these benefits, the following works by students and graduates of the Master's programme in music therapy at the National University of Colombia, an institution that has been a pillar in the development and application of music therapy in the country, are presented. These programmes prepare students to address a variety of challenges through music:

- Gómez (2015) explored how music therapy can help elderly women affected by the armed conflict redefine their self-confidence, in her work *Music Therapy in Processes of Re-Signifying Self-confidence in Elderly Victims of the Armed Conflict in Colombia*. Utilizing the Plurimodal model of music therapy, Gómez combined techniques that foster emotional expression, identity reconstruction, and self-confidence strengthening, facilitating the production of personal narratives and the development of coping strategies in a safe space for exploring and expressing emotions. Gómez highlighted that music therapy not only alleviates emotional distress but also strengthens the sense of belonging and support networks among participants, promoting both emotional and physical well-being for deep and lasting recovery.

- Salgado Vasco (2015) investigated how music therapy can be an effective tool for psychosocial repair in his work *Pilot Programme of Music Therapy as a Tool to Foster Coping with Difficult Situations in the Life Projects of Adolescent Victims of the Colombian Armed Conflict*. The programme used the four main methods of music therapy: receptive, re-creative, improvisation, and composition (Bruscia, 2007). Salgado Vasco aimed for an integral intervention to help adolescents affected by violence in Colombia face difficult situations and consider their life projects. The results showed that music therapy improves the ability to cope with these situations by developing skills such as breathing management, generating positive thoughts, and expressing negative feelings. It also helps project future expectations by visualizing personal and professional goals. Salgado Vasco concluded that music therapy is a valuable tool for psychosocial repair, supporting emotional management and strengthening coping skills, contributing to building a more hopeful future for adolescents and enhancing their ability to plan and visualize their future with confidence.

- Gómez Montoya (2015) conducted research on a music therapy intervention for young victims of the armed conflict in Colombia. The study focused on adolescents and children of displaced families living in the peripheral neighbourhoods of Soacha, south of Bogotá, Colombia. The intervention, developed with the foundation Arte Sin Fronteras of the Academia de Artes Guerrero, combined music therapy methods (Bruscia, 2007) with elements of the Pagamento ritual, a traditional ceremonial practice of the indigenous peoples of the Sierra Nevada de Santa Marta and the Muisca communities of the Cundiboyacense highlands. The integration of these methods aimed to improve participants' quality of life, addressing their emotional and social needs. Gómez Montoya applied a qualitative methodology with an emphasis on the ethnographic method, allowing for a deep understanding of the cultural and social context of the youth, enriching the intervention. Gómez Montoya supported the inclusion of ritual elements in the Ethnomusic therapy approach, adapting traditional healing practices to therapeutic contexts. This combination facilitated participants' connection with their cultural roots and improved their ability to envision a promising future. The results indicated that the intervention had a positive impact on interpersonal relationships, adaptability, and the development of the youth's life projects, demonstrating the effectiveness of combining music therapy methods and traditional ceremonies in improving their quality of life (Gómez Montoya, 2015).

- The Community Music Therapy for Social Cohesion Construction in the Post-conflict Process project, coordinated by the Master's programme in music therapy at the National University of Colombia and supported by the National Extension Solidarity Call, was carried out in 2018. With the support of the National University of Colombia, the Government Agency for Reincorporation and Normalization (ARN), and the Master's programme in music therapy team, the project was implemented in public spaces and ARN offices in the Kennedy locality of Bogotá and in the Soacha municipality of the Cundinamarca Department. In Kennedy, participants included people in the reintegration process (PPR) from illegal armed groups, their families, and members of the Corporación Tiempo de Mujeres. In Soacha, participants were members of the FARC (now the political party Fuerza Alternativa Revolucionaria del Común) and their families. The project also included the local civil community in the execution areas (Luna et al., 2020). The main objective was to use community music therapy strategies to generate collective knowledge and rebuild social cohesion. Luna et al. (2020) reported that activities focused on improving co-existence through organization, mobilization, sensitization, and awareness, promoting creative processes that strengthened leadership, communication, and self-management. The project facilitated participants' empowerment through community music therapy meetings, significantly contributing to the strengthening of social cohesion and peace in the post-conflict period. Besides detailing the work carried out, the document provides a conceptualization of community music therapy and establishes the basis for its application in the Colombian context (Luna et al., 2020).

- Martínez Durán (2019) investigated the use of community music therapy (Pavlicevic & Ansdell, 2004) to strengthen popular knowledge and empower the indigenous Jitnu community, affected by the armed conflict and located in the illegally established shanty town Bello Horizonte in Arauca-Colombia. Music therapy proved to be an effective tool for empowerment, promoting intuitive expression through music and facilitating behaviours and narratives that foster social networks, cultural revitalization, and the strengthening of the community's and individuals' self-concept and self-esteem. Martínez Durán highlighted that music contributed to modelling community behaviours and cultural empowerment, acting as a central axis in intercultural and intergenerational dialogue and promoting popular knowledge as practical knowledge. Through continuous musical practice in Arauca, the music therapist served as a bridge between the Jitnu community and the dominant culture, facilitating reflection on issues such as gender violence, upbringing, and silence, while promoting social networks and strengthening participants' self-concept and self-esteem. The musical interaction not only allowed a better understanding of the Jitnu culture but also promoted empowerment and cultural resistance. Flexibility in planning and community participation were crucial to avoid burnout and ensure a positive impact (Martínez Durán, 2019).

- Ruiz Fandiño (2019) worked from a community music therapy perspective with adolescents displaced by the armed conflict in Colombia, aiming to facilitate meetings among them, rebuild their identity, and improve their co-existence and quality of life. Participants from peasant families relocated to the Benposta Nation of Youth Organization experienced a reframing and resignification of their identity despite the ruptures caused by forced displacement. The intervention mainly used improvisation and composition methods of music therapy (Bruscia, 2007). Improvisation allowed adolescents to explore and express their feelings, build relationships, and create unity through interactive activities such as question-and-answer work. This method promoted a free space that facilitated personal and group connections. Composition, though challenging, helped consolidate the improvisations and reflect the evolution of relationships. Participants created two groups that produced compositions about peace and love, highlighting the drum as a central element in their songs and in the making of instruments, which fostered empathy and trust. The process facilitated self-knowledge and acceptance, transformation of feelings, and individual and collective expression. It also addressed feelings of anger and aggression, promoting tolerance, respect, and group work, while strengthening the bond with their roots and valuing both their original and current contexts (Ruiz Fandiño, 2019).

- Cervera Osorio (2020) proposed an innovative integration between law and music therapy for the symbolic reparation of victims of forced displacement. Her study, conducted in 2018 with displaced women in the Ciudad Bolívar locality of Bogotá, explored how music therapy can be crucial in this process, highlighting the deficiencies of the symbols constructed by the Third Section of the Colombian State Council, which are responsible for offering reparation to conflict victims. Victims in Colombia have the right to reparations, which include both material and symbolic benefits. Material benefits encompass economic subsidies, health assistance, compensation for material damages, education and training, psychosocial rehabilitation, infrastructure reconstruction, and legal assistance. Symbolic benefits include recognition ceremonies such as public events, commemoration and remembrance brought to the community through museums, memory centres, and monuments, participation in forums and discussion groups, and artistic and cultural projects such as theatre and documentaries that reflect their experiences.

Cervera Osorio suggested that these symbols do not effectively fulfil their reparative function and argued that community music therapy offers a more effective alternative. The author proposed that music therapy provides a space to construct narratives of truth and memory, allowing victims to express and process their experiences meaningfully, contributing to their emotional and psychological dignity. It also fosters empathy and reconciliation by facilitating reflection on experiences and promoting mutual understanding in the community. Cervera Osorio suggested a review of the criteria used to design reparation symbols, advocating for a deeper integration between therapeutic and legal approaches to adequately address the aftermath of forced displacement. Her proposal defended a more effective combination of therapeutic and legal methods to achieve real symbolic reparation for victims in Colombia.

- Cardozo Ruiz (2023) evaluated the impact of community music therapy on strengthening social cohesion in the Asociación de Afectados por el Proyecto Hidroeléctrico El Quimbo (Asoquimbo). This association defends the social, economic, cultural, and environmental rights of communities affected by the El Quimbo dam, promoting resistance against the extractive model. The Asoquimbo population, composed of peasants, fishermen, and day labourers, faces unemployment and food insecurity while preserving their peasant identity. The research was conducted between November 2022 and June 2023 in rural areas of the Huila Department of Colombia, in a context of socio-environmental conflict. The results indicated that community music therapy improved integration, participation, empathy, and communication within the community, strengthening the sense of identity and belonging. An increase in participation in decision-making and the creation of common agreements was also observed. However, the process faced challenges due to the negative effects of the El Quimbo Hydroelectric Project and the structural limitations of the organization. Cardozo Ruiz concluded that community music therapy is a valuable tool for strengthening social cohesion but emphasized the need to adapt therapeutic approaches to the specific realities and needs of affected communities in Colombia (Cardozo Ruiz, 2023).

KEY ELEMENTS OF MUSIC THERAPY PRACTICE

In Colombia, music therapists (Cardozo Ruiz, 2023; Cervera Osorio, 2020; Gómez, 2015; Gómez Montoya, 2015; Luna *et al.*, 2020; Martínez Durán,

2019; Ruiz Fandiño, 2019; Salgado Vasco, 2015) primarily use the four methods of music therapy defined by Bruscia (2007):

- Improvisation, which involves the spontaneous creation of music by the therapist and participants;

- Composition, focused on creating new songs, lyrics, or musical pieces during the session;

- Receptive, which consists of listening to music selected or created live by the music therapist; and

- Re-creative, which refers to the interpretation of existing musical pieces.

Most studies (Cardozo Ruiz, 2023; Cervera Osorio, 2020; Gómez Montoya, 2015; Luna *et al.*, 2020; Martínez Durán, 2019; Ruiz Fandiño, 2019) adopt a community music therapy approach that is relevant for the type of population they worked with. According to Stige (2002), this practice takes place in communities of interest. This term describes a group of people with a common interest or passion and links to considerations around the specific social and cultural context of each group.

A notable example is the work of Gómez Montoya (2015), who integrated indigenous ceremonial practices, such as the Pagamento ritual. This ritual, an ancestral spiritual practice that varies by community, may focus on music, thought, silence, or the use of materials such as stones and crystals. Originating in the Sierra Nevada de Santa Marta and adapted by the Muisca communities, the Pagamento is performed not only in sacred places like mountains and lagoons but also at specific times related to natural cycles and for significant life events, such as births and harvests.

The Pagamento ceremony is divided into three stages. The first is preparation, which includes a strict diet and physical, mental, and emotional engagement. The second stage is the ritual act, which also consists of three phases: cleansing (bringing to mind difficult aspects of life with the purpose of cleansing them), *poner la medicina*[1] (after cleansing, wishes for health and well-being in all aspects of life are evoked and enhanced, accompanied by singing and dancing), and offering (the symbolic offering of the newly cleansed aspects of self). The third stage consists of subsequent procedures,

---

[1]   *Poner la medicina*: In the context of the Pagamento ceremony, 'putting the medicine' refers to a ritual moment where a substance or symbolic element with spiritual, healing, or protective significance is used. This may involve the use of plants, prayers, chants, sacred objects, or any other element considered 'medicine' in the spiritual and cultural sense within the ritual.

which focus on maintaining and actualizing the desired changes through continuous reflection and community practice.

This ritual aims to restore spiritual and physical balance, reflecting a deep connection between the individual, the community, and the natural environment. In the research, some elements of the ritual were adapted to make them accessible and useful for the youth in Soacha, simplifying the process to facilitate their understanding and application. Additionally, concepts from Ethnomusic therapy (Moreno, 1995) were incorporated, adapted to their needs without strictly following the theory.

Ethnomusic therapy is understood as the study of indigenous music in healing practices, highlighting its role in ritual contexts. Although the intervention with youth in Soacha was based on this model, it deviated from shamanic practices, focusing the Pagamento ritual on introspection and personal relationships rather than spiritual trance. The study emphasizes that Ethnomusic therapy can include techniques from other traditions and be adapted to clinical and community contexts, using methods such as musical composition to enrich the music therapy practice.

MUSICAL INSTRUMENTS

In terms of musical instruments that may be used in music therapy, the variety in Colombia is extensive. Percussion instruments are the most commonly used in sessions, including the tambor alegre, made of wood and leather with a stretched membrane that produces a deep sound; the tambor de bomba, similar but larger and deeper; maracas, made from gourds or plastic containers filled with seeds that create a rhythmic sound when shaken; guacharaca, a hollow cane or wood that is scraped to produce a characteristic sound; caja, with a rectangular wooden structure and a leather membrane; and redoblante, smaller and cylindrical, emitting a high-pitched tone.

Colombia's cultural richness is also reflected in the music used in sessions, with each region contributing unique styles and rhythms. In the Caribbean region, *vallenato*, known for its melodic narratives, and *cumbia*, famous for its vibrant rhythms of drums and maracas, are predominant. The Pacific region stands out with *bomba* and *marimba*, offering deep rhythms and resonant sounds. In the Eastern Llanos, *joropo* is characterized by its fast tempo and the virtuosity of the cuatro, a guitar-like instrument and harp, while in the Cundiboyacense highlands, Andean music is expressed through the tiple, a 12-stringed guitar known for its complex melodies. In a music therapy group, the presence of people from diverse regions enriches the musical experience by merging local genres and traditions, presenting a stimulating challenge for music therapists.

CONCLUSIONS

Music therapy has proven to be an invaluable tool in addressing the emotional and social aftermath of the armed conflict in Colombia. Its practice has evolved significantly, adapting to the diverse realities of the country and demonstrating its ability to foster resilience, identity reconstruction, and the strengthening of social cohesion. Through methods and techniques such as improvisation, composition, and the integration of traditional cultural elements, music therapy has contributed to the health and empowerment of affected communities. However, the number of music therapists and the availability of these services are still limited compared to the magnitude of the problem, which affects nearly 9 million displaced victims. Despite these challenges, the positive impact and value of music therapy in emotional and social repair are undeniable, and its evolution continues to show its potential as a crucial component in the national strategy to address the aftermath of displacement and promote peace and social cohesion in Colombia.

The works conducted have addressed various life stages (from adolescence to older adults), populations (individuals in post-conflict reintegration, the indigenous Jitnu population, displaced urban women, and rural communities affected by socio-environmental conflicts, among others), and genders, reflecting the breadth of experiences.

FUTURE DIRECTIONS

The practice of music therapy in Colombia, particularly in the context of displacement and armed conflict, has proven to be a powerful tool for working with affected communities. However, to expand its impact and reach, it is crucial to develop strategies that strengthen this emerging discipline. One of the main future directions is the expansion of training and education for music therapists in the country. This includes not only the creation of more specialized academic programmes in music therapy but also the offering of workshops and continuing education courses for practising professionals. The integration of intercultural practices and evidence-based techniques will better equip music therapists to address the diverse needs of communities affected by conflict.

Additionally, it is essential to establish interdisciplinary collaborations with other fields of knowledge, such as psychology, sociology, and law, to design effective interventions. Collaborative research can provide a deeper understanding of the mechanisms through which music therapy impacts emotional and social health, thereby improving existing practices. The implementation of longitudinal studies and rigorous evaluations will allow for more precise measurement of the impact of music therapy in different contexts and populations, generating data that can influence public policy and resource allocation.

Another important direction is the expansion of music therapy services to rural areas and communities that currently have limited or no access to this type of intervention. This can be achieved through the creation of community outreach programmes. The inclusion of music therapy in health and education systems as part of comprehensive care protocols is also fundamental to ensuring that more people can benefit from its therapeutic effects.

It is vital to promote awareness and understanding of music therapy among communities, health professionals, and policymakers. Awareness and education campaigns can help demystify music therapy and highlight its proven benefits, facilitating its acceptance and support. By strengthening the visibility and recognition of music therapy as a valuable therapeutic practice, new opportunities will open for its integration into national health and wellness strategies, thereby contributing to the reconstruction of social cohesion and the promotion of peace in Colombia.

Finally, Colombia, with its experience in applying music therapy to address the aftermath of forced displacement and armed conflict, stands as a global reference for music therapy professionals seeking to develop and train in this area. The rich variety of approaches, methods, and techniques implemented in the country, combined with the unique contexts of displacement and post-conflict, offers valuable lessons and innovative practices for the global field. The Colombian experience demonstrates how music therapy can adapt to complex and multifaceted contexts, providing effective and culturally sensitive solutions. Thus, international music therapists can find in Colombia an inspiring model and a living laboratory to learn and refine their skills in therapeutic intervention in humanitarian crises.

REFERENCES

Batuta. (2003). Fundación Batuta. www.fundacionbatuta.org/quienes-somos.
Bienestar Colsanitas. (n.d.). Fundación Batuta. www.bienestarcolsanitas.com/articulo/fundacion-batuta.
Bruscia, K. (2007). *Musicoterapia: Métodos y prácticas*. Editorial Pax México.
Cardozo Ruiz, O. l. (2023). *Proceso piloto de musicoterapia comunitaria para el fortalecimiento del tejido social comunitario de integrantes de la asociación de afectados por*

el proyecto hidroeléctrico El Quimbo (Asoquimbo) (Tesis de maestría). Universidad Nacional de Colombia.

Cervera Osorio, M. C. (2020). *Reparación simbólica y desplazamiento forzado: Parámetros a partir de un caso de musicoterapia comunitaria en la localidad de Ciudad Bolívar de Bogotá* (Tesis de maestría). Universidad Externado de Colombia.

Comisión de la Verdad. (2022). *Hay futuro si hay verdad: Informe final de la Comisión para el Esclarecimiento de la Verdad, la Convivencia y la No Repetición* (primera edición). Bogotá.

Comisión Interamericana de Derechos Humanos. (2004). *Informe sobre la situación de los derechos humanos en Colombia.* www.cidh.org/countryrep/colombia04sp/informe3.htm.

Defensoría del Pueblo. (2023). *Durante el 2023 en Colombia, cerca de 121.000 personas fueron víctimas de desplazamiento forzado masivo y confinamiento.* https://defensoria.gov.co/-/durante-el-2023-en-colombia-cerca-de-121.000-personas-fueron-victimas-de-desplazamiento-forzado-masivo-y-confinamiento.

Fundación Nacional Batuta. (2015). Música para la Reconciliación, un compromiso con las víctimas del conflicto armado y en situación de vulnerabilidad. Correo Cultural. https://correocultural.com/2015/11/musica-para-la-reconciliacion-un-compromiso-con-las-victimas-del-conflicto-armado-y-en-situacion-de-vulnerabilidad.

Fundación Nacional Batuta. (2024). *Música para la reconciliación: una experiencia del Centro Musical Lisboa como apuesta de construcción de paz en Bogotá.* https://fundacionbatuta.org/musica-para-la-reconciliacion-una-experiencia-del-centro-musical-lisboa-como-apuesta-de-construccion-de-paz-en-bogota.

García, G. A. (2010). Trayectoria del paramilitarismo tras los acuerdos de paz. En G. A. Aguirre (ed.) *Trayectoria del paramilitarismo tras los acuerdos de paz* (pp.18–19). Corporación Conciudadanía.

Gómez, J. H. (2015). *La musicoterapia en procesos de resignificación de la autoconfianza en personas mayores víctimas del conflicto armado en Colombia* (Tesis de maestría). Universidad Nacional de Colombia.

Gómez Montoya, C. A. (2015). *La incorporación del ritual del pagamento en una intervención de musicoterapia, para contribuir a la calidad de vida del grupo de jóvenes desplazados de la fundación Arte Sin Fronteras del municipio de Soacha* (Tesis de maestría). Universidad Nacional de Colombia.

Indepaz. (2013). *El Caguán: Un proceso de paz en Colombia* (Documento PDF). www.indepaz.org.co/wp-content/uploads/2013/04/El_Caguan.pdf.

Internal Displacement Monitoring Centre. (2022). *Global report on internal displacement 2022.* https://api.internal-displacement.org/sites/default/files/IDMC_GRID_Report_2022_ES_LowRes.pdf.

Jurisdicción Especial para la Paz. (2016). Acuerdo final para la terminación del conflicto y la construcción de una paz estable y duradera. www.jep.gov.co/Marco%20Normativo/Normativa_v2/01%20ACUERDOS/Texto-Nuevo-Acuerdo-Final.pdf?csf=1&e=0fpYA0.

Luna, C. B., Güiza, D. A., Urrea, N. E., & Salgado Vasco, A. F. (2020). Community Music Therapy for Constructing Social Cohesion in the Post-Conflict Process. In B. Hesser & B. L. Bartleet (eds) *Music as a Global Resource: Solutions for Cultural, Social, Health, Educational, Environmental, and Economic Issues Compendium* (fifth edition, p.205). New York, NY: Music as a Global Resource.

Luna, C. B. & Salgado Vasco, A. F. (2023). Desarrollo de la musicoterapia en Colombia. Nacimiento y evolución. En V. A. Cannarozzo & V. Díaz Abrahan (eds) *Desarrollos disciplinares de la musicoterapia. Construyendo redes desde y hacia el Sur* (pp.19–29). Universidad Nacional de La Plata.

Martínez Durán, L. A. (2019). *Musicando el conuco. Musicoterapia comunitaria para el empoderamiento de comunidad jitnu víctima del conflicto armado* (Tesis de maestría). Universidad Nacional de Colombia.

Moreno, J. (1995). Ethnomusic therapy: An interdisciplinary approach to music and healing. *The Arts in Psychotherapy*, 22(4), 329–338.

Pavlicevic, M. & Ansdell, G. (2004). *Community Music Therapy*. London: Jessica Kingsley Publishers.

Programa de las Naciones Unidas para el Desarrollo. (2010). Arte y deporte para la vida. *Hechos Del Callejón*, 56(15).

Red. (1998). *Red de escuelas de música de Medellín*. https://redmusicamedellin.org.

Registro Único de Víctimas. (2024). Víctimas por hecho victimizante – Fecha corte 31/05/2024. www.unidadvictimas.gov.co/es/registro-unico-de-victimas-ruv.

Ruiz, N. Y. (2011). El desplazamiento forzado en Colombia: Una revisión histórica y demográfica. *Estudios Demográficos y Urbanos*, 26(1), 141–177.

Ruiz Fandiño, S. M. (2019). *Musicoterapia comunitaria en la construcción de la identidad en adolescentes desplazados del conflicto armado, en su actual contexto, en el Colegio Benposta de Cundinamarca* (Tesis de maestría). Universidad Nacional de Colombia.

Ruud, E. (1998). *Music Therapy: Improvisation, Communication and Culture*. Gilsum, NH: Barcelona Publishers.

Salgado Vasco, A. F. (2015). *Programa piloto de musicoterapia como herramienta para favorecer el afrontamiento de situaciones difíciles en función del proyecto de vida de adolescentes víctimas del conflicto armado colombiano* (Tesis de maestría). Universidad Nacional de Colombia.

Salgado Vasco, A. F. & Güiza, D. A. (2018). *Musicoterapia comunitaria en Colombia*. In Cantare.

Stige, B. (2002) *Culture Centred Music Therapy*. Dallas, TX.: Barcelona Books.

Turner, V. (1969). *El proceso ritual*. Taurus.

SECTION 3

CO-CREATING CULTURAL CONNECTIONS

CHAPTER 10

The Songwriters' Democracy

DANNY D. KORA

SETTING THE SCENE

As all authors in this publication will agree, the displacement of any population from their homeland is difficult. Challenges can include finding short-/long-term shelter and work; integrating with the local population's language and culture; managing the impact of past and present situations on mental health; helping children to adapt to the new environment and school system; dealing with bias from the host population; and rebuilding a life with positive prospects. While there are many possible reasons for mass displacement, I will focus here primarily on migration due to war and armed conflict, particularly regarding Syrians who fled to Türkiye (formerly known as Turkey) from war in Syria (Güney *et al.*, 2018; Kora, 2023) and Rohingyas who fled to Bangladesh from armed conflict in Myanmar (Güney & Lundmark, 2019).

I will explore the process of cross-cultural communication and songwriting in music therapy. This is based on my experiences working as a music therapist through a range of projects involving forced migration across Asia and Europe. These programmes were designed by multidisciplinary teams of creative arts therapists, who co-developed programmes for both participants and interdisciplinary support teams. Using approaches that utilized humanistic, person-centred, existential, cognitive behavioural, and developmental methodologies, they worked to build a sense of hope for those who participated in the projects through arts-inspired coping mechanisms using evidence-based methods.

I will reflect on the use of music therapy alongside other creative arts therapies such as dance movement and visual art. My experience is that when multimodal approaches are used to manage challenges displaced persons may face, they can support developing skills in being expressive, they can harness inspiration and may bring about a sense of hope. The educational value of such programmes is explored as well, along with the creative use of songwriting activities to engage group members through group discussion and decision-making.

Regarding my own background, in 2007 I graduated with a Bachelor's degree in Music Therapy from Berklee College of Music, choosing to then move to Türkiye in 2008 after completing my music therapy internship. Having been born and raised mostly in Los Angeles, I was excited to be closer to my mother's side of the family and was intrigued to learn more about my family roots and Turkish culture. I also saw an opportunity to utilize and promote my music therapy skills in a place that had the potential for growth within the field of music therapy.

THE PROJECTS

In 2014, I was invited to join a project involving Syrian refugees in Istanbul. This took place when there were several million Syrians who had escaped the war and fled to cities around Türkiye. As mentioned earlier, they faced many challenges trying to create new lives and integrate with the host community. The vision for our project was to design a programme comprised of elements from dance movement therapy, art therapy, and music therapy to provide psychosocial support for Syrian children living in Türkiye. The programme found broad support, and the organization put together a team of volunteers and translators while securing a space for activities. Along with the other creative arts therapists, we implemented three iterations of the project, which formed the bedrock for a series of other related programmes that have helped many Syrian refugee children across Türkiye over the years.

In 2018, we implemented a second project led by a small team including the same dance movement therapist (who would later become my wife), myself, and a visual storyteller to provide psychosocial support for training staff and Rohingya participants living in Bangladesh. The project included a Trainer of Trainers (ToT) programme to teach local staff techniques to utilize creative arts methodologies. These staff then applied these methodologies with the support of supervision offered by me and the other trainers in the project. The ToT model typically first places participants in a training role, observing and learning from an experienced trainer, before practising the techniques in the field with supervision from the trainers. An advantage to this approach is that the same skills are shared and delivered to an ever-widening group of trainers, increasing the capacity for the delivery of the work. Our training programme took place in the city of Cox's Bazar, while the practice programme was held inside what was then the world's largest refugee camp, Kutupalong, just outside the city.

A third project I was involved in took place in Germany between 2016 and 2018. It involved a large group of people from a range of different professions and fields, all working to support refugees settling into societies throughout Europe and beyond. The team was divided into subgroups, according to the interests and skills of individual members, with each group tasked with devising their own goals and outcomes. Each group might, for example, create a game or an activity, with the aim of furthering the integration of refugees into their host cities. These educational tools and outcomes were then distributed across a range of countries that partnered with the project, with translations of materials into Turkish, English, German, Arabic, and more.

Overall, each of these projects gave me important insights regarding the challenges and potential solutions for working with people who have been displaced. They also demonstrated how powerful a multifaceted and interdisciplinary approach could be in supporting the psychosocial needs of a population facing many challenges. Within my own approach, I utilized songwriting techniques. These were highly effective in facilitating group discussion and allowing participants to experience a goal-oriented process of producing a song together. They also appeared to help participants develop coping mechanisms for dealing with trauma, by encouraging socialization and discussion with their peers.

RESILIENCE AND COPING AFTER TRAUMATIC EVENTS

I learned throughout these projects how many of the participants had experienced horrific incidents, such as losing friends or family members during the conflict in their home countries. Some had been physically wounded or sexually assaulted, and others told of how they had had to run for their lives. While facilitating groups, I became aware that some participants displayed symptoms of post-traumatic stress disorder (PTSD), including signs of hyperarousal and hypoarousal. Several participants indicated feelings of negative self-worth, reported experiencing nightmares, and demonstrated dissociation and/or strong emotional outbursts, all of which the American Psychiatric Association (APA) (2013) regards as symptoms of PTSD. On average, for every 15 participants in a group, at least three or four participants showed symptoms of PTSD. This also meant that about two-thirds of the participants did not exhibit overt signs of trauma. A study by Fino *et al.* (2020) notes that encouraging the development of coping strategies in such situations results in a better response to symptoms of PTSD. Another study by Veronese *et al.* (2021) notes that 'Syrian children who successfully maintained good social competence and functioning were associated with membership of the high resilience cohort' (p.2582). These findings support the use of social activities such as group music-making and songwriting to build on strengths and increase resilience.

CROSSING THE CULTURAL BRIDGE: MUSIC, DANCE, AND ART

We noticed through the projects that people had different preferences as to how they engaged with the creative arts. Some were more interested in music, some in art, and some in dance. In the context of our projects, many participants found themselves favouring certain disciplines, with some reporting it was the first time they had ever played an instrument, danced, or drawn pictures. Thus, music, dance, and art therapies not only provided multiple avenues for expression but were also educational in their content, offering opportunities for learning new things. Participants were able to explore different possibilities, be inspired, and make choices. Windows into other worlds were opened through engagement in the creative arts.

It is my experience that music has a universal quality which allows it to be internationally recognized. This trait is not found in music alone, for where there is music, there is dance. And where there is dance, there is form, motion, and movement. The same can be said of visual art, of course, with colour and imagery being aspects of this. These three mediums offer powerful ways to express thoughts and feelings for people throughout the world. We felt that it seemed only natural that these same methods be used to offer a bridge between people of different languages and cultures. We wondered if, considering the challenging circumstances experienced by people who have been displaced, the creative arts also offered a healthy outlet for difficult thoughts and emotions and could ignite one of the most powerful feelings in the world: hope.

THE POWER OF SONGS IN MY LIFE

On a personal note, I have been writing and recording my own songs since I was a teenager. Doing so helped me overcome much of the adversity I faced early in my life. It felt so good to write down my thoughts, to mould them into poetic phrases, to link those words with notes and fit them into rhythmic locks. The words didn't have to be true; I had the freedom to fly on paper, to create with no bounds, to express my inner world to the outside and revel in my creations. At that time, I had bought a little four-track cassette recorder, and that was where I began painting my sonic canvas. It was at that point I also learned how powerful it was to listen back to the songs I had created. No matter the mood I was in, the act of listening to my own creation was something like magic, and it helped me deal with the problems in my life. I'll spare the details about my strife, but there were multiple significant challenges I had to face growing up, the combination of which I now understand made me an extra unique person in the world. I once had two different psychologists tell me that my experiences made me an interesting 'case study'. How fantastic.

Once I had graduated with my music therapy degree in 2007 and moved back to Türkiye, I began working with kids and adults using songwriting in groups. It was at this point that I began to hone my own group songwriting techniques.

CONNECTING WITH MUSIC: MY VISION
FOR A DEMOCRACY OF SONGWRITERS

There is a common misconception that songs can only be written by people who have a talent for music or poetry. I believe this is not true and is a rather restrictive perspective which ignores the combined power of creativity and inspiration. Examples of spontaneous music-making abound: a mother making up a song for her child; a man whistling an idea from the top of his head at work; a teenager creating words to an existing melody to help them remember the periodic table. These are but a few examples where the power of songwriting can take place in daily life. During these moments, each person became a songwriter when inspiration came knocking.

On the other hand, writing a song with the aim that it should be sung more than once could take a lot of time, with multiple edits back and forth in search of the 'perfect' lyric. I found that during a group songwriting exercise, participants' ideas and needs could complicate or enrich the process, sometimes making it difficult to build and play an originally composed song together. I also had to consider time constraints; with sessions finite and limited in scope, it helped to have a streamlined approach. I began to realize that there was a raft of decisions to be made from beginning to end. For instance: would the song have words? If so, what would the words be about? Would there be a rhyming scheme to the words, and if so, what would the scheme be? Was explicit language appropriate for the song? Was there a common theme linking the words together? What language(s) should the words be in? What instruments, if any, would be used? Should the song be in a major or a minor key? Which chords would support the melody? Should the tempo of the song be fast, slow, or medium? What meter would the song be in?

As a musician, I was aware of the myriad options available during the songwriting process. However, participants often had little or no experience with music. I came to realize that it was my role as a facilitator to light the way but let them walk the journey (Kora, 2023). I believe that songwriting with a group should involve a democratic process. This meant that I encouraged group members to gather ideas and then slowly sift through, making choices together. This meant that it was ideas collectively chosen by the group that were included in the song. I hoped to encourage group participants to be open to creative interpretations. I felt that there were therapeutic benefits from participants listening to each other's stories, feeling heard and mixing and matching different ideas together. We seldom used every contribution from group members. Facilitating the group process to keep only what they found valuable resulted in not only better communication between group members, but eventually a better, more memorable song. By building a discussion about what worked and what did not, group members were able to communicate together and ultimately decide the final form of the song.

While language may not matter so much when improvising music instrumentally, it felt more important when discussing how to build a song with others in each group. It was further complicated by language differences, which in the case of working with displaced persons was a reality. In each of our projects, it was necessary to have translators involved to facilitate effective communication. The translators in our sessions were a valuable part of the process, allowing for greater verbal expression and understanding from both sides. They were asked to provide transparent translations while remaining as neutral in presence as possible. They played a critical role in bridging communication between the participants and the team members in all our projects. They helped me to build a productive and thoughtful atmosphere, as outlined in the vignette below.

A VIGNETTE OF A SONGWRITER'S DEMOCRACY

The following is what a typical songwriting session of mine looked like.

A group of participants entered a room. Through a translator, I asked them to sit in chairs, and led them through a series of short physical and vocal warm-up activities. This helped not only to get their body systems moving and vocals ready, but also synchronized the group and began a process for increasing comfort with the idea of expressing themselves within the group. A brainstorming session was then initiated, with ideas written on a board in three columns: the original word in their native language; the same word but with phonetic spelling; and an English translation of the word. As the song was ultimately to be written in the participants' native language, the phonetic spelling was key to helping me aid in the making of the song. It should be noted that multiple participants throughout my sessions could not read or write, so the very act of writing things on a board was intellectually and emotionally evocative, demonstrating the power of writing as a tool to share and ruminate on our individual ideas together as a group.

When all the words were voiced (which was dictated either by time constraints or made as a decision by the group, whichever was shorter), we then moved on to the next phase – piecing the words into meaningful phrases. To keep the creative path 'clear', I reminded participants they could add words to their phrases if needed, which were not found on the board. Depending on time limits, the previous three-column writing procedure was reduced to two or even one column, with translated words being first to be deleted, followed by the phonetic spellings if necessary. It was more important that the translator read back phrases to the group, rather than I understand or be able to say any of the phrases at this particular stage in the songwriting process.

Once all the phrasing ideas were complete, then came the pruning and organizing phase. It was at this point that I explained to participants that not all the words and phrases they had contributed would be included in the song; rather, the group would vote on each phrase, and the top phrases would then be organized into a meaningful form that would eventually make up the lyrics of the song. This was a great way to put forward only the favourite collectively chosen ideas, as group members raised their hands after each phrase was read aloud by the translator, with the number of votes each phrase received written down. The group then discussed the appropriate order for the top choices, after I advised them to keep the most powerful phrasing for the chorus.

With the lyrics almost fully set, it was time to begin turning the lyrics into a song. When preparing to work with any population, I tried to make myself familiar with each group's cultural musical style. For example, Syrian music has common elements with Turkish music, such as complex rhythms with percussive instruments like the darbuka and stringed instruments like the oud. Rohingya music places less emphasis on rhythmic complexity, focusing more on the storytelling and melodic aspects of songs, often using a mandolin-style instrument to convey intricate melodic sequences influenced by Arabic, Urdu, Hindi, and Bangla music. I also had at least one group who chose to use more contemporary styles like rock and hip-hop.

It was at this point that I asked for a phonetic spelling of the lyrics to be written, so I could begin using my music skills to guide the group. When I started singing the words in their native language, there were smiles from participants as I did my best to pronounce everything correctly. I asked them for any rhythmic or melodic ideas they had and worked to explore them with the group, with proposals being rejected or accepted through collective agreement.

Eventually, after making any small tweaks necessary, the song was finally finished! With the time remaining, we sang the song at least a couple of times. Participants sang the lyrics together, while I supported them musically, often using my guitar but being flexible to include other instruments if necessary and possible. Some also joined in with instruments and vocal improvisations, building on what they had collectively created. This was the crescendo, the reward for all their effort, patience, and perseverance. We savoured the moment.

If it was appropriate and permitted in these sessions, we could also make an audio recording so the song could be saved and replayed by participants when needed, as a reminder of the creative process. As the session was wrapping up, I opened a short discussion on their thoughts and feelings regarding the songwriting activity. One participant expressed surprise at what we had done, while another said they felt proud about their creation. After we said goodbye, I could hear some participants singing the song to themselves as they left the room.

CLOSING THOUGHTS

I have used this songwriting method countless times with different populations of all ages and backgrounds over the years. I call this the Songwriters' Democracy Method (SDM). There has always remained a consistent flow to the process. During the brainstorming period, there is a lack of coalescence. As the lonely words on the board slowly develop into phrases, the ideas become increasingly tangible, but are still not solidly defined until the very end, when the melody, rhythm, and lyrics finally come together. Participants appear to similarly begin the sessions as several individual pieces, and end by becoming a shared structure. This method can be applied for a wide range of groups in both educational and therapeutic settings, and perhaps most significantly, across cultural and linguistic differences.

I believe that the act of songwriting itself and the SDM offer a way to provide the structure and support that groups of displaced persons may need to be creative. Songwriting can offer safe structures within which participants can share, explore, and develop ways of managing their traumatic life experiences. Providing projects and opportunities such as these is of vital importance to displaced persons worldwide.

REFERENCES

American Psychiatric Association. (2013). *Diagnostic and Statistical Manual of Mental Disorders. Fifth Edition*. Washington, DC: American Psychiatric Association.

Fino, E., Mema, D., & Russo, P. M. (2020). War trauma exposed refugees and posttraumatic stress disorder: The moderating role of trait resilience. *Journal of Psychosomatic Research*, 129, 109905. https://doi.org/10.1016/j.jpsychores.2019.109905.

Güney, S. S., Atik, L. A., & Lundmark, D. S. (2018). Holding Hope: Rehabilitation of Syrian Refugee Children through Art, Music and Dance Movement Therapy. In T. Colbeand & C. Bent (eds) *Working Across Modalities in the Arts Therapies: Creative Collaborations* (pp.95–108). London: Routledge.

Güney, S. S. & Lundmark, D. S. (2019). Dance Movement Therapy for Social Change: Working with Syrian and Rohingya Asylum Seekers. In I. A. Serlin, S. Krippner, & K. Rockefeller (eds) *Integrated Care for the Traumatized: A Whole-Person Approach* (pp.59–71). Lanham, MD: Rowman and Littlefield.

Kora, D. D. (2023). Songwriting with a Group of Syrian Refugee Children in a Multi Disciplinary Creative Arts Therapy Program in Turkey. In A. Heiderscheit & N. Jackson (eds) *Clinical Decision-Making in Music Therapy* (pp.43–57). Glen Rock, PA: Barcelona Publishers.

Veronese, G., Pepe, A., & Giordan, F. (2021). Child psychological adjustment to war and displacement: A discriminant analysis of resilience and trauma in Syrian refugee children. *Journal of Child and Family Studies*, 30, 2575–2588. https://doi.org/10.1007/s10826-021-02067-2.

Music for Displaced Dyads (M4DD)

A Music Therapy Feasibility Study for Displaced Ukrainian Parents and their Pre-School Children

ELIZABETH COOMBES, LETITIA SLABU, ANTHONY MANGIACOTTI, TAMAR HADAR, AND FABIA FRANCO

This chapter describes and discusses aspects of a music therapy feasibility study, Music for Displaced Dyads (M4DD), for displaced Ukrainian parents and pre-school children undertaken in the Spring of 2023 in London. A feasibility study is a way to find out if a project plan has the potential to be successful as a bigger project. As this was the first project plan where the team was aware of using these measures and protocols, a feasibility study seemed the best way to test the thinking behind the project. The chapter will consider the range of data collected and their relationship to each other, and discuss findings.

The study was a collaboration between Middlesex University and the University of South Wales. It aimed to explore whether music therapy could help Ukrainian parents reduce their own stress and improve bonding with their pre-school children. Group music therapy sessions, each 45 minutes long, were delivered weekly over eight weeks, with two groups receiving the intervention. Of vital importance to the work were the participants who gave of their time not just for sessions, but also to complete the study's measures and interviews and participate in a film. It is such generosity, including insights shared with the team in the qualitative data, which has been invaluable to the study.

THE BACKGROUND

As of November 2024, 6.8 million Ukrainians had fled the ongoing war with Russia, of which over 251,836 entered the UK by 12 November 2024 (UNHCR, 2024). Given Ukraine's introduction of martial law on 24 February 2022, these refugees are mostly women, often mothers. They are frequently exposed to profound and multiple traumas, including war, losses relating to housing and jobs, physical and sexual violence, and long and dangerous journeys. They continue to encounter barriers and hardships even after arriving in the host community. Some of these are due to long waiting periods during asylum processes, language and cultural barriers, poverty, acculturation difficulties, racism, and discrimination. These factors exacerbate the vulnerability of this population as major mental health stressors (Michelis *et al.*, 2024). Evidence identifies a prevalence of elevated risks of general psychological distress and psychiatric disorders among refugees that is alarmingly higher than in age-matched general populations in high-income countries (Fazel *et al.*, 2005). A systematic review suggested that depression and post-traumatic stress disorder (PTSD) affect on average one out of three asylum seekers and refugees (Turrini *et al.*, 2017). There is an established evidence base for a link between refugee caregivers' psychopathology and poor mental health in their children (Eruyar *et al.*, 2017). In fact, studies indicate that maternal trauma, anxiety, depression, and stress experienced in refugee and migration contexts, as well as parent-child separation periods, can impair a child's emotional regulation by increasing their sensitivity to anxiety (Gottman *et al.*, 1997). Being both a parent and a refugee comes with its own set of competing challenges:

- Grappling with one's own mental health issues while understanding the potential impact this may have on one's own children's cognitive and emotional development.

- Endeavouring to support one's own children in adjusting to a new environment while also addressing their mental health concerns.

Several studies have stressed that children with mental health problems are also confronted with lower academic achievement (Deighton *et al.*, 2018), increased risk of psychological problems as an adult, and a substantially reduced income (Smith & Smith, 2010).

There is a growing consensus (Murray *et al.*, 2010) about the need to move beyond the focus on individual-level work by developing interventions tailored not only for the caregivers but also for their children. This could reduce hardships and costs for these two generations simultaneously as well as the hosting society at large. Music-based interventions and music therapy could be a step in this direction. There are, however, few studies that use a mixed methods dataset to explore the impact of this work. Many rely on anecdotal evidence (Coombes, 2018; Orth, 2005). Some music and music therapy studies in other areas of work, however, have provided an evidence base for this topic in music therapy, such as alleviating symptoms of depression (including postpartum) and PTSD and improving mental health in individual refugees (Erkkilä *et al.*, 2011; Fachner *et al.*, 2013; Fancourt & Perkins, 2018a; Fancourt & Perkins, 2018b). Such studies show higher retention rates compared to other standard care (Beck *et al.*, 2021; Rudstam *et al.*, 2017). However, studies that evaluate the benefits of music therapy interventions with refugee families are still scarce (Bernard & Dvorak, 2023; Hettich *et al.*, 2020). M4DD aims to add to the evidence base for this work.

THE M4DD TEAM

The M4DD team consisted of a number of professionals and students as detailed in Table 11.1. Included in the table is a film-maker. To show the impact of the work and to share the project more widely, Tom McGorrian, working with students from Buckinghamshire New University, created a film telling the story of the project prior to any data collection (Middlesex University, 2023). This added an interesting layer to the work and has proved a very important way of sharing the project. Team members and participants were eager to share their experiences of the project during filming, with the film being available on social media platforms as well as being used to disseminate pre-analysis thinking about the work and for teaching in a range of subjects such as music therapy, sociology, and psychology. In addition to this, the range of skills and expertise in the project team has enriched the potential of the study and enabled the team to see multiple aspects of the work, making links between them as the data and themes emerged.

Table 11.1: Project team

Name	Profession	Role
Dr Fabia Franco (Middlesex University)	Music psychologist and developmentalist	Joint principal investigator overseeing all aspects of the study
Dr Letitia Slabu (Middlesex University)	Social psychologist	Joint principal investigator overseeing all aspects of the study
Dr Anthony Mangiacotti (Middlesex University)	Cognitive-neuro psychologist and neuroscientist	Providing support in collecting and analysing quantitative data

Dr Tamara Fedotiuk (Middlesex University)	Psychologist and Council for At-Risk Academics (CARA) Fellow	Providing support and interpretation in groups, conducting interviews
Dr Elizabeth Coombes (University of South Wales)	Music therapist and researcher	Devising the shape of sessions and providing clinical supervision, analysing qualitative data
Dr Tamar Hadar (University of Haifa)	Music therapist and researcher	Interviewing the student music therapist, analysing qualitative data
Ellie Matthews (University of South Wales)	Student music therapist	Leading the music therapy groups
Nidhi and Abigail (University of Middlesex)	Music students	Providing support in music therapy sessions
Dr Tom McGorrian (Buckinghamshire New University)	Film-maker	Creating a film of the project with student film-makers: *Music 4 Displaced Dyads*

M4DD used a mixed methods approach to provide qualitative and quantitative data. The qualitative data, gathered through interviews with the participants and Ellie Matthews, the music therapy student leading the groups, helped build a picture of the constructed reality of their experience. The data from quantitative measures was from an objective standpoint. These two types of evidence were analysed separately and then looked at together to obtain a more pragmatic view of the data and study. Pragmatic approaches recognize that there are many different ways of interpreting human experience and give a sense of how these multiple realities need to be represented in research (Leech, 2014). Using mixed methods in this study offered the opportunity to capture a wide range of data that could lead to findings that could be very important for music therapy and refugee dyads.

Oldfield *et al.* (2019) describe an increasing demand from funding bodies and music therapy service providers for outcome measures being used in music therapy to provide an evidence base for music therapy practice. In the TIME-A Randomised Control Trial (RCT) where the effectiveness of improvisational music therapy for autistic children was explored using mixed methods (Geretsegger *et al.*, 2012), discrepancies were shown between qualitative and quantitative data. The qualitative data was positive in its findings, whereas the numerical data did not show any difference in the study participants' post music therapy intervention. This clash of evidence proved a heavy blow to the leverage that music therapy had always had in working with autistic children. It showed the music therapy community that considerable care needed to be taken when designing research protocols and determining which measures would resonate with the methods and techniques employed by music therapists. In Oldfield *et al.* (2019) the authors remind music therapists that it is important to look at the whole picture of the datasets taken together; it could be that quantitative results alone do not give us the entirety of experience.

The M4DD study team was composed of practitioners and researchers with expertise in quantitative and qualitative data collection and analysis. A purely quantitative data viewpoint assumes that there is 'one truth' and objective reality, while a qualitative position may link to a belief system that all knowledge is constructed through human experience. The team was curious as to whether findings emerging from these datasets would support each other and generate new knowledge at this early stage of the work. In light of the TIME-A study mentioned above, it could be said that the music therapists approached the quantitative measure results with some trepidation; would these resonate with or support the qualitative data, or would there be once more a clash of evidence? It is fair to say that there was some anxiety as well as excitement as the project progressed as to the outcomes that would be found.

THE MUSIC THERAPY GROUPS

The feasibility study tested an eight-week-long music therapy group intervention. Groups took place weekly and lasted 45 minutes, with the student music therapist Ellie receiving clinical supervision from Dr Elizabeth Coombes. The intervention aimed to reduce negative outcomes of displacement due to conflict in the homeland and also provide a supportive community with other mothers who shared experiences of culture and displacement simultaneously in two generations: caregivers and pre-school children. The sample included two groups of five or six dyads of Ukrainian parents. The project aimed to develop a comprehensive and effective music therapy protocol, originally devised by Dr Elizabeth Coombes based on her earlier work with displaced dyads (Coombes, 2018). This methodology was selected due to the positive feedback from previous dyads, with the addition of a Ukrainian children's song to incorporate familiar sounds of home into the sessions.

Each session was meticulously structured to include several key components designed to foster engagement and therapeutic benefits. The sessions began with a greeting song, which set a welcoming tone and helped participants transition into the therapeutic environment. This was followed by a variety of engaging activities, including movement exercises to music, interactive action songs with handheld instruments, improvisation with voice, body movement, and percussion, a song from the participants' native land, and soothing lullabies. Each session concluded with a farewell song, providing closure to the experience and reinforcing positive interactions.

To ensure consistency and stability, the same structure was maintained each week. This predictability was crucial for the dyads, as it provided a stable and reliable framework that enhanced their comfort and engagement.

QUANTITATIVE DATA

A range of measures was used to generate data for this study. These measures focused on PTSD symptoms and aspects of mental health and daily functioning. Each participant completed these, with the respiratory sinus arrhythmia measurements being administered by a trained operator. Table 11.2 gives a list of the measures.

Table 11.2: Quantitative measures

Measures	When administered	How completed	Outcome
Post-traumatic stress disorder checklist (PCL-5, Weathers et al., 2013)	Pre and post intervention	Self-rated	Significant reduction of PTSD symptoms
Patient Health Questionnaire (PHQ-9, Spitzer et al., 1999)	Pre and post intervention	Self-rated	Significant reduction of depression and anxiety symptoms
Generalized anxiety disorder (GAD-7, Spitzer et al., 2006)	Pre and post intervention	Self-rated	Marginally significant reduction in anxiety symptoms
Short Warwick-Edinburgh Wellbeing Scale (SWEMWBS, Stewart-Brown et al., 2009)	Pre and post intervention	Self-rated	Marginally significant improvement in well-being

cont.

Measures	When administered	How completed	Outcome
Respiratory sinus arrhythmia (RSA) measurement	Before the second session and at the seventh session	Administered by a trained operator	Significant improvement in autonomic regulation over time was observed more in parents than in infants

As the RSA aspect of the data showed a significant effect, there is a detailed description of this method here, as many music therapists and others interested in this work may not be aware of RSA measurement. The equipment used provides a way of measuring physiological regulation, something that is important in exploring people's mental health. It focuses on parasympathetic functioning as this reflects emotional reactivity and regulation (Beauchaine, 2015; Berntson *et al.*, 2007; Blandon *et al.*, 2010). Parasympathetic functioning refers to a network of nerves that relaxes the body after periods of stress or danger. A reliable method for studying the regulation of the parasympathetic nervous system is through the analysis of RSA within cardio-respiratory measures. RSA measurement notes cardiac vagal activity, reflecting fluctuations in heart rate throughout the breathing cycle. During inhalation there is acceleration due to sympathetic activity, and deceleration during exhalation due to parasympathetic activity (Berntson *et al.*, 1997; Grossman *et al.*, 1990). Studies have linked higher RSA to increased vagal regulation, promoting social engagement and relaxation in safe environments (Patriquin *et al.*, 2013). Evidence suggests that mothers holding their infants close also exhibit increased RSA in response to tonal music, indicating a potential for co-regulation between mother and infant (Van Puyvelde *et al.*, 2014).

To measure RSA, the operator collected three-minute resting-state electrocardiogram (ECG) and respiration measurements before and after the second (T0) and seventh (T1) music therapy sessions to understand whether the activities could lead to short-term changes in parasympathetic activity. These were chosen to avoid meaningful sessions corresponding to the establishment of the therapeutic relationship (i.e. session one), and the ending of the therapy group (i.e. session eight). ECG and respiration measures were obtained using the portable BioRadio™ system (Cleveland Medical Devices, Inc., OH). For both parents and children, the positive electrode was placed on the lower left side of the chest while the negative one was on the upper right side. A grounding electrode was placed on the upper left side of the parent's chest. Both caregiver and child were tested at the same time and were asked to relax and to remain as still as possible. RSA values were processed, as detailed in Van Puyvelde *et al.* (2014). Before further discussing these findings, some aspects of the qualitative data analysis will be shared. It is important to note that there was a significant and strong effect size in these measurements, although it should be considered that the sample size was small (N=11 parents). Nevertheless, this was an exciting piece of evidence to uncover and, linked with the improvements as outlined in Table 11.2, showed that the music therapy groups appeared to have important effects on participants.

QUALITATIVE DATA

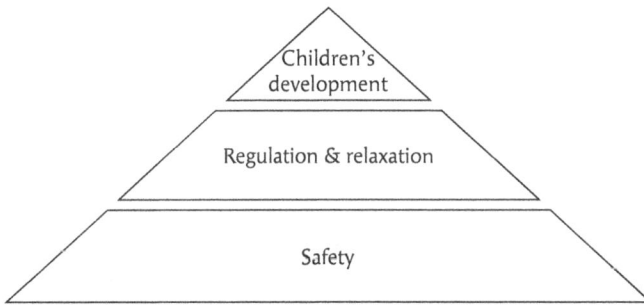

Figure 11.1: A layered musical process

All parents were interviewed at the end of the project in their native language by the Ukrainian psychologist, Tamara. Interviews were recorded, transcribed, translated into English, and thematically analysed with a range of emerging themes (Braun & Clarke, 2022). Subsequently, the music therapist Ellie was also interviewed about her experience, and some of her experiences have been added to this data to show links between her thoughts and those of the participants. Due to the vast amount of data generated, the team has selected a few relevant main themes that emerged for the writing of this chapter. The interviews with the parents and Ellie revealed several themes and subthemes that shed light on their experiences as individuals and as an evolving community. The analysis emphasized parents' feelings of safety and belonging on the one hand and the children's social, emotional, and verbal development on the other hand. In addition, the analysis revealed a layered process, demonstrating the interconnection and dependence of one theme on another. It became evident that once the music therapy groups were established as a safe place for families, they could use the group as a source of relaxation and regulation, to foster community building, and support children's development (see Figure 11.1). Each layer of this model is expanded on below, with quotes provided to support these claims. Additionally, there is an exploration of how the musical environment facilitated the group's process. It is notable throughout this section how the information obtained from Ellie's analysis complemented the participants' interviews, emphasizing the close relationship formed between the group facilitator and the participants.

Safety, structure, and regulation

The interviews showed that the music therapy sessions acted as a safe haven for parents, allowing them to shift from the reality of war towards being able to adapt to a new country. Several parents described how relocating to London created for them a sense of safety and helped them to loosen up a little after being extremely anxious for a long period of time. As one parent explained, an indicator of them being less stressed relates to their reduced reaction to traumatic triggers:

> 'I feel secure and comfortable in London. It's a truly pleasant city. Since relocating, my mental state has become less strained. I used to be on edge at the slightest sound. Interestingly, on one occasion, we were heading home and there was an explosion – a child burst a balloon – and I didn't react at all.'

As the music therapy sessions became a safe space, they also contributed to the regulation and stability of both parents and infants. This was also reflected in Ellie's interview:

> 'The group was a designated time which they felt was different from sitting in a cafe or sitting outside somewhere. Their whole being was kind of tuned into this. Yeah, a safe zone and also an intimate place.'

The parents highlighted how the music sessions became a safe refuge for the family, often linked to their own and their child's increased sense of regulation. Importantly, all parents highlighted the regulating and relaxing aspects of the group:

> 'Music therapy became a refuge here. A place that was convenient and comfortable. My boy and I enjoyed attending it.'

> 'From the second or third lesson, I thought: "Oh! Cool!" We already knew what to expect, what we would do. When the brain knows what to expect, even in an adult, then you are in the comfort zone and there is no danger.'

'At the moment, at the end of music therapy, I feel much better, optimistic. My anxiety has decreased, my fears have disappeared.'

'With the beginning of the war, the brain was tuned to other stimuli. I came and mentally rested. And I left after classes with pleasant feelings.'

'But then it's as if you come to some mini-family and you can just relax there, not think about anything, somehow relax morally and psychologically... Perhaps the most surprising thing is that it is such a relaxed form.'

This theme was also emphasized by Ellie, who explained how the group's structure was carefully designed in order to model modes of regulation for the dyads. This can be seen in the short description of the group structure.

'So the way it was structured was that, obviously, we had the Hello song. And then we did movement that was kind of encouraging them to be a bit more energetic to really engage with each other physically and musically, through a familiar song, just to ease them into the session. And then we did a musical improvisation. And then we did a lullaby. It was a really nice way of structuring the sessions because it facilitated that emotional regulation.'

The important role of allowing a safe and predictable space for the therapy to take place was affirmed when an unplanned change of setting brought up anxiety and disturbance among group members, especially the children, as elucidated by Ellie:

'I think the biggest challenge in parts was some limitations we had in terms of the actual space. So there were a couple of times when we had to move to different rooms. They had to move us and probably didn't realize the impact this would have on the group. But it really affected the children as we went into this room. The walls were red, no windows, no seats to sit on. It was so dark, really. And that was really hard. Everyone became a little bit unsettled and a little bit destabilized.'

A group evolution – from parents' hesitance to cohesion and independence, and towards becoming a community

Ellie's interview described the parents' initial struggle to join the group and freely participate in the activities:

'It potentially felt like a kind of mother-baby group to start with in terms of experience. It was very much, we're gonna sit back and watch the kids play with the music. [Later on], the parents definitely became a lot more involved with physically playing.'

Ellie shared how she focused on allowing a slow, gentle, and attuned process with the parents, one that would allow them to gradually bring their war-induced guards down.

> 'I think taking the approach of allowing them to come into the group and to come into the playing, as opposed to being really encouraging to them, actually served a really good purpose... They're not sure. Are they allowed to do this? Is this okay? They didn't necessarily feel overly comfortable with letting their child just do whatever. But it was that real, gentle approach. I think that really helped.'

In response to Ellie's attentive introduction to the music therapy, in their interviews parents emphasized her attuned and personal approach towards the families' emotional states and needs:

> 'And during MT, I saw that maybe due to the fact that everything is happening all the time, it is safe, that everyone enveloped you in love...all this had an effect on calming down. It's nice that they pay attention to you and your feelings.'

> 'Everything was directed towards us personally. Usually, when you come with a child, you are given tasks, but no one even cares what your name is and what the child's name is. And you come with your mother and leave with your mother, and no one cares what you are and how you are.'

Consequently, as observed by Ellie, the parents and children started pacing their way towards being more active in the sessions:

> 'It was really nice to see this kind of progression of really not necessarily sitting in the process but leading it. It kind of felt as if I was pulling them along, maybe, or indicating this is what we're doing now, this is what we're doing next. Very directive and constantly informing and encouraging. Towards the end of the therapy...the anticipation of "oh, we've got this next" and the children would start getting the next toys and they would know, have a... sense of ownership and leadership... I could hear them singing one of the songs as they were coming up to the session.'

According to Ellie, being more active in the sessions enhanced the level of communication and interaction in the group, between the group members as well as between participants and herself:

> 'There was a lot more musical communication between the dyads towards the end than there was at the beginning. There was a lot more eye contact between myself and the parents towards the end.'

This ultimately increased the level of communication and participation among the group members, and it enabled the parents to have a shared experience of fluidity and group cohesion. According to Ellie:

> 'It also encouraged them potentially to experience that as a group as well. It created some kind of sense of fluidity. Some children would sit on their mum's lap kind of hiding, others would run around the room. You know, there was a lot going on.'

Feelings of belonging and shared experiences were also highlighted by the parents, who marked the significance of meeting others who shared the same language and life circumstances, and had children the same age as theirs:

> 'The group played a part in this as well, as I engaged with fellow Ukrainians who had children of the same age.'

> 'Attending the group has been beneficial for me both in terms of social interaction and as a way to distract myself: keeping occupied with something.'

The group's influence on children's play, development, and sense of empathy

All parents highlighted how the music therapy group acted as an agent of change inside and outside sessions, in several developmental domains. One prominent aspect mentioned by parents was language development:

> 'He has already started speaking. Maybe music therapy has sped up the language. I remember that when we started the project, he did not speak. And now he speaks two to three words. He was not two years old. And only two months have passed.'

> 'When she now hears the sounds of music and the rustling of instruments, like there were rattle eggs for the song "Shake Shake", she reacts. And this is thanks to music therapy.'

Moreover, it seems that the children's social skills developed due to the music therapy sessions and these skills were revealed either in the group, at home, or generally, as mentioned by both the parents and the instructor:

> 'He learned how to work more together with his mother. He has more persistence. To sit with his mother and play. Before, he had no interest in that. He could play for two or three seconds and that was it. He wants me to sit down with him and play with him.'

> 'She started sharing toys with pleasure. And she likes it. This was not the

case before. Because she usually doesn't share toys. And now she has begun to share with other children on the street.'

Ellie emphasized children's development of togetherness and empathy when recalling one specific incident:

'It was a really, really sweet moment in that, you know, this one child who was very intense to start with, and wasn't really overly aware or mindful of the other children's responses to him, was playing with them. They were establishing friendships and relationships.'

Music as a central agent for change

All parents discussed the qualities of the musical experiences and their contribution to the safe and enabling environment created in the group. One central aspect raised by parents relates to the music being played live in the sessions, enhancing relaxation and parents' attentiveness.

'I enjoyed live music. Live music has a very good effect on a person. Now I'm talking about it and tears are coming to my eyes. Because it is very touching.'

'Live music is very important.'

'It is live music that causes such relaxation. The music playing in the column [referring to the wifi speaker] does not have such an effect. I think it was the live music that switched me on.'

Several participants mentioned Ellie's guitar as enabling a more intimate relationship with the music as well as the importance of engaging with 'real' musical instruments:

'He fell in love with the guitar there. Of all the musical instruments, he chose the guitar.'

'I liked that it was played on a real instrument, that Ellie played the guitar.'

Relating to the theme of regulation and predictability, it seems that the greeting and goodbye songs were very important to the group, as well as additional elements emphasizing routine and familiarity:

'I really like the welcome song. It is very touching for me. More than other songs. Here is a song that was specifically addressed to every mother and child, and when our names were called, it was very emotional.'

'Greetings and farewells, at first he was happy, and when they said goodbye, he was sad. Well, it's a ritual, probably.'

Connected to the emerging theme of parents learning to take authority and leadership in the group, it seems that Ellie's improvisatory approach contributed to the parents' sense of agency:

'In Ukraine, we had a slightly different method of working with children. And on a practical level, maybe subconsciously, I thought that it would be the same. In Ukraine we do not give time for improvisation. We interact with children according to our script. And for me, probably, this moment was a positive surprise.'

As the group evolved, parents wished to expand their musical journeys into their home environments, adding musical instruments and singing to their new homes:

'I even made a homemade shaker at home and the children play with it.'

'It seems to me that after those classes he wanted to listen to music more. We even bought him some small rattles – maracas. He showed more interest in music at home. It was also interesting for him to play with musical instruments at home.'

'I'm thinking about buying different musical instruments for my home, and to conduct such sessions at least once a week at home, to play and involve the children in music.'

'When we go to bed in the evening, my middle son sings, dances, shows various things he did in the choir. So now A has started joining these performances and the two of them are already showing, singing, and dancing. A feels freer musically.'

This also supported parents in incorporating singing into their daily routines as a means for communication, organization, and responding to their children's needs:

'You can say "go to bed" or "go brush your teeth", or you can sing it. I went up in the morning and started singing to them "Hello, V", the song that the teacher sang to us when she greeted us: "Hello, V! Nice to see you." I started singing this song to them and they started to stand up. And they began to get up with pleasure, smiling, joyful.'

'I liked that I could see how my child was feeling and how he was reacting.'

DISCUSSION

The preliminary quantitative findings of the feasibility study demonstrate statistically significant improvements on several mental health outcomes such as post-traumatic stress disorder, depression, anxiety, and well-being in displaced caregivers. Additionally, the RSA findings show that the music therapy intervention study exerted a parasympathetic influence. This is particularly noteworthy, given that existing studies have demonstrated the beneficial effects of music therapy on decreasing the levels of anxiety and depression in different clinical contexts (Ribeiro *et al.*, 2018) as well as mothers undergoing Caesarean sections (Weingarten *et al.*, 2021) or with preterm infants in neonatal intensive care units (Ribeiro *et al.*, 2018). Crucially, the current feasibility study, supported by mixed methods data, is the first to show the benefits of a music therapy intervention on mental health outcomes for refugee caregivers, according to the team's understanding.

PTSD, depression, and anxiety are chronic disorders challenging to treat through pharmacological means alone. Using medication can generate a range of side effects and often leads to long-term treatments. However, music therapy is increasingly recognized as a valid means of treatment of these particular mental health disorders as referenced above. It often has lower attrition rates compared to traditional pharmacological/individual treatments, with some theory of change research showing that aspects of music therapy work, such as the therapeutic relationship, creativity, and trying new things, are core aspects of this intervention that those who access it find very supportive (De Witte *et al.*, 2021).

Arnon *et al.* (2006) and Standley (2012) have documented the calming effects of music on preterm infants, and as an extension, our music therapy sessions may have similarly contributed to the observed decrease in stress level over time, consequently impacting the RSA values. This links to parents telling us that the music therapy groups were a safe space, where dyads felt at ease and relaxed. They were able to focus on their child, feeling that Ellie was able to provide a safe space where they could really explore music with their child and be together. This is clearly an important finding in this study.

Moreover, the study by Van Puyvelde and colleagues (2014) provides valuable insights into the potential mechanisms underlying the observed improvement in RSA values. Their findings suggest that music with qualities reminiscent of mother-infant vocal interactions can elicit positive physiological responses in both mothers and infants, fostering co-regulation. Given the nature of our music therapy sessions, which aimed to replicate these intimate vocal interactions as part of the session, it is plausible that the increased RSA levels observed among parents holding their infants close during the sessions reflect enhanced co-regulation between parent and child. Elevated RSA is also linked to favourable behavioural reactivity, suggesting a correlation between appropriate vagal regulation and behaviour and emotion regulation (Doussard-Roosevelt *et al.*, 2003). These results can potentially be explained by the multifaceted nature of the music therapy activities: listening to music (Schäfer & Sedlmeier, 2010; Van Puyvelde *et al.*, 2014), singing play-songs and lullabies (Kostilainen *et al.*, 2021), and play-ing instruments, in conjunction with the affect-matching hypothesis. This latter posits that cognitive benefits occur when the perceived emotional expression of the music and the listener's affective state match (Franco *et al.*, 2014). From our RSA results, it seems that the music therapy protocol utilized in this study exerts a parasympathetic influence that may reflect a relaxation phenomenon in participants' bodies (Patriquin *et al.*, 2013).

What was not explored in the quantitative data were aspects of the children's development, nor of their families beginning to see the benefits of music in the home and more generally in their lives. It would be possi-ble for this to be explored in a range of child development measures and potentially Politimou *et al.*'s (2018) Music@Home. This might seem rele-vant considering the participants reporting using music-related activities at home. It would also be valuable to investigate whether the use of music activities at home was sustained even after the music therapy sessions, and how this continued to affect the social, emotional, and developmental aspects of the families' lives.

Having completed this study, the team's next step is to produce rec-ommendations for a viable intervention scalable to a larger diverse refugee population, with the aim of identifying key contributors to the improve-ment of mental health, cognitive functioning, and parenting. These rec-ommendations would ultimately be used in a fully developed RCT testing the transformational impact of music therapy in contexts of displacement and integration in different countries, with culturally informed adaptations.

CONCLUSION

The wide range of data collected provides an interesting picture in which links between datasets can be made. The RSA data appears to align with what participants shared in interviews with the research team about their experiences with music therapy. This was of huge interest and significance to the team. They described it as a safe place where they could relax and experience a different kind of time with their child. The impact of the work on the participants can be seen not only in the qualitative data analysis, but also in the film created alongside the project. Interviews with mothers show how they felt at ease, accepted, and able to engage freely in the music therapy. Aspects of the development of children in terms of social, verbal, and emotional domains were unanticipated, but were very exciting to witness and experience in the work. It may be that a future iteration of the work would consider these aspects also and find a way of exploring them.

As of mid-2024, the team is running a scaled-up version of the project – Music Therapy for Displaced Dyads East and West. This study has recruited Ukrainian and Afghan dyads to try to understand, through co-production of the music therapy protocol and broader set of measures, if any adjustments to the study may be needed when widening group participation criteria. The team looks forward to exploring these datasets at the completion of the study, and to further develop thinking around this important work. What is certain already is that music therapy group work with displaced dyads holds an important role in the support provided to families. The team hopes that similar initiatives will be developed and expanded so that more families can experience the benefits of music therapy.

REFERENCES

Arnon, S., Shapsa, A., Forman, L., Regev, R., *et al.* (2006). Live music is beneficial to pre-term infants in the neonatal intensive care unit environment. *Birth*, 33(2), 131–136. https://doi.org/10.1111/j.0730-7659.2006.00090.x.

Beauchaine, T. P. (2015). Respiratory sinus arrhythmia: A transdiagnostic biomarker of emotion dysregulation and psychopathology. *Current Opinion in Psychology*, 3(509), 43–47. https://doi.org/10.1016/j.copsyc.2015.01.017.

Beck, B. D., Meyer, S. L., Simonsen, E., Søgaard, U., *et al.* (2021). Music therapy was non-inferior to verbal standard treatment of traumatized refugees in mental health care: Results from a randomized clinical trial. *European Journal of Psychotraumatology*, 12(1), 1930960. https://doi.org/gk979t.

Bernard, G. & Dvorak, A. L. (2023). Using music to address trauma with refugees: A systematic review and recommendations. *Music Therapy Perspectives*, 41(1), e30–e43. https://doi.org/10.1093/mtp/miac013.

Berntson, G. G., Quigley, K. S., & Lozano, D. (2007). Cardiovascular Psychophysiology. In J. T. Cacioppo & L. G. Tassinary (eds) *Handbook of Psychophysiology* (pp.182–210). Cambridge: Cambridge University Press.

Berntson, G. G., Thomas, B. J., Eckberg, D. L., Grossman, P., *et al.* (1997). Heart rate variability: Origins, methods, and interpretive caveats. *Psychophysiology*, 34(6), 623–648. https://doi.org/10.1111/j.1469-8986.1997.tb02140.x.

Blandon, A. Y., Calkins, S. D., Keane, S. P., & Brien, M. O. (2010). Contributions of child's physiology and maternal behavior to children's trajectories of temperamental reactivity. *Developmental Psychology*, 46(5), 1089–1102. https://doi.org/10.1037/a0020678.

Braun, V. & Clarke, V. (2022). *Thematic Analysis: A Practical Guide*. Thousand Oaks, CA: Sage Publications.

Coombes, E. (2018). We all came from somewhere. *Voices: A World Forum for Music Therapy*, 18(1). doi: 10.15845/voices.v18i1.915.

Deighton, J., Humphrey, N., Belsky, J., Boehnke, J., Vostanis, P., & Patalay, P. (2018). Longitudinal pathways between mental health difficulties and academic performance during middle childhood and early adolescence. *British Journal of Developmental Psychology*, 36(1), 110–126. doi: 10.1111/bjdp.12218.

De Witte, M., Karkou, V., Orkidi, H., Zarate, R., *et al.* (2021). From therapeutic factors to mechanisms of change in the creative arts therapies: A scoping review. *Frontiers in Psychology*, 12. https://doi.org/10.3389/fpsyg.2021.678397.

Doussard-Roosevelt, J. A., Montgomery, L. A., & Porges, S. W. (2003). Short-term stability of physiological measures in kindergarten children: Respiratory sinus arrhythmia, heart period, and cortisol. *Developmental Psychobiology: The Journal of the International Society for Developmental Psychobiology*, 43(3), 230–242. https://doi.org/10.1002/dev.10136.

Erkkilä, J., Punkanen, M., Fachner, J., Ala-Ruona, E., *et al.* (2011). Individual music therapy for depression: Randomised controlled trial. *British Journal of Psychiatry*, 199(2), 132–139. https://doi.org/10.1192/bjp.bp.110.085431.

Eruyar, S., Maltby, J., & Vostanis, P. (2017). Mental health problems of Syrian refugee children: The role of parental factors. *European Child & Adolescent Psychiatry*, 27(4), 401–409. doi: 10.1007/s00787-017-1101-0.

Fachner, J., Gold, C., & Erkkilä, J. (2013). Music therapy modulates fronto-temporal activity in the rest-EEG in depressed clients. *Brain Topography*, 26(2), 338–354. https://doi.org/10.1007/s10548-012-0254-x.

Fancourt, D. & Perkins, R. (2018a). The effects of mother–infant singing on emotional closeness, affect, anxiety, and stress hormones. *Music & Science*, 1. https://doi.org/10.1177/2059204317745746.

Fancourt, D. & Perkins, R. (2018b). Effect of singing interventions on symptoms of postnatal depression: Three-arm randomised controlled trial. *The British Journal of Psychiatry*, 212(2), 119–121. https://doi.org/gczvdv.

Fazel, M., Wheeler, J., & Danesh, J. (2005). Prevalence of serious mental disorder in 7000 refugees resettled in western countries: A systematic review. *Lancet*, 365, 1315–1320. doi: 10.1016/S0140-6736(05)61027-6.

Franco, F., Swaine, J. S., Israni, S., Zaborowska, K. A., *et al.* (2014). Affect-matching music improves cognitive performance in adults and young children for both positive and negative emotions. *Psychology of Music*, 42(6), 869–887. https://doi.org/10.1177/0305735614548500.

Geretsegger, M., Holck, U., Carpente, J. A., Elefant, C., Kim, J., & Gold, C. (2012). Common characteristics of improvisational approaches in music therapy for children with autism spectrum disorder: Developing treatment guidelines. *Journal of Music Therapy*, 52(2), 238–262.

Gottman, J. M., Katz, L. F., & Hooven, C. (1997). *Meta-Emotion: How Families Communicate Emotionally*. Mahwah, NJ: Lawrence Erlbaum Associates.

Grossman, P., Beek, J., & Wientjes, C. (1990). A comparison of three quantification methods for estimation of respiratory sinus arrhythmia. *Psychophysiology*, 27(6), 702–714. https://doi.org/10.1111/j.1469-8986.1990.tb03198.x.

Hettich, N., Seidel, F. A., & Stuhrmann, L. Y. (2020). Psychosocial interventions for newly arrived adolescent refugees: A systematic review. *Adolescent Research Review*, 5(2), 99–114. https://doi.org/10.1007/s40894-020-00134-1.

Kostilainen, K., Partanen, E., Mikkola, K., Wikström, V., *et al.* (2021). Repeated parental singing during kangaroo care improved neural processing of speech sound changes in preterm infants at term age. *Frontiers in Neuroscience*, 15, 686027. https://doi.org/10.3389/fnins.2021.686027.

Leech, G. (2014). Methods of data collection: Empirical pragmatics. *The Pragmatics of Politeness*, Oxford Studies in Sociolinguistics (2014; online edition, Oxford Academic). https://doi.org/10.1093/acprof:oso/9780195341386.003.0009.

Michelis, I., Makepeace, J., & Reis, C. (2024). Who is centred in the humanitarian response to gender-based violence? A critical discourse analysis of the survivor-centred approach. *Violence Against Women*. https://doi.org/10.1177/10778012241231783.

Middlesex University. (2023, 10 November). *Music 4 Displaced Dyads* [video]. YouTube. www.youtube.com/watch?v=16T3k-vTy6o.

Murray, K. E., Davidson, G. R., & Schweitzer, R. D. (2010). Review of refugee mental health interventions following resettlement: Best practices and recommendations. *The American Journal of Orthopsychiatry*, 80(4), 576–585. http://doi.org/10.1111/j.1939-0025.2010.01062.x.

Oldfield, A., Blauth, L., Finnemann, J., & Casey, O. (2019). Clinical Trials: Are Music Therapists Deluding Themselves? In H. Dunn, E. Coombes, E. Maclean, H. Mottram, & J. Nugent (eds) *Music Therapy and Autism Across the Lifespan: A Spectrum of Approaches* (pp.35–56). London: Jessica Kingsley Publishers.

Orth, J. (2005). Music therapy with traumatized refugees in a clinical setting. *Voices: A World Forum for Music Therapy*, 2. http://dx.doi.org.10.108008098131.2011.571276.

Patriquin, M. A., Scarpa, A., Friedman, B. H., & Porges, S. W. (2013). Respiratory sinus arrhythmia: A marker for positive social functioning and receptive language skills in children with autism spectrum disorders. *Developmental Psychobiology*, 55(2), 101–112. https://doi.org/10.1002/dev.21002.

Politimou, N., Stewart, L., Müllensiefen, D., & Franco, F. (2018). Music@Home: A novel instrument to assess the home musical environment in early years. *PloS One*, 13(4), e0193819. http://doi.org/10.1371/journal.pone.0193819.

Ribeiro, M. K. A., Alcântara-Silva, T. R. M., Oliveira, J. C. M., Paula, T. C., *et al.* (2018). Music therapy intervention in cardiac autonomic modulation, anxiety, and depression in mothers of preterms: Randomized controlled trial. *BMC Psychology*, 6, 57. https://doi.org/10.1186/s40359-018-0271-y.

Rudstam, G., Elofsson, U., Söndergaard, H. P., Bonde, L. O., & Beck, B. D. (2017). Trauma-focused group music and imagery with women suffering from PTSD/complex PTSD: A feasibility study. *Approaches: Music Therapy and Special Education*, 9(2), 202–216. http://approaches.gr/wp-content/uploads/2017/12/2-Approaches-9-2-2017-rudstam-a20171222.pdf.

Schäfer, T. & Sedlmeier, P. (2010). What makes us like music? Determinants of music preference. *Psychology of Aesthetics, Creativity, and the Arts*, 4(4), 223. https://doi.org/10.1037/a0018374.

Smith, J. P. & Smith, G. S. (2010). Long-term economic costs of psychological problems during childhood. *Social Science & Medicine*, 71(1), 110–115. doi: 10.1016/j.socscimed.2010.02.046.

Spitzer, R. L., Kroenke, K., & Williams, J. B. (1999). Patient Health Questionnaire Primary Care Study Group: Validation and utility of a self-report version of PRIME-MD: The PHQ primary care study. *Journal of the American Medical Association*, 282(18), 1737–1744. doi: 10.1001/archinte.166.10.1092.

Spitzer, R. L., Kroenke, K., Williams, J. B. W., & Löwe, B. (2006). A brief measure for assessing generalized anxiety disorder: The GAD-7. *Archives of International Medicine*, 166(10), 1092–1097. doi: 10.1001/archinte.166.10.1092.

Standley, J. (2012). Music therapy research in the NICU: An updated meta-analysis. *Neonatal Network*, 31(5), 311–316. doi: 10.1891/0730-0832.31.5.311.

Stewart-Brown, S., Tennant, A., Tennant, R., Platt, S., Parkinson, J., & Weich, S. (2009). Internal construct validity of the Warwick-Edinburgh mental well-being scale (WEMWBS): A Rasch analysis using data from the Scottish health education population survey. *Health Quality Life Outcomes*, 1(7), 1–8. https://doi.org/10.1186/1477-7525-7-15.

Turrini, G., Purgato, M., Ballette, F., Nosè, M., Ostuzzi, G., & Barbui, C. (2017). Common mental disorders in asylum seekers and refugees: Umbrella review of prevalence and intervention studies. *International Journal of Mental Health Systems*, 11, 51. https://doi.org/10.1186/s13033-017-0156-0.

UNHCR. (2024, 18 November). Ukraine refugee situation. Retrieved 26 November 2024, from https:/data2.unhcr.org/en/situations/Ukraine.

Van Puyvelde, M., Loots, G., Vanfleteren, P., Meys, J., Simcock, D., & Pattyn, N. (2014). Do you hear the same? Cardiorespiratory responses between mothers and infants during tonal and atonal music. *PloS One*, 9(9), e106920. https://doi.org/10.1371/journal.pone.0106920.

Weathers, F. W., Litz, B. T., Keane, T. M., Palmieri, P. A., Marx, B. P., & Schnurr, P. P. (2013). *The PTSD Checklist for DSM-5 (PCL-5)*. Scale available from the National Center for PTSD. www.ptsd.va.gov.

Weingarten, S. J., Levy, A. T., & Berghella, V. (2021). The effect of music on anxiety in women undergoing cesarean delivery: A systematic review and meta-analysis. *American Journal of Obstetrics & Gynecology*, 3(5), 100435. doi: 10.1016/j.ajogmf.2021.100435.

CHAPTER 12

Our Humanity

Creating a Music Video with an Asylum Seeker While He Was in Mandatory Offshore Detention

EMMA O'BRIEN WITH GUEST CONTRIBUTIONS
FROM BLAIR HARRIS AND CRAIG PILKINGTON

The Universal Declaration of Human Rights Article 14 states:

> 1. Everyone has the right to seek and to enjoy in other countries asylum from persecution. (United Nations, 1948)

INTRODUCTION

This chapter explores the logistics and experiences of connecting with a Kurdish asylum seeker across multiple barriers such as 12ft high barbed wire fences and across seas, while he was in offshore detention. It describes how we found ourselves in a virtual space to support him and deliver a music video of his original song, all within a music therapy framework over four months in 2017. It draws on three perspectives, my own as a music therapist (Emma O'Brien) who coordinated the overall music video project and edited the video, a sound engineer/music producer who worked closely with me to weave all the elements of the song together (Craig Pilkington, founder and director of Audrey Studios, Melbourne, Australia), and a cellist who added the unique melodic line to the song (Blair Harris, professional musician), responding to the emotional content and the songwriter's text. The asylum seeker/songwriter has chosen not to share his side of the experience in this publication other than the song itself, and the music video, as he will be writing from his own perspective in another format with other aspects of his story. I have met him several times in person over the years after he came to the Australian mainland, and I continue to catch up with him. Due to the public nature of the music video clip and how it has been subsequently used in protests and in a movie, it is impossible to keep the asylum seeker/songwriter's identity entirely separate from this chapter. We will refer to him by his name, Moz.

This experience took place in Australia in a very socio-politically charged time at the height of government-sanctioned mandatory offshore detention of asylum seekers. This is now under multiple investigations, including human rights challenges. There were several other people involved in the different stages of this project; they are all on the credits of the music video clip, cited in this chapter, and available to watch on YouTube. All participants in this project volunteered their time and expertise. The other main character in this chapter is the music video of the song, and its progression is woven in throughout.

It would be unusual to start at the end of the story, but we invite you now to do exactly that. Please take some time now to watch and listen to 'All the Same' by scanning the QR code or visiting https://www.youtube.com/watch?v=fq85xln6Kf4.

BRIEF OVERVIEW OF THE LITERATURE

In Australia, music therapists are working with asylum seekers and refugees to assist in resettling refugees and building connections with communities. Some projects are run by community musicians for immigration transit centres (Lennette *et al.*, 2015) and others by music therapists or refugee community leaders (Winsor, 2018). There are online sites such as Music for Refugees,[1] offering resources and contacts for those who wish to be part of this work, with instruments being donated to detention centres for use. There are group and individual sessions held in community centres and schools. The focus in school sessions with music therapists is integration, using music therapy interventions as means of connection,

---

1   https://musicforrefugees.org

understanding, self-expression, and healing (Jones *et al.*, 2004; Baker & Jones, 2005). The role of music in social and emotional support and assisting in addressing complexities of trauma is also highlighted in music therapy research, particularly with teenagers and children (Wiess & Bensimon, 2019; Enge & Stige, 2022). There is little written about working directly with asylum seekers in detention, and this may be due to multiple barriers that may be experienced. However, in Germany, there is evolving literature about working with refugees in transitional care and in an early intervention model in music therapy practice, to reduce the impact of trauma for high-risk children and young adults (Mallon & Antick, 2021).

SONGWRITING IN THIS CONTEXT

As Moz had already workshopped his song with other people before we came to work on it with him, strictly speaking the song was not created in a music therapy context. However, music therapy principles of Guided Original Lyrics and Music (GOLM), a therapeutic songwriting method of verifying and reflecting (O'Brien, 2005, 2006, 2014), was applied in the recording of the tracks, arrangement of the song, producing of the song, and in the editing of music video clips. At no point was Moz ever in the same room as us. All our communication was over Messenger, often at unusual hours of the night as he was in mandatory offshore government detention, on Manus Island, having committed no crime, but seeking asylum as a refugee.

Posselt *et al.* (2020) have cautioned about the vicarious trauma that health professionals in Australia can experience when working within the asylum seeker offshore detention centre system. This can arise due to the stories they hear from the clients and patients they treat, compounded by complexities and politicization and often the under-resourced environment. Some medical professionals go as far as to question the value of supporting the system by working within it, and have protested by refusing to do so (Berger & Miles, 2016). There are ongoing concerns for the ethical conflicts that health professionals face daily as they seek to care for asylum seekers and refugees in offshore detention and mandatory detention in Australia, but the health professionals are often finding themselves in the impossible position of having to go against evidence-based practice due to multiple constraints (Dudley *et al.*, 2021). There is a call by the later authors for health professional organizations to step in on behalf of their members and negotiate for better care for all.

BACKGROUND

This background information on Moz's asylum-seeker journey is available in the public domain. Moz spent six years in offshore detention in closed and open settings on Manus Island. Moz was transferred to Australia in 2019 on medical grounds and spent 14 months in a hotel under what was officially called Alternative Places of Detention (APOD) without receiving appropriate medical treatment for the conditions he was 'medevaced' for. He was released from the APOD in Melbourne in January 2021 (Amnesty International, 2024). This chapter focuses on the music video's creation and time in 2017. However, I continued to follow up (virtually) with Moz after the release of the music video, for several years. I visited him when he was medevaced to Australia in 2019 at APOD hotels, and once he was released in 2021.

MANUS ISLAND DETENTION CENTRE

The Manus Island Detention Centre was located on the Papua New Guinea Navy Base Lombrum (previously a Royal Australian Navy Base called HMAS Tarangau) on Los Negros Island in Manus Province, Papua New Guinea. Originally intended to house 500 people, at its peak it housed 1500 people. It had various private service/security contractors over the years and many have been under investigation for various reasons. Initially, men, women, and children who were seeking asylum were sent there from 2012 to 2013 but eventually only men were sent to Manus. They lived in very basic shacks in shared spaces and the litany of mistreatment and abuse is still being reported on and investigated. In October 2017, the centre was being closed and the UN refugee agency warned that Australia's withdrawal from Manus Island could create a humanitarian emergency. Human Rights Watch urged Canberra to consider sending police to assist with the transition. At that time, hundreds of refugees and asylum seekers refused to leave the centre, citing fears for their safety in the local community, as water and electricity were disconnected. Moz was part of that protest. It was a few weeks after his music video was completed. Manus Island Detention Centre was closed in 2019.

TIMELINE FOR CONTEXT

This timeline covers the time span from when Moz first arrived as an asylum seeker in 2013 up until when the video was released in 2017. The main time points and data have been sourced from Human Rights Law Centre (2020) and are not exhaustive of all significant events relating to asylum seekers, offshore detention, or Moz's personal journey. Some of the data listed in this timeline may be disturbing to the reader. They have been signposted for the reader for the socio-political context leading up to our collaboration with Moz and events that occurred during our collaboration up until 2017. Sadly, people are still being held in offshore indefinite detention by the Australian Government despite ongoing protests, changes of leadership, the humanitarian crisis, and international criticism.

JULY 2013
The Labour Prime Minister (Kevin Rudd) at the time announces that no person seeking asylum by boat in Australia will ever be allowed to settle. A 'Regional Resettlement Arrangement' with Papua New Guinea is announced to detain and process protection claims there.

NOVEMBER 2013
Liberal Tony Abbott becomes Prime Minister of Australia. Operation Sovereign Borders, a military-led border security operation designed to prevent boats carrying asylum seekers from arriving in Australia, begins.

FEBRUARY 2014
The UN Refugee Agency reports on conditions in the offshore processing facilities in Nauru and Manus Island. It is found that men, women, and children are being held in arbitrary detention in conditions that do not meet international standards.

MARCH 2014
Following the death of Reza Barati, a 24-year-old Iranian man, during protests at the Manus Island Regional Processing Centre in February, detention staff are accused of his murder.

SEPTEMBER 2014
Department of Border Protection releases the Moss Review into allegations of sexual abuse on Nauru. United Nations Special Rapporteur on Torture finds that various aspects of Australia's asylum-seeker policies violate the Convention Against Torture and Other Cruel, Inhuman or Degrading Treatment or Punishment. Men held in Manus Island Detention Centre begin a two-week hunger strike.

MARCH 2015
The Australian Border Force Act 2015 takes effect. Secrecy provisions in the Act make it a crime punishable by two years' imprisonment for medical

professionals, teachers, and other people employed in offshore detention centres to disclose information about conditions in detention.

JULY 2015
The Human Rights Law Centre and Human Rights Watch launch a report on their inspection of Manus Island, The Pacific Non-Solution, highlighting that more people have died than been resettled.

SEPTEMBER 2015
The #LetThemStay movement begins, a campaign to ensure that people, including babies, at risk of return to Manus or Nauru are allowed to stay in Australia.

FEBRUARY 2016
Victorian Premier (Labour) Daniel Andrews writes to then Liberal PM Malcolm Turnbull asking him to let the 267 people stay in Australia (other premiers shortly follow suit).

Lady Cilento Children's Hospital refuses to discharge one-year-old Baby Asha without a government guarantee that she won't be returned to detention in Nauru.

Immigration Minister Peter Dutton responds to public pressure and releases Baby Asha into the Australian community.

APRIL 2016
Hamid Kehazaei, a 24-year-old Iranian man, dies in a Brisbane hospital from septicaemia contracted on Manus Island after cutting his foot.

Asylum seeker Sayed Ibrahim Hussein drowns when he is caught in a rip swimming in the Galab channel off Nauru.

TIMELINE FOR MAY 2016 TO NOVEMBER 2017

MAY 2016
Omid Masoumali dies in Australia after self-immolating on Nauru.

One day later the Manus Island Detention Centre becomes an 'open centre' in response to being judged by the Papua New Guinea Supreme Court.

Ten days later a 22-year-old Somali refugee sets herself on fire in offshore detention and is evacuated to Australia with life-threatening burns.

AUGUST 2016

The Human Rights Law Centre and GetUp! launch the report *Association with Abuse*.

A Bangladeshi man, Rakib Khan, dies in Nauru of a suspected suicide.

Kamil Hussain, a 34-year-old Pakistani man, dies on Manus Island.

OCTOBER 2016

The Guardian Newspaper releases the 'Nauru files' – the largest cache of documents to be leaked from within Australia's asylum-seeker detention regime. It details assaults, sexual assaults, and self-harm.

NOVEMBER 2016

Amin Afravi, an Iranian refugee on Manus, attempts to set himself on fire for the second time in five weeks.

Refugee and former aid worker Masoud Ali Shiekh is hospitalized with serious head injuries after an unprovoked attack by persons unknown with rocks near the transit centre at East Lorengau, Manus.

DECEMBER 2016

The Australian Government announces that some refugees detained on Manus Island and Nauru will be resettled in the United States.

JANUARY 2017

Faysal Ishak Ahmed, a 27-year-old Sudanese man, dies in Brisbane. Faysal had fallen and had a seizure at the Manus Detention Centre. Before his death, Fayseal was denied medical assistance numerous times.

MARCH 2017

The Australian Government issues an apology to Save the Children employees and pays them compensation following Scott Morrison's accusations of 2014 that Save the Children staff on Nauru were 'coaching' people seeking asylum to self-harm, which had prompted their exit in 2016.

AUGUST 2017

The Australian Senate Committee publishes a report containing serious allegations of abuse, self-harm, and neglect of asylum seekers in offshore detention.

Iranian man Hamed Shamshiripour dies of suspected suicide on Manus Island after failing to receive appropriate mental health treatment.

● **OCTOBER 2017**
The first group of refugees from Manus Island leave for the US under the resettlement deal.

Hundreds of refugees and asylum seekers refuse to leave Manus Island, citing fears for their safety in the local community, as water and electricity are disconnected at the centre.

Sri Lankan asylum seeker Rajeev Rajendran dies of a suspected suicide on the grounds of Manus Hospital.

OUR EXPERIENCES
Emma's context and experience
I was approached by a long-time music therapy colleague, Catherine Threl-fall, to coordinate this project and edit the video as she was aware that I had created music video projects in my music therapy practice. However, she wasn't aware that I grew up in Thailand and volunteered with my mother at inner city refugee camps in the late 1970s as an assistant in teaching basic English as a Second Language (ESL) with standard cue cards for refugees transitioning through Thailand destined for Australia. It is a very powerful childhood memory for me: walking into the makeshift refugee camps in open shelters, with each person assigned to a single mat on the ground; singing songs with the children to help with basic ESL skills; wondering why they had so little and listening to stories of displacement, loss, and injustice, but perhaps not really understanding the politics behind it all.

My mother was a refugee advocate all her life, and later in life she was part of the Grandmothers Against Children in Detention, now known as Grandmothers for Refugees. She has also published articles advocating for refugee rights.

> Since the 1990s consecutive Australian Federal Governments have had a penchant to render asylum seekers invisible to the general public. Our political leaders, working on the assumption that out of sight will mean out of mind, have prevented the media from having access to camps on the mainland or on Manus Island and Nauru. Kevin Rudd brought this to new lows with his 'PNG Solution', a policy which has now been adopted by Tony Abbott. It's difficult to relate to stories of personal human suffering while we accept or embrace policies which deliberately exclude us from witnessing or hearing about them. While asylum seekers remain an anonymous group, rather than individual men, women and children with names and life stories, they and their sufferings remain invisible. (O'Brien, 2013, paragraph 1)

I am grateful to my mother's guidance to always look for truth and question all narratives in the name of compassion and humanity.

The collective shame that many Australians feel about the mistreatment of asylum seekers by governments and policies with mandatory offshore detention is an ongoing conversation culturally in many aspects of Australian life. Like our colonial past, it has many horrors, mistruths, complications, and entrenched wounds that require truth-telling, compassion, healing, and active change for a better, more equitable future for all. It should also be noted that not all Australians share this shame, and these conversations remain very contentious issues locally and internationally in a continually fractious world. However, the collective motivation of individuals in this project was one of wanting to contribute in some small positive way to Moz's experience and song. We all shared a humanistic, creative human rights paradigm and believed in the power of music for self-expression and compassion.

Despite my history of working with my mother in refugee settings and her advocacy work, my chosen music therapy speciality was in healthcare settings. I wonder, however, if this is why I welcomed the opportunity to support Moz, not entirely sure of what it was going to entail logistically, and how many threads were already part of the project. But I was happy to volunteer and see if I could aid his vision of turning his song into a music video.

The enthusiasm of all the musicians wanting to assist in building Moz's song was heartening and allowed us to stage the process. Moz had already established multiple external connections with refugee advocates through the Julian Burnside KC Asylum Seeker Letter Writing Campaign (2016) which was a call to compassionate Australians to write to people in the mandatory detention centres in Nauru or on Manus Island. Julian Burnside KC has an Order of Australia Medal, is a well-known refugee advocate and human rights activist, and is a lawyer who has tirelessly campaigned for refugees' rights in Australia and internationally. It was through a significant connection Moz made, through a letter that he opened from a woman moved by Burnside's campaign called Jane McCracken, that he became connected to us all.

Establishing our collaboration

My first phone call with Moz was both inspiring and difficult as there were many people on the call, and he had limited time. There was a move to remove mobile phones from all asylum seekers by authorities to diminish their ability to communicate their conditions to the outside world and in essence to silence their voices. In hindsight, it was an extraordinary feat that we were able to receive such a powerful evocative vocal and such moving imagery from Moz for the music video and on his smartphone at such a contentious time.

I agreed to run the project and work on this song with Moz. As he had already sketched elements of his song, we spent a bit of time ensuring we understood the overall structure of his piece. Other parties had worked with him on this, and my role was to clarify and verify that we were not pushing the song in any direction that disempowered Moz. It was vital that we were following his vision and responding to his creativity, not our own. His living situation had become increasingly dangerous and powerless, and he was experiencing high levels of physical and emotional trauma. The authorities onsite were trying to decommission Manus Island Detention Centre, and at the same time, there was no clear plan or programme for the detainees.

Our discussions remained focused on his song, with me supporting his emotional experiences as best I could using my music therapy skills and, where possible, seeing if there were local services that could support him. It was a very distressing time, but from my perspective, the frustration and powerlessness I was experiencing were proportionally very small compared to Moz's lived experience. I did my best through trauma-informed practice to provide virtual care for Moz. At times I provided guided relaxation music as well as positive messaging around his song and the progress of the music video. We worked to a very tight timeline. Moz wanted the clip to be launched as a special preview for the Writing Through Fences group, hosted by Jane Galbraith (another great advocate for refugees) as part of the Queensland Poetry Festival in August 2017. We also hosted a website for the clip and posted it on YouTube with a September release. An important part of my role as the lead was to ensure that none of the musicians in the project disempowered him in our processes. This was a core value for us in every stage and with every person involved.

THE SONG
The lyrics
Moz sent us the lyrics directly with a sketch of the song on voice and guitar. He immediately said he wanted a band sound with drums, electric guitar, and, if possible, some 'strings'.

'Our Humanity': Lyrics and music by Moz (2017)
Verse 1:

> Australians Pay Attention
> It's Moz from Manus who's been stuck in the hell
> since four years without any reason!

Listen to me for a minute 'por favor'
Just want you to be aware about what all the rats have done to me.

Liberal and Labour are lying to you
I'm not a terrorist, I'm not perilous
But they have put my youth in a horrible cage
For their cheating money and running their bloody policy

Pre-chorus:

So want you to get your [sh*t] together and sort out this mess
or you'll always be known as 'Australia's next Hess'.

Chorus:

Help us keep our sanity
Remember our Humanity
I am, you are, we are all the same

Verse 2:

Do you know if you don't put pressure on them,
they will abandon me in limbo
No worries when I hear sorry from you,
But you know your silence brings them a strength and happiness,
Your governments treat us like animals
While the UN says we're not criminals
Peter Dutton, Malcom Turnbull, hang your heads in shame
It's a crime you have committed in Australia's good name.

Pre-chorus
Chorus

HONOURING MOZ'S VOICE
Emma's reflections

Once the structure was clear we were able to send Moz a basic backing track for him to sing to. It is always difficult to build a simple clear music guide for a song when someone has an idea of an arrangement in their mind. It is important to spend time explaining that it is the bare bones of the song that will be layered later in the process, even when working with a client/patient who is in the room with you. I always ensure that I talk about the listening and experiencing of the basic guide before and after listening to it, so people are aware that these are the building blocks of a song. It is much easier in person than remotely, plus adding to this was Moz's highly traumatizing situation, which was escalating daily. But he was committed to finishing the song and music video clip and he was open to the support I offered.

We then embarked on virtual vocal coaching sessions so Moz could use his mobile phone to sing each vocal line clearly into voice notes while listening to the backing track on his fellow asylum seeker and friend's mobile phone with earphones. This also assisted Moz in refining any vocal lines, adding further nuances. This detail enabled Craig, the sound engineer who joined the project at this stage, to have vocal recordings that were as clear as possible to then add to the mix from Moz. All the music mixes and vocal notes were sent back and forth via Messenger.

Craig's reflections

I happily agreed when Emma asked me to help on this project to support Moz. Apart from attending protests, there was little we could do about our Federal Government's cruel policy of punishing those seeking asylum with indefinite offshore detention. Both parties had endorsed it, so it didn't seem to matter who you voted for. Being given the opportunity to contribute with my sound engineering and production skills to Moz's song 'All the Same' was a great way to show solidarity for Moz, to show compassion, to show our humanity, and to help Moz spread his message.

Moz had recorded his vocals on his Samsung phone to a clean basic backing track set to a click. This meant we could mix and match his multiple takes to get the best possible combination. We wanted to ensure the most positive outcome musically for Moz and his song. We were able to programme beats and record instruments in the same key and beats per minute with the basic backing track to bring the song to life.

The biggest challenge was to bring his phone vocal up to release standard. I tested many different vocal plug-ins to replicate the studio quality, so your ear would think he was on the microphone, standing there, singing his heart out. All the passion was there in his vocals and my role was to bring it virtually into the studio room. There are lots of plug-ins that can make that happen, such as reverbs that evoke different room sounds, different microphones, and tools for equalization for different voice qualities. I did a few small edits here and there, but nothing too big, because I did not want to lose the raw passion of his voice and message. Ultimately it all came together beautifully and we had a great vocal from Moz.

Emma's reflections

Once we had a complete vocal track we sent it to Moz for approval. There were a few changes made, but overall, Moz was happy with the flow of the

version Craig and I had selected and with Craig's sound engineering expertise in taking a voice note recorded on a smartphone and making it sound
as if it had been recorded in a studio. With this approval in hand, we then
moved to consider building textures around Moz's vocals. Moz had mentioned potentially wanting some strings and I had worked with Blair Harris,
an excellent, intuitive, multi-talented cellist, so I approached Blair and asked
Moz how he felt about trying to add some cello to his piece with potential
textures to enhance the emotional aspects of the song and the main melodic
themes. By this time in the process Moz and I had developed a rapport with
a creative understanding and a trusted process. He was happy for us to
explore the work with Blair on the cello using his approved vocal and send
back some ideas to him for verification.

Blair's reflections

Music has the ability to bring hope and joy into everyday life. Creating and
sharing music gives me a sense of purpose and fulfilment. I wanted that for
Moz too, so when I was contacted by Emma about Moz and his song, I felt
compelled to volunteer and support his plight. It resonated with me as a
very important message that needed to be told. I think it's vital to connect
with people, especially when they have such a moving story to share with
the world. Music is such a great way to do that. Every aspect of this song
was collaborative.

Emma's reflections

As Blair and I listened to Moz's vocals and discussed possible textures, it was
important that Blair also be given the opportunity to react spontaneously
and emotionally to the song. It is always a balancing act between being
informed and remaining creatively open. Moz had consented to me sharing
his situation with Blair, which was vital to inform Blair's musical choices
as well as the song itself.

Blair's reflections

Moz's situation, lyrics, and imagery naturally conjured up haunting and
evocative musical lines for me. I found myself responding to them in several
different takes and landing on ones that I kept repeating, which I know that
Emma brought together with Craig to create something so powerful. The
idea of conversation and togetherness was the main inspiration for how the
cello would be incorporated into Moz's work. We played with the idea of the
cello and the voice talking to each other, sometimes in a call-and-answer
framework and other times in unison. When Moz calls out 'Australians Pay

Attention' – I answer and then join him melodically on 'I'm not perilous...'
It is yet another example of how music can bring people together to speak
a common language regardless of their background or circumstances.

Emma's reflections

Selecting from such rich musical material for the song arrangement and textures that Blair provided was a real privilege. Moz told me that he approved
of all the cello parts: the timbre, the melodic lines, the dialogue between
the cello and the voice. I also found that the cello lines helped to inform
the timing of the visual edit in the next phase of the project.

Craig's reflections

Once we had found the placement of cello motifs, the powerful opening
melodies, and the natural musical dialogue between Moz and Blair, the
whole arrangement of the song began to settle. We began to really experience the musical representation of our solidified message of support for
Moz. It inspired me to add some trumpets to the piece, to add my call for
the release of the detainees on Manus Island. I also sourced some Kurdish
drum textures for the piece, as a sign of respect to Moz's culture. It was a
privilege to work with all the other support musicians who contributed to
Moz's song, and then to see the song come even more to life in the music
video clip was inspiring. Reflecting on this process has really invigorated me
to keep pushing back against the injustices that are still happening today.

Manus Island through Moz's and his fellow asylum seekers' eyes

As we were working on a short timeline, we kept processes moving in par-
allel. Once Moz had his complete vocal, he then set about filming different
elements for the music video clip. This was a very difficult time. In newspa-
pers the then Minister for Immigration was threatening to remove access
to mobile phones for all asylum seekers in offshore detention. Protests were
happening across Australia and inside Manus Island Detention Centre, and
the Papua New Guinea Government and the private businesses operating
the centres were simultaneously closing down the spaces. Many of the asylum seekers were going on hunger strikes and staging sit-in protests. It was
neither my agenda to stop Moz from proceeding with the filming nor insist
that he continue. It was his choice alone to make. We were all committed
to supporting his autonomy throughout the process. I did, however, give
him the option of postponing, of course, as I was deeply concerned, but he
wanted to pursue the music video. So, we continued to support him and

sent him what he needed to do. His friend, also credited in the music video, filmed him on his smartphone as Moz lip-synced to the agreed final vocal cut. We also discussed atmospheric shots he could take, and advised him where possible to send any still photos as well.

When images or video footage are sent via Messenger or WhatsApp they are compressed and become lower quality. We were concerned about this aspect of receiving images as Moz wanted to present his music video on a large screen as part of a major poetry festival. Through a unique process that I am not privy to, but grateful for, we were able to receive the footage in a higher quality format than we anticipated. It is important to note that no one was injured or reprimanded because of the footage reaching us.

Emma's reflections

I received multiple takes of the song, photos, atmospheric footage of the detention centre, stills of Moz, and some very fine arthouse filming styles by Moz's friend and fellow asylum seeker on his smartphone. When I uploaded the footage and imagery to Final Cut Pro video editing software I was overwhelmed by the power of the imagery. I had originally thought of filming the recording process of the cellist and placing that with Moz, which I suggested to him, but this footage needed to stand alone. I spoke to Moz about it, and he agreed.

We also discussed where to place which photos, the use of the colour tint on the footage, and which words we would highlight in the music video clip. Moz understood that I had to make samples of the best quality takes from what I received and at times that meant reusing certain images, which is a standard technique in music video editing of the pop genre. Again, we had established trust and rapport in the process, and I was always bringing the process back to the Guided Original Lyrics and Music (O'Brien, 2005, 2006, 2014) therapeutic principles of verification and reflection, and whenever logistically possible giving Moz complete agency and control over the process.

When progressing through the visual edit, I followed Moz's story, the beat of the song, and the duo melodies from Moz and the cello for the cuts. They were both musically embedded together in the final product. It was increasingly difficult to send Moz versions of the music video, so I described the stages on Messenger where possible as by this stage things were becoming even more complicated and desperate in the detention centre. Throughout this period, I sought external supervision to ensure that I was dealing with the vicarious trauma and responding appropriately to Moz. We were all very committed to finishing his music video. It kept us all going.

THE MUSIC VIDEO RELEASE

The music video was first played at the Queensland Poetry Festival, launched as part of the Writing Through Fences sessions on 25 August 2017 and the formal media launch and on YouTube on 30 August 2017. The excerpt below is from the media launch and was sent out to all major TV and radio stations:

> Kurdish refugee Mostafa 'Moz' Azimitabar today released a music video and song he recorded from his detention on Manus Island. Moz, 31, has been detained for four years. The vocals for his song, 'All the Same', were recorded on a mobile phone and, with the footage, the song found its way out to artists in Australia. In the clip, Moz sings into the camera, surrounded by tall wire fences, and implores all Australians to 'help us keep our sanity, remember our humanity'. Moz said the song was created to bring attention to the plight of himself and other refugees. 'We have been left in political limbo for four years now. The conditions are hellish and how they treat us is deplorable. I hope people who are listening to my song will understand our desperation, frustration and fear'... Moz has dedicated 'All the Same' to all of those in their refugee plight, to those who have lost their lives at Manus Island and especially to his friend and fellow musician Hamed, who was recently found deceased. Moz and Hamed would often play guitar together.

The music video's release preceded a series of protests within the detention centre by the asylum seekers as they feared for their lives if they were to be transferred to other facilities. Moz was proactive in many of these protests, suffering great physical and mental trauma. His song and the music video were used as a call to action by refugee advocates across Australia in local protests calling on the release of all refugees and resettlement for all of them in Australia. Across 2017 and 2018, when I was walking through the city I heard the song playing at protests and I also attended marches. Often at these they would play recordings of Moz that we had hosted on our website (no longer available) and that had been used in radio interviews and at the Queensland Poetry Festival.

THE MUSIC VIDEO'S LIFE
Emma's reflections

When we released the song it received local community radio play, was used in multiple protests by refugee advocates across Melbourne, sampled online, featured in the website and Facebook page (Our Humanity) we hosted, and used as a fundraiser to support mobile phone purchases for people in mandatory detention. Even the footage was later sampled in a feature film, launched in 2023 (but not cited). Our role was of course not media promotion but to enable the production of the video. We did want to share far and wide, but we had our limits, and as it turned out, the music video had a life of its own and it is still used today.

Craig's reflections
The result surpassed our wildest dreams. It became an anthem at many freedom rallies protesting indefinite detention. We believe that music is a fantastic medium to spread messages of peace, love, and solidarity which continues to be Moz's offering to the world. The 'All the Same' music video continues to have a life of its own.

CONCLUSION
Writing this chapter for this book and reflecting on this time has been a powerful experience. Originally, we were hoping to also share Moz's words and personal reflections alongside our own, but we respect his decision to do so in another format. These are my recollections of Moz and my interactions, and I hope I have honoured the process as best as I could.

Moz has gone on to become a public figure, a celebrated visual artist, a character in a documentary feature film, and a humanitarian advocate. Despite the trauma he has experienced, I am constantly in awe of his ability to show compassion, his capacity for forgiveness, and his generosity.

I still work very closely with Craig, the sound engineer and music producer, on regular Scrub Choir projects, and we often reflect on how this intense process taught us both so much about our own craft. I also have gone on to work with the cellist Blair in further collaborations. We hope that we have been able to give a small insight into the work and time and acknowledge that there are many other people who were part of this music video song recording, listed below and credited online. And of course, Moz and I are still in contact and have remained so consistently across the years. I look forward to having a cup of tea with him very soon.

Credits for 'All the Same'
Sung by Moz; words and music by Mostafa Azimitabar; onsite filming by Farhad Bandesh.

Artists living in Australia who contributed to 'All the Same' – Blair Harris (cello), Ryan Fullerton (electric guitars), Stephan Skov (sound engineer and guitars), Craig Pilkington (sound engineer/producer and trumpet), Dr Emma O'Brien OAM (music therapist, video editor, co-arranger and producer). Thanks to Catherine Threlfall (music therapist initial song support), Janet Galbraith (Writing Through Fences), Jane McCracken (Burnside's Letter Writing Campaign), Carol Quilter (initial poetry support), and Chris Lassig and Stefan Delatovic (media).

REFERENCES

Amnesty International. (2024). Full federal court bench set to hear Moz Azimitibar's appeal against APOD ruling. www.amnesty.org.au/full-federal-court-bench-set-to-hear-moz-azimitabars-appeal-against-apod-ruling.

Baker, F. & Jones, C. (2005). Holding a steady beat: The effects of a music therapy program on stabilising behaviours of newly arrived refugee students. *British Journal of Music Therapy*, 19(2), 67–74. https://doi.org/10.1177/135945750501900205.

Berger, D. & Miles, S. H. (2016). Should doctors boycott working in Australia's immigration detention centres? *BMJ*, 352, i1600. https://doi.org/10.1136/bmj.i1600.

Dudley, M., Young, P., Newman, L., Gale, F., & Stoddart, R. (2021). Health professionals confront the intentional harms of indefinite immigration detention: An Australian overview, evaluation of alternative responses and proposed strategy. *International Journal of Migration, Health and Social Care*, 17(1), 35–51. https://doi.org/10.1108/IJMHSC-08-2020-0083.

Enge, K. E. A. & Stige, B. (2022). Musical pathways to the peer community: A collective case study of refugee children's use of music therapy. *Nordic Journal of Music Therapy*, 31(1), 7–24. https://doi.org/10.1080/08098131.2021.1891130.

Human Rights Law Centre. (2020). #ElevenYearsTooLong. www.hrlc.org.au/timeline-offshore-detention.

Jones, C., Baker, F., & Day, T. (2004). From healing rituals to music therapy: Bridging the cultural divide between therapists and young Sudanese refugees. *Arts in Psychotherapy*, 31, 89–100.

Lenette, C., Weston, D., Wise, P., & Sunderland, N. (2015). Where words fail, music speaks: The impact of participatory music on the mental health and wellbeing of asylum seekers. *Arts & Health*, 8(2), 1–15. doi: 10.1080/17533015.2015.1037317.

Mallon, T. & Hoog Antink, M. (2021). The sound of lost homes – Introducing the COVER model – theoretical framework and practical insight into music therapy with refugees and asylum seekers. *Voices: A World Forum for Music Therapy*, 21(2). https://doi.org/10.15845/voices.v21i2.3124.

Music Feeds (2017, 4 September). Asylum Seeker Releases Music Video From Inside Manus Island Detention Centre. https://musicfeeds.com.au/news/asylum-seeker-releases-music-video-inside-manus-island-detention-centre.

O'Brien, E. (2005). Songwriting with Adult Cancer Patients in Oncology and Clinical Haematology. In F. Baker & T. Wigram (eds) *Songwriting: Methods, Techniques and Clinical Applications for Music Therapy Clinicians, Educators and Students* (pp.180–205). London: Jessica Kingsley Publishers.

O'Brien, E. (2006). Opera therapy: Creating and performing a new work with cancer patients and professional singers. *Nordic Journal of Music Therapy*, 15(1), 82–96.

O'Brien, E. (2014). *The Effect and Experience of Therapeutic Songwriting on Adult Cancer Patients' Quality of Life, Mood, Distress Levels and Satisfaction with Hospital Stay*. PhD thesis, University of Melbourne.

O'Brien, M. E. (2013). Invisible Icarus and asylum seekers. *Eureka Street Magazine*, 23(20). www.eurekastreet.com.au/article/invisible-icarus-and-asylum-seekers.

Our Humanity: Lyrics and music by Moz. (2017, 29 August). 'All the Same.' Moz. YouTube. https://youtu.be/fq85xln6Kf4?si=tg_BfX5WirF7neJ4.

Posselt, M., McIntyre, H., Ngcanga, M., Lines, T., & Procter, N. (2020). The mental health status of asylum seekers in middle- to high-income countries: A synthesis of current global evidence. *British Medical Bulletin*, 9, 134(1), 4–20. doi: 10.1093/bmb/ldaa010. PMID: 32409820.

United Nations. (1948). *Universal Declaration of Human Rights*. New York, NY: United Nations General Assembly.

Wiess, C. & Bensimon, M. (2019). Group music therapy with uprooted teenagers: The importance of structure. *Nordic Journal of Music Therapy*, 29(2), 174–189. https://doi.org/10.1080/08098131.2019.1695281.

Winsor, M. (2018, June). *On World Refugee Day 2018 a record 68.5 million forcibly displaced last year.* ABC News. https://abcnews.go.com/International/world-refugee-day-2018-record-685-million-forcibly/story?id=56026315.

CHAPTER 13

Songs of Travel

Songwriting with Children Displaced by War:
A Biopsychosocial Model, Methodology, and Possible
Taxonomy – Music and Transformation

NIGEL OSBORNE

This chapter is about songs written by children and others displaced by war. The title is a reference to Ralph Vaughan Williams' song cycle 'Songs of Travel' composed between 1901 and 1904, set to words drawn from a collection of Robert Louis Stevenson's poems of the same name, eventually published posthumously in 1908.

For Stevenson, travel was an ambiguous affair. He may in earlier years have identified himself as a 'romantic' traveller. But he had been forced to travel first and foremost in search of warm and dry climates to help him deal with the debilitating effects of sarcoidosis and other illnesses. Vaughan Williams set the poems when he was a young man, sometime before his life was also to take him on harrowing journeys. In 1914, he volunteered for the Royal Army Medical Corps and was a stretcher bearer in France in some of the bloodiest battles of the early First World War. And then came the horrors of Gallipoli, followed by gruelling service as an artillery officer.

The songs of displaced children and others we shall discuss – like Stevenson's journeys and like some of Vaughan Williams' life experiences – are overshadowed by suffering and war. They are songs of trauma, loneliness, deep sadness, extreme discomfort, and the pain of displacement. But they are also songs of the children's and others' life journeys, including resilience and defiance, memories of joyful times, and moments of stunning beauty and ecstatic happiness.

This is not a scientific study. It is a historical and anecdotal account of the use of songwriting to support children and others who have been displaced by conflict, primarily in the Balkans, Middle East, and Ukraine, but with reference to projects spread across four continents.

The songwriting projects form part of a wider 'community arts' intervention using music and creative arts to support children and others who are victims of war. The intervention began in early 1993 in Sarajevo, Bosnia and Herzegovina. There were no communications in the city, so workshops were organized in safe cellars and coordinated through a bush telegraph system with parents and families. In 1994, work also started in the Mostar region (Osborne, 2017a, 2015, 2009). By 1997, the project enjoyed support from War Child London and War Child Netherlands, and the Pavarotti Centre had been built and had opened in Mostar, housing a clinically supported music therapy department (Lang *et al.*, 2002; Woodward, 2012a, 2012b). Schools were now being rebuilt and were re-opening, so we were able to negotiate with the education authorities to take over the 'hours' for creative arts in the school curriculum (Journeyman Pictures, 2007).

In 1998, work began in Kosovo, in collaboration with War Child Netherlands, Médecins Sans Frontières (MSF), and World Child; in Georgia with the Gift Festival, the Georgian non-governmental organization (NGO) Atinati, and the Tbilisi Academy of Music; and in Chechnya with the then Chechen/Russian Little Star. This was followed in the early 2000s with work in Palestine, with The Children of Amal and the Palestinian Union of Social Workers and Psychologists, and in East Africa with the local NGO Art for Community Development, and the Ruwenzori Foundation. Further projects were to follow in South America, India, and South East Asia, with organizations such as Opera Circus, the Aurobindo Foundation, the Indian Head Injury Foundation, Yayasan Hasanah, Silpakorn University, and the Princess Galyani Vadhana Institute of Music in Bangkok (Osborne, 2011; Trevarthen *et al.*, 2014).

In recent years, projects have begun with Syrian refugees in Lebanon with SAWA for Development and Aid and Edinburgh Direct Aid International (Osborne, 2017b), and in Ukraine with Art Dot/Art Therapy Force, children's hospitals and shelters, and a consortium of universities including the Ukrainian Catholic University in Lviv, the Lviv Ivan Franko National University, Kharkiv University of the Arts, the Central Ukrainian Pedagogical University in Kropyvnytskyi, the University of Ivano-Frankivsk, and music colleges in Cherkasy and Uzhhorod.

Where the chapter is written in the first-person plural, 'we' refers to the relationships and collaborations listed above, and collectively to the many students and volunteers who joined us in our work.

SARAJEVO AND MOSTAR

The methodology evolved as the projects grew (Osborne, 2017a). The intervention began with the humblest of objectives: primarily the provision of musical and creative activities to distract children from negative experiences and the horrors of the war around them. But our team found that there were positive responses to creative work and the exploration of emotions and that musical activities could help regulate both hyperactive and sluggish behaviours among the children. Similarly, we found that musical activities could help promote trust, loss of fear, communication, joy, self-confidence, self-belief, self-respect, and socialization.

An important turning point came in 1995 in Sarajevo. The intervention was assessed by members of what remained of the Bosnian Ministry of Health. They described it as an effective 'therapeutic programme' and suggested it should be scaled up and rolled out in other parts of Bosnia. We had been careful not to use the word 'therapy' as we did not as yet have the necessary clinical conditions or support – these were to come later with the opening of the Pavarotti Centre and the founding of the clinical music therapy department. Although we were happy and proud to use the term 'therapeutic', we realized we had a responsibility to explain how and why we were prepared to use it.

Serendipitously, by the mid-1990s, a raft of research was emerging in music neuroscience and neurophysiology as well as in the psychology, psychobiology, and the social sciences of music that provided a valuable evidence base for our work, helped explain why we were effective, and enabled us to plot the way forwards. The evidence showed how PTSD could lead to dysregulation of the autonomic nervous system, endocrine system, movement repertoires, and breathing, how it could undermine such things as trust, empathy, cognitive development, hope, joy, self-confidence, and social communication, and how music could help regulate these systems and support these human values.

We were able to build a theoretical framework and scientific basis in tandem with the evolution of our methodology. The biopsychosocial model that emerged from this process has been described in detail elsewhere (Osborne, 2025; 2020; 2017a; 2011; 2009). It is a model both for intervention and for reflection.

The common thread running through all of these projects is that the intervention has always been 'local', has always begun as a result of invitations from local NGOs, and has usually been conducted in collaboration with local organizations.

In the early days in Sarajevo, there was a small corpus of musicians, artists, and health professionals keen to support the work and act as ani-mateurs. But in Mostar, by the end of the war, there was only one profes-sional musician left in the devastated East part of the city, and medical and psychosocial services were largely decimated. We decided to recruit and train young volunteers, including recently demobilized soldiers and young women who had been confined to cellars in one of the worst cases of shelling of a civilian population in the history of warfare. All of them had had their secondary or higher education seriously disrupted. This was a challenging undertaking, but in the long term, it worked out well. I remem-ber that the first generation of volunteers, many of whom carried their own burdens of trauma, were unable to concentrate, or sit or listen for long; they were constantly disrupting sessions and leaving the room to smoke. Within a year of patience and persistence, they had good focus, and in meetings, you could hear a pin drop (Osborne, 2014).

One activity that our young animateurs took to with passion was sing-ing. Some of them could also accompany themselves on the guitar. So songs and emotional journeys in song became an important part of the work. They helped to enliven, relax, and stimulate the children and generated an atmosphere of empathy and trust between the animateurs and the children. We made another useful discovery, or rather re-discovery: that children benefitted most when our animateurs were doing what they pro-foundly enjoyed and knew they could do well. In this way, our programme took on a doubly 'therapeutic' effect, both for traumatized children and for the young adults we had recruited in the aftermath and among the debris of war. The combination of an emphasis on creative work and singing songs led inevitably to songwriting.

We encouraged animateurs to co-create with the children in the way that was most comfortable for them – many had experience of joint com-position and co-creation from their rock and folk bands. But we also taught a 'backup' methodology that ensured that the work came primarily from the children, helped them in their cognitive and emotional development, and offered them a sense of creative ownership and achievement. We would work either individually or in small groups, but often in a hybrid of the two. Table 13.1 shows an example of a songwriting session with a small group of girls from Mostar, all with both trauma and special needs (high performing), at a summer camp by the Adriatic Sea in 1997. It is drawn in part from film footage shot at the time. It is important to note that we always insist that the children choose their own themes and subjects for songs.

Table 13.1: The songwriting process

Animateur	Children
'What colour is the sea?'	Girl 1: 'Blue'
'So do we have the first bit of our song? Blue Sea? The sea is blue?'	Silence...then Girl 1: 'Yes, I like that – blue sea'
'Are there any other colours?'	Girl 2: 'Yes'
'What kinds of colours?'	Girl 2: 'Green' Girl 3: 'And yellow and red'
'When is the sea yellow and red?'	Girl 3: 'In the evening'
'So does the first bit of the song continue: blue sea, green sea, yellow sea, red sea? Or do we add something about different times of day?'	Girl 1: 'No. It should be blue sea, green sea, yellow sea, red sea'
'So what is happening in this colourful sea?'	Girl 1: 'Fish are jumping in the sea' Girl 1 had earlier spotted a dolphin
So do we have the first part of our song now? 'Blue sea, green sea, yellow sea, red sea. Fish are jumping in the sea...?' (In Bosnian – *More plavo, more zeleno, more žuto, more crveno. Skaču ribe u more, skaču ribe u more*)	Girls together: 'Yes!' (cheering and clapping)

At this point, the animateur moves on to the melody, using a 'menu' method, offering choices of notes – and if possible, all choices at any given moment (see Table 13.2). The animateur uses her/his personal judgement to address questions of style. In Bosnia, it was fairly straightforward. The principal influences on children's musical culture were ex-Yugoslav children's songs (mostly with Western tonalities), Western classical music and Western pop, rock n roll, and jazz.

Table 13.2: Musical choices in songwriting

Animateur	Children
'What does this song sound and feel like?'	
The animateur plays several major and minor chords, and some more inventive and 'exotic' chords, and invites the girls to choose	The girls choose a simple C major chord

cont.

Animateur	Children
'Which note does it start on?' The animateur sings the notes most likely for a C major chord: mo - re mo - re mo - re	The girls choose E
'What is the next note?' The animateur sings various likely possibilities: mo-re pla - vo mo-re pla - vo mo-re pla - vo mo-re pla - vo continuing to all possibilities in C major: E B, E–C; E–D (descending), E–C, etc.	The girls choose E to G

The animateur continues in this systematic manner for every note of the song. It requires great patience, but we warn the children of this to begin with, and after one or two experiences the children realize there are rewards for their patience. As the process unfolds, it is important for animateurs to remember that this exercise helps build and rebuild cognitive capacity and emotional intelligence.

The children do not always remember all the possibilities, but they usually react to the musical interval they like when they hear it. Sometimes individual children spontaneously sing the next note or phrase, and such contributions are warmly accepted. We do not need to use musical notation in our work. Many of the animateurs we work with around the world cannot read Western notation. But they have better musical memories than most Western-literate musicians, and we usually make audio recordings of songwriting sessions. In the case of the composition 'More Plavo', beside the Adriatic Sea, there was no *a priori* rhythmic model. The rhythm emerged during composition and performance, and turned out to be a cross between a rock ballad and a show tune.

The harmony for 'Blue Sea/More Plavo' evolved in a number of stages. It was clear that the melody was in a Western style and would fit with Western-style harmony. The children were first offered the simplest harmonization:

mo-re pla-vo   mo-re ze-le-no

But the children were not inspired. They were much more interested when the animateur offered:

mo-re pla-vo   mo-re ze-le-no

And there was great excitement when they were offered a string of seventh chords – Cmajor7 – Am7 – Dm7 – G7 – with a pulsing, march-like, slow rock-ballad rhythm. The children wanted to add another verse, 'Ptice pjevaju' – the birds are singing – and thus completed a celebration of nature that we still sing every year, and a quarter of a century later, at our summer camps in Bosnia and Croatia.

mo-re pla-vo   mo-re ze-le-no   mo-re žu-to,   mo-re cr-ve-no

Ska-ču ri-be u mo-re   Ska-ču ri-be u mo-re

Over the course of more than a quarter of a century of workshops and camps, literally thousands of songs have been written by Bosnian children in this way. As we shall note later in the chapter, the songs reflect many aspects of the children's experiences. Alongside nature, home is an important theme.

For one summer camp where we had a large number of Roma children, I invited the Petrojvić Blasting Company from Los Angeles to join us – a group of talented young American brass, accordion, and percussion players who had diligently studied Roma music at the feet of the likes of Boban Marković and Taraf de Haïdouks. I also invited Misha, a gifted Russian-Australian creative musician and violinist who was later to become my composition student. Misha had a profound knowledge and love of the Eastern Roma string style. I had also, as a young man, played fiddle with a Roma band in the former Budapeszt Restaurant in Warsaw, and accompanied myself on the guitar, singing the songs of Teatr Romen in Moscow. So our theme for the camp was a 'Roma Opera'.

At the end of the camp, one of the boys who had been mooching around in the grass behind a big bonfire we had lit on a hillside told me, 'These are our sounds. I feel at home.' These were words that we would hear again and often, at different times and in different places.

LEBANON AND SYRIA

The first time I visited the Syrian refugee camps in Mar Elias, in 2015, I travelled with financial expert and philosopher Driss Ben Brahim, who had generously offered to fund the first year of the project. It was a brilliant day in early May. The Beqaa valley is 1000 feet above sea level so the spring air was fresh and intoxicating. Our NGO, SAWA for Development and Aid, had organized a 'day out' for the children of the camp in a field among walnut trees and oleanders, just a kilometre or two from the Syrian border.

I had for many years worked in Palestine (Osborne, 2011), little over 100 miles away, where the children were also refugees, spoke a very similar dialect of Levantine Arabic, and had comparable cultural and musical traditions. I imagined that work with these Syrian children would be very similar to work with the Palestinians, who in particular relished journeys around the world in music. We would sing and play songs with just one or two words and simple ostinatos and refrains that could be learned instantly: like 'Mwana Wange' or 'Pijin do mi so' from Uganda and Sierra Leone, the 'Canoe Song, Ho ho watanay' or 'This Old Hammer' from Canada and the USA, and 'Mo li Hua' or 'Sakura' from China and Japan. But in a happy atmosphere in warm spring sunshine, for the first time in my experience of many years in very many different cultures, this musical world-journey exercise fell entirely flat!

I later came to understand that there is a big difference between internally displaced children and externally displaced Syrian refugees. The Palestinian children, like those in the overcrowded Balata, Al Ain, and Askar camps in Nablus, were displaced from their ancestral homes, but were still geographically and emotionally in their 'own land'. From the perspective of life in their 'homeland' they could still relish exotic journeys around the world in song. But the Syrian children were not in their 'own land', even if they could see Syria from the flaps of their tents. As they described so eloquently in a song called 'Ana bas burah', they felt they were 'just outside' the door of their homeland. This made them yearn all the more heart-rendingly for Syria and for Syrian culture. I realized that I should base our therapeutic programme entirely on Syrian music.

With the help of the very supportive CEO of SAWA, Rouba Mhaissen, I contacted the distinguished Syrian musician Anas Abu Qaws, who was at the time living and working in Beirut. Anas is the son of one of the leading singers (if not the leading singer) of the Arabic musical world – Sabah Fakhri. Anas agreed to be our adviser and to act as my 'Syrian musical conscience'. I also made sure that among our teams of animateurs there were musicians with a profound and intimate knowledge of Syrian music. This meant that in our songwriting we would base our 'menu' of notes and rhythms on Arabic Levantine-style *maqam'at* (scales) and *iqa'at* (rhythmic modes). This proved very stimulating for the children – they were working directly with the raw materials and building blocks of their own musical culture, which they immediately recognized, understood, and cherished. Words were chosen with great care and with the extraordinary literacy cultivated by Syrian families even in the most challenging of conditions – language rich in allegory, anecdote, metaphor, metonymy, synecdoche, and simile. They were also songs full of love. When the children had finished composing the lyrics for a song, they would discuss which *maqam* they would like to use – every *maqam* is considered to have its own specific emotional character; and the rhythmic patterns – the *iqa'at* – have their own particular energies that the children would similarly discuss and then make appropriate choices.

The song 'Syria/Suria' became our 'anthem'. Ghiath, our leading musician, Abeer, a highly emotionally intelligent former air hostess-turned-art-educator, and I formed the animateur team on this occasion. The words the children composed began in an interesting way – a kind of love song to Syria, with a touch of spirituality and mystery – but then the children modulated the tone to 'memories of joy and peace', and how they felt greeted and blessed as they returned to school:

> *Syria, land of love and the righteous, a life of safety, time with family. With memories of joy and peace, and with greetings of welcome for a blessed return, we come to our school, aman, aman, aman.*

The children felt that the words had a feeling of spiritual love and mystery, qualities often associated with *maqam Hijaz*.

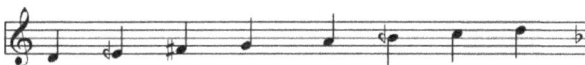

The *maqam* can have different interpretations of intonation in different contexts. Our Syrian musicians in Mar Elias always made the second degree of the scale E microtone-flat. I noticed it was the same in Palestine, although often in the Middle East, it is played closer to an equal-tempered E flat, which is actually the notation in most *maqam* textbooks, including the authoritative online *Maqam World*. Similarly, the sixth degree tends to be B microtone-flat. But I noticed in the song 'Suria' it was tuned closer to a B flat, probably because it began the second main phrase of the tune in a powerfully articulated way. The F sharp can sometimes be a microtone-flat, but in 'Suria', the children and musicians were usually closer (to my ear) to a brighter, almost equally tempered F sharp.

Maqams lend themselves to the 'menu' method of composition, because each note of the scale has a strong dynamic character. The first note of the *maqam*, the tonic, always has a powerful gravitational pull. When we gave the children the choices for the first note, for the word *Su-ri-a*, they were quick to choose the first note D, and then the second note E microtone-flat. For the word *hub* (love), they chose the bright fourth degree of the scale, then brighter still, the fifth degree for *hari* (proper, righteous), subsequently meandering downwards through the *maqam* to the tonic for *hayat aman ayla defa* (if I notated the lyrics correctly, *ayla* and *defa* – *family* and *time* – are both, as far as I know, Turkish loan words). From time to time, the children chose the rhythm, or *iqa'*, before creating the melody, in the same way as Western pop musicians set up rhythm loops to create melodies and harmonies over. But in this case, the choice of *iqa'* came later. There were two obvious choices: *Maksum* and *Baladi*; the children chose *Baladi*:

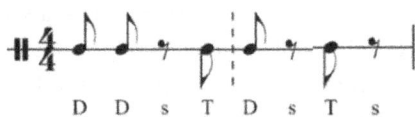

The song that was to become our anthem was now complete:

Or B
microtone-
flat

dhi-kraa fa-rah 'a-man ah-lan a-īd sa'-īd

Or E flat

za-yir ma-dra-si a- man

Or E flat Or E flat

a- man a- man

The animateur team was very touched by these lyrics. Most of our children had had no experience of a normal education until our informal schools opened. And many of them, as is sadly often the case among populations of traumatized children, were at the start highly hyperactive and destructive. Music played a large part in helping the children regulate themselves and also helped them settle down and feel 'welcome and blessed' in school. As the words of the song suggest, school had become associated with 'memories of joy and peace' and had taken on the character and feeling of Syria itself. The school had become their home, just like our camp had once become home, through music, for a young Roma boy wandering in the grass one late summer evening on a faraway hillside in Bosnia.

UKRAINE

I began work in Ukraine in September 2022, initially at the invitation of the Ukrainian NGO Art Dot, the Ukrainian Catholic University in Lviv, and the University of Arts in Kharkiv. Psychologist and psychotherapist Dr Anastasiia Shyroka, musicologist Professor Julia Nikolaevska, and I had designed a one-semester course introducing students to approaches to the theory and practice of 'Music in the Community' that would be useful in addressing the effects of the ongoing war on Ukrainian children and others. Although there are competent and skilful arts therapists working in Ukraine, there are far too few of them to deal with the magnitude of mental health problems, and there is as yet no certification or registration system. Our objective was to set up a course that would train a student workforce in simple and safe approaches to creative arts 'therapeutic' interventions. The course adopted a biopsychosocial approach very much in line with the methodology described earlier in this chapter. Other initiatives were to follow, with a course on Inclusion at the National Ivan Franko University in Lviv, and on Art Communication and Trauma-Informed Arts at both the Central Ukrainian Pedagogical University in Kropyvnytskyi and the University of Ivano-Frankivsk. In addition, training courses had begun for professional musicians, psychologists, and medical staff in hospitals in Lviv, Kharkiv, and Cherkasy. For the students, and indeed for everyone, the most important part of the courses has been supervised practical work on placement, which has included children's shelters, children's hospitals, and recently liberated front-line towns and villages (Osborne, 2023).

Over the last two years, during the course of these placements and associated camps, hundreds of songs have been composed by displaced children in shelters, villages, and hospitals. The music they have composed combines Western popular styles with Ukrainian popular and traditional styles. The lyrics have a wide variety of themes. Some of the songs the children write are valuable celebrations of experience, as in a song written by a group of five to ten-year-old children who enjoy playing percussion: Big Drum/Великий барабан/Veliykyi baraban: 'Velykyi baraban, velykyi baraban. Yaki baraban? Yaki baraban?' ('A big drum, a big drum. What drum? What drum?'). Sometimes more personal things emerge. In a group of children aged ten to twelve, a boy wrote a song, 'I don't know why I'm angry/Я не знаю, чому я злий/Ne znayu chomu ya zlyi'. Many songs from the older children are about meetings. In 'Black dog/Чорні пес/Chornyi pes', a dog is walking with his owner in the park and meets a small child.

Chor-nyi pes hulya-ye hay-da-nom u par-ku   Zu-striv ma-len-ke ko-zen-iat-ko

These songs are celebrations of normal relationships and normal lives. Here the melody is typically Ukrainian – a little melancholic, but also robust and resilient. Songs about home often feature in the work of displaced children, and these are frequently closely related to intensely patriotic songs. In a children's respite camp in the Carpathian mountains, a group of children enjoying respite from the horrors of Bakhmut wanted to write a tribute to Ukraine's soldiers, 'Our Warriors/Наші воїни/Nashi voini': 'Our soldiers are always with us, are always with us, are always with us. You risk your lives to help us, to help us, to help us. We have a song for you. Let the trenches ring with its sound, to uplift the soldiers' spirits, and help bring victory.'

A very intelligent and thoughtful-looking girl, maybe 17 years old, came to whisper in my ear. 'I would like to add – and grind the Russians to mince-meat.' The late Yevgeny Prigozhin, Putin's 'Little Chef', and head of the Wagner Corps private army, described Bakhmut as a 'meat grinder' – sadly the term caught on, on both sides. The girl's shy request raised an important moral question. We cannot censor traumatized young people's thoughts. Nor do we have the right to try to stop them from using songs to express their patriotism and resilience. But we have a duty of care to help them be true to themselves, and to help them avoid unnecessary brutalization. I told her she had every right to add these words. But I asked her to think about it first, maybe even sleep on it. Was it how she, clearly a person of humanity and dignity, would really behave? Did she really wish to mutilate her enemies? A song is forever. She came back to my workshop the next day and said without fuss that she did not wish to add the words. Our recording of the song was sent by colleagues to soldiers on the front line and became a 'hit' in the trenches.

TOWARDS A POSSIBLE TAXONOMY

While preparing this chapter, I reviewed 36 examples of children's songs from Bosnia, Lebanon/Syria, and Ukraine. In an informal way, I noted musical and verbal content, and mapped them onto both a spider graph of themes and a biopsychosocial model:

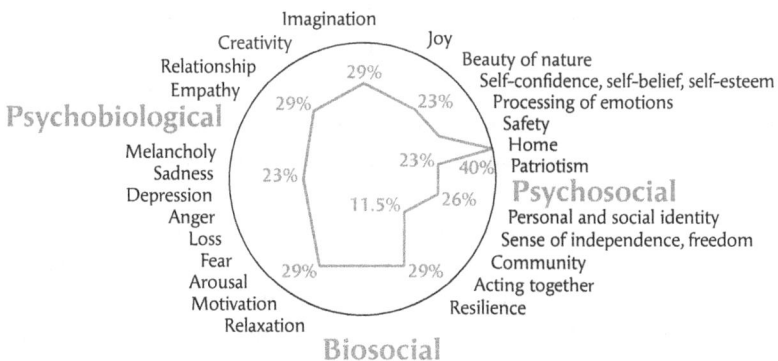

A scientifically prepared taxonomy would of course require many more examples and a more systematic approach to analysis. But this limited exercise shows some interesting and, in some ways, surprising results.

Only 11.5% of the songs allude to a sense of personal independence or freedom; 23% of songs are openly patriotic, although some songs dealing with 'home' or 'identity' also have fewer obvious patriotic undercurrents. Interestingly, 23% of songs are celebrations of nature. There seem to be two kinds of celebration: one is how children, for example from Mostar at creative camps by the Adriatic Sea, or young people from Kherson in the relative safety of the Carpathian Mountains, celebrate the nature around them in song. The other is how Syrian children who are refugees in Lebanon tend to write songs about the beauty of the nature of their former homes. For the older children, these are memories, but for the younger children who have never seen Syria, they are the paradise in their imaginations. Perhaps surprisingly, only 23% of songs have negative emotions (such as sadness, depression, fear, anger), and many that do have balancing positive emotions. Twenty-nine per cent of songs are, perhaps not surprisingly, concerned with imagination. The same percentage applies to resilience, relationships, motivation, and arousal. In purely musical terms, 40% of the songs may be regarded as 'arousing', and 60% as relaxed, simply joyful, or more mysterious or neutral.

Perhaps the most significant statistic of all for these groups of displaced children is that the most important descriptor and theme is 'home'. It is present in 40% of the songs. It is interesting that it occurs in 86% of the Syrian songs – composed by children driven out of their country, as opposed to internally displaced. It is very much the spirit of Syria, the song where children declared that the SAWA informal school in Mar Elias had become their home and the song itself their anthem. But it is no less significant that a young Roma boy in the mountains near Sarajevo – coming from a community doubly displaced, both internally and externally – should find, wandering behind a bonfire on a Balkan hillside, and listening to the strains of 'Djelem djelem' played by American brass players from Memphis and Los Angeles, an Australian Russian playing 'Čaje šukarije' on the fiddle, or 'Solnyshko' sung by an old man with a guitar from the Scottish Borders, that he had 'come home'.

The poems in the Songs of Travel collection referred to at the outset of the chapter and from which the title of this chapter is drawn were written in the last year of Stevenson's life on Samoa, during which time he was often bedridden. There are shades of the 'romantic' traveller in the writing, but the adolescent adventurer of earlier writings is left behind, and replaced by the compassionate local activist campaigning for the rights of Samoans, something that resonates to some extent with my own experience. The underlying themes of the collection are not only the joys of travel but also the grim challenges real-life travellers must face: loneliness, sadness, discomfort, despair, 'the upward and downward slope', the pain of displacement, but also resilience and defiance, as it says in Stevenson's 'The Vagabond': 'White as meal the frosty field. Warm the fireside haven. Not to autumn will I yield, Not to winter even!' When there are moments of beauty, they are not 'romantic', but rather existential: intimate glimpses of former lives, with memories of 'green days in forests and blue days at sea'. Like the displaced children's songs, these are songs of heightened experience, of travel through life, and of the essence of living. Through composing their own 'Songs of Travel', the children in turn not only begin to process difficult emotions and feelings, but also to engage with the unstoppable power of human creativity and, like Stevenson and Vaughan Williams before them, celebrate moments of intense experience, healing joy, and personal transformation.

REFERENCES

Journeyman Pictures. (2007, 16 October). *The Children of Post-War Bosnia*. YouTube. www.youtube.com/watch?v=cT-KZPVpU9M.

Lang, L., McInerney, U., & Monaghan, R. (2002). Supervision – Processes in Listening Together – An Experience of Distance Supervision of Work with Traumatised Children. In J. Sutton (ed.) *Music, Music Therapy and Trauma* (pp.211–231). London: Jessica Kingsley Publishers.

Osborne, N. (2025). The Psychobiologist Who Taught Musicians How to Sing. In J. Delafield Butt & V. Reddy (eds) *Intersubjective Minds: Rhythm, Sympathy, and Human Being*. Oxford: Oxford University Press.

Osborne, N. (2023). 'I Don't Know Why I'm Angry, I'm Angry, I'm Angry...' VAN magazine, Berlin. https://van-magazine.com/mag/music-therapy-nigel-osborne-ukraine.

Osborne, N. (2020). Imagination, Intersubjectivity, and a Musical Therapeutic Process. In A. Abraham (ed.) *The Cambridge Handbook of the Imagination* (pp.635–656). Cambridge: Cambridge University Press.

Osborne, N. (2017a). The Identities of Sevda: From Graeco-Arabic Medicine to Music Therapy. In R. MacDonald, D. J. Hargreaves, & D. Miell (eds) *Handbook of Musical Identities* (pp.722–735). Oxford: Oxford University Press.

Osborne, N. (2017b). Love, Rhythm and Chronobiology. In S. Daniel & C. Trevarthen (eds) *Rhythms of Relating in Children's Therapies – Connecting Creatively with Vulnerable Children* (pp.14–27). London: Jessica Kingsley Publishers.

Osborne, N. (2015). Running Away from Rock 'n Roll. In P. Wiegold & G. Kenyon (eds) *Beyond Britten: The Composer and the Community*. London: Boydell & Brewer. https://doi.org/10.2307/j.ctv136c1vj.

Osborne, N. (2014). The Plenum Brain. In D. Arsenijević (ed.) *Unbribable Bosnia and Herzegovina* (p.174). South East European Integration Perspectives, Nomos.

Osborne, N. (2011). Neuroscience and real-world practice: Music as a therapeutic resource for children in zones of conflict. *Annals of the New York Academy of Sciences*, 1252, 69–76.

Osborne, N. (2009). Music for Children in Zones of Conflict and Post-Conflict: A Psycho-biological Approach. In S. Malloch & C. Trevarthen (eds) *Communicative Musicality*. Oxford: Oxford University Press.

Trevarthen, C., Gratier, M., & Osborne, N. (2014). The human nature of culture and education. *WIREs Cognitive Science*, 5, 173–192.

Woodward, A. (2012a). Anger, joy and hope: Reflections of a revolutionary. An interview with Nigel Osborne. *Voices: A World Forum for Music Therapy*, 12(1). https://voices.no/index.php/voices/article/view/2040.

Woodward, A. (2012b). Arts-based practices in regions affected by war. *Voices: A World Forum for Music Therapy*, 12(2). doi: voices.v12i2.633.

A Hopeful Future

Global displacement is one of the biggest challenges of the 21st century. Conflicts around the world, some of which started last century, and some of which have only recently erupted, have repercussions that will last for decades to come. Climate-related disasters triggered more than half of new reported displacements in 2022 and experts estimate that climate change will result in further displacement of millions of people (UNHCR, 2023). In addition, countries in which people face severe economic challenges, including provision of healthcare and access to education, can experience an exodus of their population seeking improved living conditions. All of these circumstances add to what might be considered a perfect storm of displacement.

Increased numbers of music therapists and musicians in many parts of the world are rising to the challenge of working with displaced populations. There are projects and music therapists who specialize in addressing the concerns of those who have been displaced. Yet, displacement is not in itself a reason for referral to music therapy despite challenges that may be present for displaced persons. Music therapists in all settings could be working with people who have a history of displacement, sometimes without even knowing it.

Throughout the process of compiling this book, it became clear that there are in fact many music therapists and musicians around the world engaging with displaced persons, and yet the numbers are not nearly enough. This is not surprising. Displaced persons may not be attached to settings or organizations where there is a budget for services such as music therapy, or in a position for a variety of reasons to access these services.

Our vision is that this book and future developments in theory, practice, and research can provide enough evidence arguments for local and national governments, NGOs, and other relevant parties to include music and other creative arts therapies in their policies and plans of action for displaced persons. If there was a financial commitment to this also it would mean a much greater likelihood of such services being developed. We hope that this book has provided inspiration, education, and insight to those who might be working directly with displaced populations, those who might be thinking about starting a project, and those who might be occasionally encountering them in their day-to-day work.

Perhaps this book will inspire music therapists and musicians to consider turning their focus to this work and creating projects that can benefit the over 117 million displaced persons around the world. Whether it is directly working with individuals, creating interventions, conducting research, or training local leaders, this book has shown that there are many ways to support displaced persons, and there is an increasingly strong evidence base for it. This includes cutting-edge neuroscientific research, as described by Behrens in Chapter 2, strong research methodologies, such as that described by Coombes *et al.* in Chapter 11, and innovative and validated protocols, such as van Goor and Heynen described in Chapter 5. Additionally, more broader approaches to research are needed to explore the impact of programmes that train local leaders in music-based interventions, such as Coombes and Abou Amer describe in Chapter 8, and what long-term projects, such as the Bridges project explored in Chapter 6, offer.

What we can all agree on is that music and music therapy provide pathways for traversing trauma, supporting social transformation, and co-creating cultural connections. Sometimes, the communication and relational connections that music offers bring us glimpses of hopefulness and healing. Sometimes, words in a cornucopia of languages join together the harmony and melodies of home and far away to give expression to the depths of feelings that displacement creates. And sometimes, while music is but a single line in the book of the lives of displaced persons, it is one that brings its own impact to their overarching story.

So what is the way forward? It seems that the task falls on music therapists and musicians to advocate for and create more opportunities for working with displaced persons. More ongoing practice developments and research in this area are needed to further develop topics shared in this book, and the many more that are out there. Chapter 12 shows how music therapists can also support social transformations and plant the seeds for increased social justice following the lead of refugees, such as Moz, who want to use music to find a different way to raise their voices against injustice. Raising awareness can go a long way in garnering support for music therapy and music work with displaced persons. Ethical questions become of paramount importance; we hope that further debate and critical exploration of this will follow the publication of this book.

While funding remains a challenge for many projects, there is potential for music therapists and musicians to secure resources and advocate for the inclusion of their services. As the field continues to evolve, it is crucial that music therapists stay informed, collaborate, and persistently make the case for the vital role music can play in addressing the needs of displaced populations worldwide.

REFERENCE

UNHCR. (2023). *Climate change and displacement: The myths and the facts*. www.unhcr.org/news/stories/climate-change-and-displacement-myths-and-facts.

About the Contributors

Alexander F. Wormit, Prof. Dr. sc. hum. studied music therapy in Heidelberg with a doctorate from the University of Heidelberg. From 1998 to 2008 he was Research Associate at the German Centre for Music Therapy Research (Viktor Dulger Institute) DZM e.V. and, since 2008, Professor of Clinical Music Therapy at SRH University Heidelberg. He is also a member of the Scientific Advisory Board of the German Music Therapy Society (DMtG e. V.) since 2010; was Head of the Bachelor's programme in Music Therapy from 2010 to 2021; Vice Dean for Research at the Faculty of Therapy Sciences since 2021; member of the Federal Initiative Music and Dementia since 2022; and project leader for 'Bridges' since 2023. His research and publication focus is on music therapy in geriatric care and evidence-based music therapy (especially in the areas of chronic pain and palliative care).

Andrés Salgado Vasco is a Colombian music therapist, university professor, and researcher. He currently serves as a faculty member in the Master's programme in Music Therapy at Universidad Nacional de Colombia. He is the lead for community music therapy specialization, teaches theoretical and practical courses, and supervises thesis projects. As a community music therapist, he has contributed to social cohesion efforts with victims of the Colombian armed conflict and individuals in the reintegration process. He also works for SONO Music Therapy Center as a clinical music therapist at the Foundation Santa Fe University Hospital in Bogotá, in the neonatal, paediatric, and adult intensive care units, as well as in the oncology department. His experience also includes working with children and adolescents whose rights have been violated.

Anthony Mangiacotti PhD is a psychologist, neuroscientist, and consultant. He currently serves as a postdoctoral researcher for the MusiCare study, funded by the Dunhill Medical Trust at the MCCLab of Middlesex University. Anthony is a Teaching Tutor at the FISPPA Department, University of Padova, and lecturer at the Music Therapy School of Thiene, Italy. His research focuses on cognitive and music psychology, neuropsychology, and neurocognitive rehabilitation.

Bolette D. Beck has worked as Assistant Professor at Aalborg University in Denmark since 2012 (the Centre of Documentation and Research in Music Therapy). She is cand.mag. in ethnology and music therapy. She is an EAMI-registered Guided Imagery and Music therapist and trainer. She holds a PhD in music therapy (investigating Guided Imagery and Music for persons with work-related stress). Her research areas cover mixed methods studies in mental health populations and refugees, music and health studies, and music therapy pedagogics. She has special interests in music and imagery, cultural sensitivity, biomarkers (salivary hormones), embodiment and dance/movement therapy, psychedelics, shamanism, and spirituality. Currently, she is engaged in the psychological aspects of the climate crisis and the green transition, using music and imagery for the exploration of nature's embeddedness and the more-than-human. She is a consultant and music programmer for several psilocybin studies at Rigshospitalet in Denmark.

Cordula Reiner-Wormit is a qualified music therapist with a therapeutic licence for psychotherapy. She established the subject of music therapy at the Waghäusel-Hambrücken e.V. music school in 1999. In 2002, she was involved in the founding of the nationwide working group for music therapy at music schools and has since been involved in professional policy, particularly with regard to interdisciplinary and multi-professional networking with the Association of German Music Schools (VdM) and the German Music Therapy Society (DMtG). She has been a lecturer on the Early Childhood and Elementary Education programme at the Heidelberg University of Education since 2007 and also works as a composer, musician, and group analytical supervisor. Together with jazz singer Jutta Glaser, she developed the concept of Spielraum Musik in Heidelberg accommodation centres for refugees (Germany) in 2015, which expanded into the Bridges project in 2022.

Danny D. Kora graduated with a degree in Music Therapy at Berklee College of Music in 2008, and has since then been living in Istanbul, Turkey, focused on the use of music therapy for mental health, child growth and development, and trauma rehabilitation for war survivors. He led a music therapy programme at a psychiatric hospital in Istanbul for five years, working with both acute and chronic patient groups. He co-developed two separate multidisciplinary programmes for Syrian refugee children in Turkey, and Rohingya refugees in Bangladesh, and has worked with a team to support multinational refugees living in Germany. He is currently focused on using music to support children's growth and development, working at multiple schools with young learners. Artistically, Danny produces original music in various genres, using his multi-instrumental skills to create both live and electronic music. He is also known as Danny S. Lundmark.

Diane J. Pitzer, born in Thailand and raised in Germany, is a dedicated trainer and practitioner of trauma-informed bodywork. Since 2016, she has operated her own practice, offering compassionate support to individuals dealing with trauma. In 2019, she expanded her work by educating others in trauma-informed therapy. Diane is also a singer-songwriter, anti-racism trainer, and activist, bringing her unique voice and perspective to both her music and social justice efforts. She serves on the board of Migration Hub, focusing on intersectionality, colonialism, and racism. As a member of the Bridges team since 2019, Diane leads the Spielraum-Musik groups, applying her skills as a trauma-sensitive musician to foster healing and connection through music. Her work is deeply rooted in her commitment to addressing both individual and systemic trauma, making her a powerful advocate for personal and societal transformation.

Elizabeth Coombes PhD, FAMI is currently Course Director of the MA Music Therapy at the University of South Wales in the UK. She has been a music therapist for over 20 years, working primarily in the field of children, young people, and families. Since 2009, she has worked in Palestine providing support and training to people who want to use music therapeutically with those whom they educate or care for. She has published widely on a range of topics including neonatal care, liminal spaces in therapy, music therapy pedagogy, and interactive therapeutic music-making. Liz is passionate about matters of social justice; working with displaced persons and refugees is at the centre of her thinking and work. She is currently part of a mixed methods co-produced music therapy research project involving displaced mothers and pre-school children, to understand the potential benefits of this for them.

Emma Maclean is a music therapist and lecturer in music therapy in Scotland. She has worked in the National Health Service in the UK for 20 years where she is currently lead for an Arts Psychotherapies Communities Adult Mental Health Team. She has facilitated music therapy across the lifespan, working with children, adults, and older persons, including work with displaced persons when they have sought help from statutory mental health services. Emma is intrigued by different ways of knowing and sense-making that can emerge from being in relation through the arts. As a part-time lecturer at Queen Margaret University, she enjoys exploring arts therapies in context with learners and her current research interests include how we create conditions to review and agree meaningful changes across the arts therapies. She is also a musician, mother, wife, and friend and enjoys playing chamber, orchestral, traditional folk music, and tango on her violin.

Emma O'Brien PhD, RMT, OAM is the founder of music therapy at the Royal Melbourne Hospital (RMH), RMH Scrub Choir, the Global Scrub Choir, and the Global Health Choir. Emma is an internationally renowned innovator in the role of music in well-being, specializing in facilitating the creation of original songs with individuals and communities and in unique staff well-being projects. She is a singer, theatre maker, music therapist, composer, researcher, writer, video editor, and choir master. Emma was awarded a Medal of the Order of Australia in 2017 for her service to community through music therapy programmes. Emma's work has been published in peer-reviewed journals and major texts. Most recently she has been collaborating with the World Health Organization and was invited to speak at and lead the Global Scrub Choir at the opening of the 76th World Health Assembly at the United Nations in Geneva, 2023.

Eva Marija Vukich MA, MT-BC is a music therapy researcher and doctoral student at the University of Bergen in Norway. Born in rural Alaska, Eva grew up as a 'third culture kid', with a sense of fluidity among multiple homes and cultures, and finding their belonging within migrant communities. They were drawn into the field of music therapy with an interest to understand how music and arts naturally support post-conflict resilience and peace efforts in the former Yugoslavian region. They completed their Bachelor's degree in music therapy at Temple University, and Master's in Refugee Studies and Community Development at the University of East London. Their postgraduate research contributed a framework by which music therapists could sensitively engage with refugee and migrant lived experience through intersectional and ecological lenses. In 2022, Eva co-founded SADA, providing music therapy consultations for psychosocial teams in refugee care services who desire to thoughtfully integrate music into their practice.

Evelyn Heynen is Assistant Professor of Clinical Child and Youth Psychology at the Open University of the Netherlands. Her research interests centre around children and youth living in residential youth care, youth detention, or who are displaced. Evelyn has published in several peer-reviewed journals, and has contributed to national and international conferences.

Fabia Franco PhD was a developmental psychologies and lifespan music psychologist. She had expertise in environmental influences on infant communication and social development, music and early development, and music and cognitive benefits through the lifespan. She was the Director of the Middlesex Music Cognition and Communication lab, and was directing MusiCare (funded by the Dunhill Medical Trust), an RCT evaluating different types of music therapy intervention on well-being, cognitive function, and biomarkers in older adults who are healthy or living in care homes. Fabia was the Principal Investigator in M4DD. She passed away in January 2024.

Gene-Ann Behrens is a Professor Emeritus after 23 years of directing music therapy at Elizabethtown College, Pennsylvania, USA; a board-certified music therapist of 48 years; and a certified clinical trauma professional. She continues a consulting career as a workshop leader, author, lecturer, and supervisor. Her 16-year interest in neuroscience has led to giving over 90 workshops in 17 countries on a neuro-informed approach to stress and trauma, specifically working in Bethlehem, Palestine; Hargeisa, Somaliland; and Nairobi, Kenya. Gene-Ann was also invited to speak at Penn State Hershey Medical Center, USA; a NATO Security workshop in Turkey; the Mahatma Gandhi Medical College and Research Institute in India; and the ArtEZ University of the Arts in the Netherlands. She was actively involved in committees and executive boards for regional, national, and world music therapy organizations. Gene-Ann also is an avid photographer who has had exhibitions of three photography shows.

Hala Hamdan, a certified music therapist for 12 years, is also a parental counsellor and musician. Motivated by a mission to serve her community, both locally and internationally, she focuses on disadvantaged groups such as refugees and those from low socioeconomic backgrounds. For the past five years, she has worked at the Dana Children's Hospital in Tel Aviv, providing mental support to oncology patients from conflict zones like Gaza and the West Bank. Her work, addressing trauma and serious illness, has brought her significant satisfaction. Additionally, she supported refugee children at a school in south Tel Aviv and managed a mandolin ensemble in Jaffa for children from challenging backgrounds. Believing in music as a universal language that bridges cultural and social gaps, she recently co-founded SADA, a project aimed at training staff working with refugees in music therapy. As a Palestinian, she empathizes deeply with issues of belonging and identity, dedicating herself to helping others through music.

Heidi Ahonen PhD, RP, MTA, FAMI is a Professor of Music Therapy and the Co-ordinator of the Music Therapy PhD Programme at Wilfrid Laurier University in Ontario, Canada. She was born in Finland and moved to Canada in 2001. Heidi specialized in trauma psychotherapy and is a registered psychotherapist and accredited music therapist. In 2014, she graduated from the Harvard University Refugee Trauma – Global Mental Health: Trauma and Recovery Certificate Program. Heidi is also a group analyst and developed the Group Analytic Music Therapy method in 2007. She regularly conducts Refugee Trauma 101 and vicarious trauma workshops internationally. In her private practice, she works with refugees who have experienced trauma.

Letitia Slabu PhD is an experimental social psychologist with research expertise in well-being, authenticity, mindfulness, social values, and behaviour change. Her work has been covered by media outlets worldwide as it highlights how research and technology can work together to advance the study of authenticity and well-being. She is dedicated to real-world application of her work. Her recent interest is in music therapy interventions targeted at improving refugees' sense of their true self and their well-being.

Mitsi Akoyunoglou is an Assistant Professor of Music Therapy and Inclusive Music Practices at Ionian University, Greece. She completed her Bachelor's and Master's degrees in music therapy at Michigan State University, USA, and a doctorate and postdoc at Ionian University, Greece. She is the Regional Liaison for Europe (2023–2026) at the World Federation for Music Therapy, and the Country Representative of Greece to the European Music Therapy Confederation. She is a member of the scientific committee of Mousiko Pedagogika and on the editorial board of *Approaches: An Interdisciplinary Journal of Music Therapy*. She has published her work in various journals and edited volumes and has co-edited the open access resource *Music Therapy Dictionary: A Place of Interdisciplinary Encounters*. Her research interests include community music and community music therapy with refugee children and adolescents, music pedagogy and inclusion, trauma-informed music practices, informal music teaching, and Universal Design for Learning.

Nigel Osborne is a composer, Emeritus Professor of Music and Human Sciences at the University of Edinburgh, and guest professor at universities in Kharkiv, Lviv, Kropyvnytskyi, and Ivano Frankivsk. He has helped pioneer musical interventions to support children who are victims of conflict in the

Balkans, Caucasus, East Africa, Middle East, South East Asia, and Ukraine. He was recently awarded the British Academy of Songwriters and Composers Award for inspiration, and the Doubleday Medal of the University of Manchester for contributions to medicine.

Samuel Gracida is a seasoned music therapist, multi-instrumentalist, and business owner, with a global footprint in the fields of music therapy and music and medicine. With extensive experience in Germany, Colombia, Mexico, and the USA, Samuel has played a role in advancing the therapeutic role of music worldwide. As a former executive committee member of the International Association for Music and Medicine, he is deeply committed to promoting music therapy as a tool for harmony and healing, particularly for displaced persons. Currently, Samuel is an integral part of the Bridges project, delivering impactful music interventions to displaced youth in Heidelberg, Germany. Through his work, he continues to champion the global expansion of music therapy, fostering healing and well-being across diverse communities.

Sander van Goor is a Dutch music therapist specializing in trauma treatment, particularly with refugee children, youth, and their families. He developed the Safe & Sound intervention, integrating music therapy into schools for refugee children in the Netherlands. Sander also conducts training and workshops on trauma, resilience, and music therapy. As a trainer for the NGO Sounds of Change, he has guided professionals on using music in psychosocial support programmes in (post-)conflict areas, including Syria, Iraq, Lebanon, Palestine, Jordan, Bosnia and Herzegovina, Brazil, Turkey, and Greece. Additionally, he serves as a guest lecturer in several Master's and Bachelor's programmes in music therapy. Alongside his therapeutic work, Sander is a passionate musician, playing both the double bass and guitar, as well as various ethnic instruments like the ney and percussion instruments.

Saphia Abou Amer is a British Palestinian music therapist who for the past several years has been residing in Madrid, Spain. Saphia graduated from the University of Roehampton in 2017 with an MA in Music Therapy, having completed an MSc in psychology at the University of Westminster. Following her BA Hons in International Relations and Spanish, and after a period of volunteering with children in the Gaza Strip, she decided to pursue a career as a music therapist. Saphia's career as a music therapist has involved working with children and adults within the clinical areas of brain injury, dementia, adoption, and skill-sharing. In 2023, Saphia qualified as a vocal psychotherapist and has now set up her own private practice in Madrid. She also provides business support services to healthcare professionals.

Tamar Hadar PhD is a music therapist, supervisor, and lecturer at the School of Creative Arts Therapies, University of Haifa, working with children and families in an early intervention unit and in a private practice. She specializes in child-parent interventions, specifically in the context of trauma and displacement. Her research centres on the theory and assessment of clinical improvisation; music therapy for infants and preterm babies; and culturally sensitive music therapy. Currently, she is enrolled in the Nordoff-Robbins Blended Learning Certification training at NYU Steinhardt. She has originated a time-oriented model for analysing clinical improvisations. She is a professional flautist, loving spouse, and a mother to three children.

Subject Index

7 October 2023 24
  see also Occupied
    Palestinian
    Territories (OPT)

Abbott, Tony 236, 239
Abou-Amer, Saphia 166
acculturation (literature
    review) 38–9
adverse childhood
    experiences (ACEs) 127
amygdala 55, 89
anti-oppressive practice 34
Art for Community
    Development 252
Art Dot/Art Therapy
    Force 252, 261
Art and Sport for
    Life by Animarte
    programme 187
asylum seeker
    (definition) 11, 18
Atinati 252
attention modulation 131
Aurobindo
    Foundation 252
Australia
  asylum policy
    236–40, 245
  Julian Burnside KC
    Asylum Seeker
    Letter Writing
    Campaign 240
  Manus Island Detention
    Centre 235–9, 245–6
  music therapy with
    asylum seekers 233–4

see also Moz 'All
    the Same' song/
    video project
autobiographical
    memory 87
autoharp 153
autonomic nervous
    system 52
axon 51

band workshops 139–40
behaviour/motor
    modulation 132
biopsychosocial
    model 253, 263–5
Blanco, Edgar 189
body relaxation
    exercises 91
Bosnia 252
bottom-up vs. top-
    down approach 58
Brahim, Driss Ben 258
brain development 56–7
brainwave frequencies
    62
breathing exercises
    during Narrative Music
    Psychotherapy 91
  for vagal tone 60
Bridges project
    band workshops 139–40
    concerts 140–1
    'Conductor' game 137
    current team 124–6
    European grant for 141
    music lessons 138–9
    Noor and Alina (in

case studies) 126,
    130, 135–6, 137–41
  overview 123–4
  resilience in 134–6
  safe(r) spaces 130
  Spielraum Musik
    sessions 136–8
  'Stop Dance' game
    132, 137
  see also heuristic
    effect factors in
    music therapy
Burnside, Julian 240

caja 196
call-and-response
    experiences 59–60, 153
cell body 51
central nervous system 52
challenging clients 63–4
change agent (music
    as) 224–5
character (in 7 Cs
    of Resilience
    Model) 134–5
Chechen/Russian
    Little Star 252
Children of Amal 252
choice of music
    Colombia 196–7
  cultural sensitivity
    and 39–40, 178
  in intercultural
    setting 73–4
  in Narrative Music
    Psychotherapy 98–9
  prejudices about 82

rap music 36, 128
Western music 39
choice to participate
    or not 157
chord resolution 89
chronological memory 87
climate change 267
co-regulation 62–3, 128, 130
cognition modulation
    132–3
Colombia
    Art and Sport for
        Life by Animarte
        programme 187
    banditry period 184
    choice of music
        used 196–7
    Community Music
        Therapy for
        Social Cohesion
        Construction
        project 191–2
    development of music
        therapy in 188–9
    Fundación Nacional
        Batuta 187
    future directions 197–8
    integration between
        law and music
        therapy 193–4
    internal displacement
        in 184–6
    key elements of
        music therapy
        practice in 194–6
    Medellín Music Schools
        Network 187–8
    Music for Reconciliation
        programme 188
    music therapy
        with Benposta
        Nation of Youth
        Organization 193
    music therapy with
        communities
        affected by El
        Quimbo dam 194
    music therapy with the
        Jitnu community 192
    Music Therapy in
        Processes of
        Re-Signifying Self-
        confidence 190

music therapy-
    Pagamento ritual
    integration 191, 195–6
    musical instruments
        used 196–7
    peace agreements 184–5
    Pilot Programme of
        Music Therapy as
        a Tool to Foster
        Coping 190–1
    training in 189
    Unified Victim Registry
        statistics 186
colonial history (lack of
    response to) 169–70
'community arts'
    intervention 252
community music
    therapy approaches
    (literature review) 36–7
competence (in 7
    Cs of Resilience
    Model) 134–5
complex PTSD 70
composing
    in Safe & Sound
        intervention 116–17
    see also songwriting
concerts 140–1
'Conductor' game 137
confidence (in 7 Cs
    of Resilience
    Model) 134–5
connection (in 7
    Cs of Resilience
    Model) 134–5
consciousness 133
consistency 130
contribution (in 7
    Cs of Resilience
    Model) 134, 136
control (in 7 Cs
    of Resilience
    Model) 134–5
Convention Relating
    to the Status of
    Refugees 12
Coombes, Elizabeth
    166–7, 215, 216
coping (in 7 Cs
    of Resilience
    Model) 134–5
cortex area 57

cortisol levels 55–6, 89
COVER model of music
    therapy 32, 41
cultural connections
    (literature review) 37–8
cultural humility 34,
    39–40, 73, 80, 151
cultural responsiveness
    39–40
cultural sensitivity 39–40,
    73, 74–5, 106–7
cyclic sighing 60

dance, music, and art
    combined 206
daydreaming 133
decolonization 34
defences (respecting) 93
dehumanization of
    refugees 155
dendrites 51
Denmark see Music and
    Imagery (MI) method
depression 89
'developing countries'
    (ideas about) 169
developmental trauma 35
displaced persons
    definition 17–18
    diversity of 17–18, 40
    energy saved for
        settling down 26
    statistics 11, 15
dissociation 71
dopamine 89
dorsal nervous system 53
dorsal vagal freeze 129
dysregulated nervous
    system vs. regulated
    nervous system 54–5

Edinburgh Direct Aid
    International 252
educational settings
    literature review 35
    refugee children
        in 104–5
    see also Safe & Sound
        intervention
embodiment theory 129
emotional modulation
    (Bridges project) 132

empathic understanding
157
empty chair technique 97
ethical challenges
155–7, 234
Ethnomusic therapy 196
EU-Turkey deal
(2016) 146, 148
Eurocentric music therapy
practices/theories 170
eyes open/closed (when
listening) 73

facilitator training 43
Fedotiuk, Tamara 215, 219
fight or flight responses
52, 107, 128
flashbacks 92
flight phase 149–50
forced displacement 186
see also displaced
persons
Franco, Fabia 214
Fundación Nacional
Batuta 187

Galbraith, Jane 241
generalized anxiety
disorder (GAD-7)
measure 217
generative listening 40
Germany
racism in 127–8
see also Bridges project
'ghosts' metaphor 150
Gift Festival 252
Gracida, Samuel 125
Grandmothers for
Refugees 239
gratitude 76
Greece
'hotspot of Europe' 146
refugees in 145–6
'we are all refugees'
protests 147
see also SamSam groups
grounding exercises 92
Group Analytic Music
Therapy 87, 93
groups
band workshops 139–40
discussion within 93

literature review 36–7
multiple cultures in 40
narration of
trauma in 34
risks of 'othering' 38
Safe & Sound
intervention
105–6, 109–14
guacharaca 196
Guided Imagery
in Music 37
guided music listening 99
Guided Original Lyrics
and Music (GOLM)
principles 234, 246

Hadar, Tamar 215
Hamdan, Hala (story
of) 24–7
Harris, Blair 232,
244, 244–5
heart rate variability
(HRV) 60
Hebb's Theory 57
Heidelberg Bridges Project
see Bridges project
Herzegovina 252
heuristic effect factors
in music therapy
attention modulation 131
behaviour/motor
modulation 132
cognition modulation
132–3
emotional
modulation 132
interpersonal
communication 133–4
hippocampus 89
holistic models 34
home
concept of 70–1
'fighting for her house'
(vignette) 80–1
homecoming theme 82
'jinni' in 78
music as 71–2
'Music Playroom – A
Piece of Home' 124
poor housing
conditions 76–7
'hotspot' approach 146

human rights
discourses 12
humiliation 93
humming (to increase
vagal tone) 60, 72

improvisation
assumptions around 39
cathartic events
during 89
in Music for Displaced
Dyads (M4DD) 225
in Narrative Music
Psychotherapy
99–100
Indian Head Injury
Foundation 252
indicated prevention 104
insomnia 89
integration (literature
review) 38–9
interactive therapeutic
music-making (ITM-
M) groups (OPT)
overview 164, 177–9
practice considerations
169–71
projects 164–6
see also Music as Therapy
International
(MasT) training
International Covenant
on Civil and
Political Rights 12
International Trauma
Questionnaire 34
interpersonal
communication
(music as) 133–4
intersectionality lens 170
iqa'at (rhythmic
modes) 259–60
Israel Hamas war
impact of 27
professional
associations'
stances on 28
remote sessions
during 25–6
SADA project 25

'jinni' 78, 79–80

Kosovo 252

language acquisition
  literature review 36
  Music for Displaced
    Dyads (M4DD) 223
  Safe & Sound
    intervention
    (Netherlands) 106
  and successful
    integration 127
Lebanon songwriting
  project 258–61
limbic system 57
liminal spaces 150
literature review
  cultural responsiveness/
    humility 39–40
  group working 36–7
  integration and
    acculturation 38–9
  language acquisition 36
  overview 31–3
  search criteria 31
  skill sharing 41–2
  social transformations
    and increased
    cultural
    connections 37–8
  stepped approaches
    40–1
  themes (overview) 33
  trauma and PTSD
    in educational
    contexts 35
  trauma and PTSD
    in healthcare
    settings 33–4
  trauma-informed
    practice and
    establishing trust
    through musical
    connections 35–6
Lummi sticks 59

McCracken, Jane 240
McGorrian, Tom 215
Mangiacotti, Anthony 214
Manus Island Detention
  Centre 235–9, 245–6
maqam'at (scales) 259–61
maracas 196

Matthews, Ellie 215,
  216, 219, 221–3
Médecins Sans Frontières
  (MSF) 252
Medellín Music Schools
  Network 187–8
medical models 34, 75
melatonin 89
memory
  body's 89
  trauma 87
Mhaissen, Rouba 259
mirror neuron network 60
Mostar songwriting
  project 252,
  253–8, 254–8
motor/behaviour
  modulation 132
Moz 'All the Same' song/
  video project
  credits 248–9
  establishing the
    collaboration 240–1
  honouring Moz's voice
    in production
    process 242–6
  life of the video 247–8
  link to 233
  lyrics 241–2
  Moz's background 235
  participants 232–3,
    239–41
  release of video 247
  songwriting context 234
  timeline (for
    context) 235–9
music (as central agent
  for change) 224–5
music, dance, and art
  combined 206
Music for Displaced
  Dyads (M4DD)
  as agent for change 224–5
  background 213–14
  film about 214
  group evolution 221–3
  groups in 216–7
  improvisatory
    approach 225
  language development
    during 223
  qualitative data 219–25
  quantitative data 217–19

safety, structure,
  and regulation
  theme 220–1
social skills development
  223–4
study design 215–16
study discussion 225–7
team 214–16
Music and Imagery
  (MI) method
  overview 72–3
  session structure 73
  vignette 1: the sorrow
    of a mother 76–7
  vignette 2: feeling safe at
    home alone 77–80
  vignette 3: fighting for
    her house 80–1
music lessons (Bridges
  project) 138–9
Music for Reconciliation
  programme 188
Music Taxonomy 82
Music as Therapy
  International
  (MasT) training
  changes made to 171–2
  distance learning
    programme 172–7
  impact in OPT 171–2
  personal and
    professional
    influence 175–7
  projects 41–2, 165, 168–9
  therapeutic stance 174–5
Musicians Without
  Borders 172
musicking 37, 156
myelin sheath 51

narrative approach 12–13
Narrative Exposure
  Therapy 96
Narrative Music
  Psychotherapy
  choice of music 98–9
  chronological life
    journey: 'sounds
    of pain and hope'
    intervention 96–7
  guided music
    listening 99

Narrative Music
  Psychotherapy *cont.*
  'if I were a tree'
    intervention 94-6
  improvising with
    client 99-100
  induction image 98
  instruments in 90
  'my future...'
    intervention 97
  'my refugee journey'
    intervention 94
  overview 87
  processing: storytelling
    with music 93-4
  psychoeducation in 93
  session structure
    90-1, 97-100
  stabilization: grounding
    and relaxation 91-2
neoliberalism 34
nervous system
  autonomic 52
  central 52
  co-regulation of 62-3
  dorsal 53
  micro view of 51-2
  parasympathetic 52-4
  peripheral 52
  regulated vs.
    dysregulated
    54-5, 55-6
  somatic 52
  structure of 52-4
  sympathetic 52
  vagal nerve 53-4
  ventral 53-4
Netherlands *see* Safe &
  Sound intervention
neuroception 72
neurogenesis 56
neuroplasticity 58-60
neuroscience perspective
  application of 49-50
  brain development 56-7
  maturational changes 57
  neuroplasticity 58-60
  repetition and synaptic
    change 57
  resiliency 61
  vagal tone 60-1
Nikolaevska, Julia 261
norepinephrine 55

'nothing about us without
  us' movements 28

O'Brien, Emma 232,
  239-40, 242-3, 243-4,
  244, 245, 246, 247-8
Occupied Palestinian
  Territories (OPT)
  history 167-8
  ITM-M projects in 164-6
  see also Music as Therapy
    International
    (MasT) training
Opera Circus 252
othering (risks of) 38

Pagamento ritual
  191, 195-6
Palestine *see* Occupied
  Palestinian
  Territories (OPT)
Palestinian Union of
  Social Workers and
  Psychologists 252
parasympathetic
  functioning
  measurement 218
parasympathetic nervous
  system 52-4
participants' voices 170-1
Patient Health
  Questionnaire
  (PHQ-9) 217
patriarchal structures 75
Pavarotti Centre
  (Mostar) 252
peripheral nervous
  system 52
Petrojvic Blasting
  Company 257
phenomenological
  approach 34
Pilkington, Craig 232,
  243, 245, 248
Pitzer, Diane Jeeranut 125
polyvagal theory 72
post-traumatic
  stress disorder
  complex 70
  in educational
    contexts (literature
    review) 33-4

in healthcare settings
  (literature
  review) 33-4
  varying prevalence of 70
post-traumatic stress
  disorder checklist
  (PCL-5) 217
potentially traumatic
  events (PTEs) 107
power imbalance 75
predictability of
  musical structures
  35, 71-2, 89, 220-1
'presentification' 71
professional associations'
  stances on Israel
  Hamas war 28
psychoeducation 93, 117
Psychological First Aid
  (PFA) principles 151

Qaws, Anas Abu 259
Queensland Poetry
  Festival 241, 247
questionnaires
  Frankfurt Acculturation
    Scale 34
  generalized anxiety
    disorder (GAD-7)
    measure 217
  Harvard Trauma
    Questionnaire 34
  International Trauma
    Questionnaire 34
  Patient Health
    Questionnaire
    (PHQ-9) 217
  post-traumatic stress
    disorder checklist
    (PCL-5) 217
  Riverside Stress
    Acculturation
    Inventory 34
  Short Warwick-
    Edinburgh
    Wellbeing Scale
    (SWEMWBS) 217

racism
  in Germany 127-8
  in Scandinavia 74
rap music 36

Rap and Sing Music
    Therapy 128
receptive music theory 82
redoblante 196
reflexivity prompts 28–9
refugee
    definition 11, 17, 146
    term used to label and
        marginalize 155
refugee children
    definition 146
    impact of forced
        migration on 149
'refugee crisis' (2015-
        2016) 146
refugee experience
    flight phase 149–50
    'survival' stage 148–9
regulated nervous system
    in Music for Displaced
        Dyads (M4DD)
        220–1
    resilience and 136
    vs. dysregulated nervous
        system 54–5, 128
Reiner-Wormit,
    Cordula 125
relaxation exercises
    (in Narrative Music
    Psychotherapy) 91
remote sessions 25–6
repetition and synaptic
    change 57
research protocols
    design 216–17
resilience
    7 Cs Model 134–6
    in Bridges project 134–6
    components of 134
    neuroscience perspective
        (resiliency) 61
    Syrian refugees 205–6
respiratory sinus
    arrhythmia (RSA)
    measurement
    218–19, 226–7
Riverside Stress
    Acculturation
    Inventory 34
Rohingya (Trainer
    of Trainers
    programme) 204
Rudd, Kevin 236, 239

Ruwenzori
    Foundation 252

SADA project 25
Safe & Sound intervention
    case example:
        Amir 117–19
    culture-sensitive
        approach 106–7
    group sessions
        105–6, 109–14
    indicated prevention 104
    individual sessions 105–6
    learning Dutch 106
    overview 32, 41,
        103–5, 119
    phase 1: establishing
        safety 109–11
    phase 2: composing
        116–17
    phase 3: integration 117
    psychoeducation in 117
    selective prevention 103
    trauma-sensitive
        approach 107–8
safe space (definition) 156
safe(r) spaces 130
safety
    feeling safe at home
        alone 77–80
    keeping the therapy
        safe 97–100
    sense of 61–2
    theme in Music for
        Displaced Dyads
        (M4DD) 220–1
    see also Safe & Sound
        intervention
SamSam groups
    creation of 151
    implementation 152–3
    outcomes 154–5
    supports for the
        team 153–4
    training of team 152
Sarajevo songwriting
    project 252, 253–8
SAWA for Development
    and Aid 252, 259
selective prevention 103
self-care 100, 154
self-regulation

    and resilience 136
    see also regulated
        nervous system
shame 93
Short Warwick-Edinburgh
    Wellbeing Scale
    (SWEMWBS) 217
Shyroka, Anastasiia 261
skill sharing 41–2, 163
    see also training
Slabu, Letitia 214
social capital 36–7
social engagement
    system 52, 128
social justice approach
    166, 170
social transformations
    (literature review) 37–8
solidarity, act of
    standing in 147–8
solution-focused
    questions 117
somatic nervous system 52
Song Seeking projects 38
'Songs of Travel'
    251, 264–5
songwriting
    censoring during song
        creation 263
    as democratic
        process 207–10
    Guided Original Lyrics
        and Music (GOLM)
        principles 234, 246
    iqa'at (rhythmic
        modes) 259–60
    Lebanon songwriting
        project 258–61
    maqam'at (scales) 259–61
    Mostar songwriting
        project 252,
        253–8, 254–8
    musical choices in 255–7
    power of 206–7
    process of (Mostar
        project) 255
    in Safe & Sound
        intervention 117
    Sarajevo songwriting
        project 252, 253–8
    Syrian refugees
        songwriting
        project 258–61

songwriting *cont.*
taxonomy of
themes 263–4
Ukranian refugees
project 261–3
vignette 208–10
see also Moz 'All
the Same' song/
video project
Spielraum Musik
sessions 124, 136–8
stepped approaches 40–1
Stevenson, Robert
Louis 251, 264
'Stop Dance' game 132, 137
storytelling
storyteller-listener
relationship 86–7
trauma storytelling 88–9
see also Narrative Music
Psychotherapy
supervision 154
support for practitioners
153–4
'survival' stage 148–9
sympathetic nervous
system 52
synapses 51–2, 57
Syrian refugees
projects overview
204–5, 252
resilience of 205–6
songwriting project
258–61

tambor alegre 196
tambor de bomba 196
Tbilisi Academy of
Music 252
terminology
asylum seeker 11, 18
displaced persons 17–18
refugee 11, 17
therapeutic process (seven
dynamic phases of) 90
therapeutic relationship 35

therapeutic self-
representation
(music as) 87–8
Threlfall, Catherine 239
top-down vs. bottom-up
approach 58
Trainer of Trainers (ToT)
programme 204
training
in Colombia 189
facilitator 43
MasT training
projects 165
qualifications
required 43
Ukraine student
workforce 261–3
of young volunteers
(Mostar) 254
see also Music as Therapy
International (MasT)
training; skill sharing
trance-like states 133
transit camps (temporality
of life in) 149–50
transitional identities 36
trauma
in educational contexts
(literature review) 35
in healthcare settings
(literature
review) 33–4
impact on brain 58
potentially traumatic
events (PTEs) 107
see also post-traumatic
stress disorder
trauma memory 87
trauma storytelling 88–9
trauma-focused Music
and Imagery (tr-
MI) 32, 33, 39
trauma-informed practice
establishing trust 35–6
Safe & Sound
intervention 107–8

SamSam group 151
traumatic dissociation 71

Ukrainian refugees
songwriting project
252, 261–3
trauma experienced
by 213
see also Music for
Displaced Dyads
(M4DD)
unconditional positive
regard 175–6
Universal Declaration
of Human Rights 12

vagal nerve 53–4
vagal tone 60–1, 72, 128
Vaughan Williams,
Ralph 251
ventral nervous
system 53–4
vicarious traumatization
100, 234
Vukich, Eva Marija
(story of) 27–8
vulnerable group
representation 28

War Child London 252
War Child
Netherlands 252
'we are all refugees'
protests 147
Western music 39
white saviour
perspective 170
woman-to-woman
encounters 74–5
World Child 252
Wormit, Alexander
F. 125–6
Writing Through Fences
group 241, 247

Author Index

Aarø, L. E. 12
Abdeen, Z. 168
Abdulbaki, H. 71
Adu, J. 146, 147
Agbaria, N. 168
Ahonen, H. 32, 34, 37, 42, 87, 88, 90, 93, 97, 100
Ahonen-Eerikainen, H. 87, 88
Akoyunoglou, M. 151, 158
Al-Krenawi, A. 168
Albanese, F. 28
Allen, M. 60
Altschuler, J. 158
American Psychiatric Association 205
Amnesty International 18, 235
Ansdell, G. 192
Arnon, S. 226
Artuch-Garde, R. 136
Arvanitis, E. 150
Azab, I. 49
Azevedo, F. A. 52

Baak, M. 155
Bager, L. 127
Baines, S. 34
Baker, F. 233
Balban, M. Y. 60
Bartleet, B. 163
Bashir, M. 127
Bath, H. 13
Batuta 187
Bayeck, R. Y. 155
Beauchaine, T. P. 218

Beck, B. 20, 31, 33, 34, 35, 39, 40, 41, 42, 69, 72, 73, 74, 214
Behrens, G. A. 128
Beld, M. H. M. 104, 109, 115
Bemman, B. 74
Benessaieh, A. 16
Bensimon, M. 104, 132, 158, 234
Berger, J. 71, 234
Bernard, G. 31, 33, 35, 39, 214
Berntson, G. G. 218
Bienestar Colsanitas 187
Blackmore, R. 104
Blandon, A. Y. 218
Boccagni, P. 71
Boer, F. 107
Bogic, M. 104
Bolger, L. 33, 42, 169, 170, 171
Bonde, L. O. 82
Bongard, S. 34
Bonini, L. 60
Bonny, H. 71, 72
Bornstein, M. H. 62
Bosman, M. 59
Braun, V. 173, 219
Bremner, J. D. 56
Brett, M. 59, 63
Brough, M. 127
Brown, E. D. 129
Brown, S. 89
Bruscia, K. 190, 191, 193, 195
Bullock, L. M. 149

Bustamante Duarte, A. M. 156

Cacioppo, J. T. 59
Cacioppo, S. 59
Callister, A. H. 146
CAMTI Collective 34, 169, 170
Carastathis, A. 146
Cardozo Ruiz, O. l. 194, 195
Carnevali, C. 32, 36, 42
Center for Substance Abuse Treatment 104
Cervera Osorio, M. C. 193, 194, 195
Chanda, M. L. 90
Chantah, J. 32, 34, 37, 38
Charura, D. 166, 170
Cherry, K. 52
Chu, J. B. 87
Clark, S. 49
Clarke, V. 173, 219
Cleveland Clinic 60
Cloitre, M. 34
Cobussen, M. 157
Codrington, R. 18
Colquitt, J. A. 177
Comisión de la Verdad 185, 186
Comisión Interamericana de Derechos Humanos 184
Comte, R. 33, 34, 39, 169
Coombes, E. 32, 35, 40, 41, 42, 43, 71, 163, 164, 165, 168, 170, 171, 214, 216

Coppens, L. 107, 114
Courtois, C. A. 87
Cover Three 52
Crenshaw, K. 170
Crepet, A. 104
Crooke, A. H. D. 156
Curtis, S. 12

Dana, D. 52, 53, 54, 55, 60, 61, 62, 63
Dangmann, C. 149, 150
Davies, B. 155
Davis, K. M. 158
de Cruz, M. 169
de Freitas Girardi, J. 152
De Quadros, A. 32, 36, 37, 38, 39, 42
De Witte, M. 226
Defensoría del Pueblo 186
Deighton, J. 213
Desautels, L. 59
DeZIM 127
Diaz, E. 33, 36, 40, 43
Dieterich-Hartwell, R. 71
Dileo, C. 156
Dokter, D. 127
Douglas, P. 146
Doussard-Roosevelt, J. A. 227
Dudley, M. 234
Dvorak, A. 31, 33, 35, 39, 214

Edele, A. 127
Edwards, D. J. 61
Edwards, J. 34, 40, 73, 151
Else, B. A. 151, 152
Encyclopaedia Britannica 79
Enge, K. E. A. 32, 33, 35, 36, 37, 39, 40, 42, 158, 234
Erkkilä, J. 214
Eruyar, S. 213
Esposito, G. 62
Evers, S. 89

Fachner, J. 214
Fancourt, D. 61, 214
Fazel, M. 70, 213
Felsenstein, R. 19
Fino, E. 205
Fischer, J. 129

Ford, J. D. 87
Franco, F. 227
Frankl, V. E. 88
Fredrickson, B. L. 59
Froemke, R. C. 59
Fröhlich-Gildhoff, K. 134
Fruhholz, S. 89
Fukuie, T. 59, 63
Fundación Nacional Batuta 188

Gamma, E. 59
Gangrade, A. 89
Garcia, R. 185
Garrido, S. 158
Gaul, M. 156
Geretsegger, M. 215
Gever, V. 32, 33, 34, 43
GGZ Standaarden 103, 104, 105, 117
Giang, V. 59
Ginsburg, K. R. 134
Gkionakis, N. 147, 152
Gómez, J. H. 190, 194
Gómez Montoya, C. A. 191, 194, 195
Gonzales, M. 151, 152
Good, A. 59
Gottman, J. M. 213
Grabbe, L. 58
Grahn, J. A. 59, 63
Grebosz-Haring, K. 156
Greenberg, M. 50, 54
Gregory, S. Y. 56
Groβ, D. 61
Grocke, D. 72, 73, 82
Grossman, P. 218
Güiza, D. A. 189
Güney, S. S. 211
Gwyn, R. 22

Haas, B. W. 57
Hanson-Abromeit, D. 129, 168
Harré, R. 155
Harrod, E. G. 61
Hebb, D. O. 57
Heidelberg 124
Helsing, M. 89
Henderson, S. 31, 37, 39, 42
Herman, J. 73, 87, 90, 130
Hermosilla, S. 152

Hesser, B. 163
Hettich, N. 214
Heynen, E. 32, 33, 35, 36, 38, 39, 40, 41, 42, 43, 103, 104, 105, 113, 158
Hieronymi, O. 149
Hillecke, T. K. 123, 129, 131
Ho, H. Y. 72
Holley, L. C. 156
Hoog Antink, M. 32, 41, 42, 71, 234
Horeweg, A. 105, 109, 115
Hotulainen, P. 57
Human Rights Law Centre 235
Huq, E. 150

Idemudia, E. S. 104
Indepaz 185
Internal Displacement Monitoring Centre 186
Iqbal, A. 18

Jablow, M. M. 134
Jalonen, A. 148
Jefferson, A. 157
Jensen, S. 149, 150
Jensen, T. K. 149, 150
Jin, S. 32, 37, 42
Johnson, J. 61
Jones, C. 233
Jones, K. L. 56
Jones, P. B. 57
Journeyman Pictures 252
Jurisdicción Especial para la Paz 185
Juslin, P. 72, 89

Kaczmarek, B. 59
Kale, A. 71
Katsanidou, Al. 147
Kenny, A. 32, 38, 40, 42
Khalidi, R. 167, 168
Khanal, P. 57
Kim, K. 70
Klein, R. 87, 90
Klyve, G. P. 12
Koch, S. C. 71
Koelsch, S. 72, 89
Kohlmann, C. W. 61
Koike, A. 130

Kok, B. E. 59, 60
Kok, M. 130
Kora, D. D. 203, 208
Körlin, D. 78
Kostilainen, K. 227
Krüger, V. 12, 33, 36, 40, 43
Kumar, A. M. 89

La Corte, P. C. 148
Lamb, D. G. 60
Lang, L. 19, 252
Layne, C. M. 127
Leech, G. 215
Lefkofridi, Z. 147
Lenette, C. 71, 158, 233
Levine, P. 74, 87
Levitin, D. J. 90
Lieberman, M. 62
Lim, A. 80
Lindauer, R. 107
Lobo, F. M. 62
Loo, F. Y. 72
Luke, C. 49, 50
Luna, C. B. 189,
    192, 194, 195
Lundmark, D. S. 203
Lunkenheimer, E. 62
Lupien, S. J. 56
Lutz Hochreutener, S. 130

McInerney, U. 19
MacKinnon, L. 59, 63
Malloch, S. 168
Mallon, T. 32, 41,
    42, 71, 234
Mansvelt, N. 171
Marley, C. 105
Marsh, K. 32, 35, 38, 39, 42
Martin-Saavedra, J. S. 72
Martínez Durán, L.
    A. 192, 194, 195
Marusak, H. A. 104
Mauki, B. 105
Mediendienst
    Integration 128
Mendoza-Halliday, D. 62
Merriam-Webster 156
Messel, C. 31, 33,
    35, 39, 40, 41
Meyer, S. 31, 33, 34, 39, 41
Michelis, I. 213
Middlesex University 214

Miles, S. H. 234
Millar, O. 158
Miller, K. K. 151
Miller, M. J. 34
Miller-Karas, E. 58
Miraftab, F. 150
Moe, T. 73
Mohammed, S. 149
Mollica, R. F. 34, 86,
    87, 88, 90, 94
Mongillo Desideri,
    A. 32, 34, 37, 42
Moodley, R. 166
Moore, K. S. 129
Moreno, J. 196
Moss, H. 163
Murphy, M. 169, 170, 171
Murray, K. E. 213

National Institute of
    Neurological Disorders
    and Stroke 51
Nelson, C. A. 57
Nersessian, N. J. 155
Nielsen, N. 157
Noe, R. A. 177

O'Brien, E. 234, 246
O'Brien, M. E. 239
Ogden, P. 129
Oldfield, A. 215, 216
Orth, J. 19, 214
Osbeck, L. M. 155
Osborne, N. 19, 252,
    253, 254, 258, 262

Paida, S. 151
Papadopoulos, R. 148,
    149, 156, 158
Papastathopoulos,
    S. 149, 150
Papataxiarchis, E.
    146, 147, 148
Parker, D. 32, 34, 36,
    37, 40, 41, 42, 43
Patel, S. G. 149
Patriquin, M. A. 218, 227
Pavlicevic, M. 192
Pedersen, I. N. 73
Perkins, R. 214
Perry, B. D. 56, 57

Pieloch, K. A. 155, 156
Pinna, T. 61
Pino Gavidia, L. A. 146, 147
Politimou, N. 227
Porges, S. W. 53, 54,
    55, 60, 61, 72, 128
Porter, S. 168
Posselt, M. 234
Power, J. D. 57
Präger, U. 150
Programa de las Naciones
    Unidas para el
    Desarrollo 187
Punamaki, R. L. 168
Puras, D. 34

Quin, A. 163

Ramadan, A. 150
Ramirez, M. 151
Rauchbauer, B. 60
Red 188
Registro Único de
    Víctimas 186
Reiner-Wormit, C. 136
Ribeiro, M. K. A. 226
Richter, K. 149
Roeder, S. S. 56
Rogers, C. 169, 174
Rogers-Sirin, L. 127
Rolvsjord, R. 13, 136
Rom, R. B. 156
Rönnau-Böse, M. 134
Rossetti, A. 128
Rothschild, B. 89
Rowland, C. 163
Rudstam, G. 214
Ruiz Fandiño, S.
    M. 193, 195
Ruiz, N. Y. 186
Russell-Chapin,
    L. A. 50, 64
Russo, F. A. 59
Ruud, E. 189

Salgado Vasco, A. F.
    189, 190, 195
Salimpoor, V. N. 89
Schäfer, T. 227
Schauer, M. 87, 88, 96
Schermer, V. 87, 90

Schlaggar, B. L. 57
Schlaug, G. 60
Schmidt, S. N. L. 60
Schottelkorb, A. A. 112
Scrine, E. 130
Sedlmeier, P. 227
Segal, J. 18
Sena Moore, K. 168
Shaffer, J. 49
Shafir, T. 58
Sharif, A. 56
Shrubsole, B. 163
Sirin, S. 127
Skewes McFerran,
    K. 33, 42, 82
Skinner, C. 32, 36
Small, C. 37, 164
Smets, P. 70
Smith, G. S. 213
Smith, J. P. 213
Solberg, Ø. 104
Sommers-Flanagan, R. 157
Soulsby, L. K. 168
Souzas, N. 146, 147, 148
Speranza, L. 59
Spitzer, R. L. 217
Stanat, P. 127
Standley, J. 226
Steiner, S. 156
Stern, D. N. 169
Stewart-Brown, S. 217
Stige, B. 12, 32, 33, 35,
    36, 37, 39, 40, 42,
    158, 195, 234
Storsve, V. 19, 168
Strange, J. 163
Suhr, B. 89
Sunderland, N. 71, 158
Sutton, J. 39, 168

Thomas, M. 149
Thomason, M. E. 104
Tiems, J. 104
Tierney, A. L. 57
Tombs-Katz, M. 32, 41,
    43, 163, 165, 170, 171
Tosto, V. 19
Trevarthen, C. 168, 252
Trondalen, G. 157
Tsiris, G. 158
Tsolka, E. 170
Tsoni, I. 150
Turner, S. 150
Turner, V. 189
Turrini, G. 213

Uhlig, S. 128
Ungar, M. 111
UNHCR 11, 15, 17, 49, 123,
    145, 146, 148, 213, 267
United Nations 12, 227
United Nations
    Conference on Trade
    and Development 167
United Nations Relief
    and Works Agency for
    Palestine Refugees 167

Vaghri, Z. 158
Vaillancourt, G. 12
van Blooijs, D. 56, 57
van den Ouwelant,
    A. 107, 108
van der Hart, O. 71, 82
van der Kolk, B. 50,
    54, 55, 56, 58, 87
Van der Veer, G. 93
Van Eck, F. 168

Van Gennep, A. 150
Van Langenhove, L. 155
van Oudheusden, H. 105
Van Puyvelde, M. 218,
    219, 226, 227
Vandamme, N. 105, 111
Veronese, G. 205
Vu, K. T. 32, 36, 37,
    38, 39, 42

Waldschmidt, A. 28
Wang, F. 170
Wanner, M. 52
Wärja, M. 82
Warren, J. R. 156
Warwick, I. 158
Weathers, F. W. 217
Weingarten, S. J. 226
Wentling, B. 128
Wiess, C. 104, 158, 234
Wigram, T. 169
Wilker, F.-W. 123, 131
Wilkinson, R. G. 170
Williams, K. E. 129
Winsor, M. 233
Winter, A. L. 166, 170
Woitsch, K. 128
Woodward, A. 252
World Health
    Organization 12, 38, 70

Yayan, E. H. 104
Yinger, O. S. 127, 129, 130
Young, L. J. 59

Zambonini, J. P. 19
Zatorre, R.J. 89
Zolkoski, S. M. 149